China that was 1985-1989

Through the eyes of an expat resident

Hector Mc Leod

Balboa Press books may be ordered through booksellers or by contacting:

Balboa Press
A Division of Hay House
1663 Liberty Drive
Bloomington, IN 47403
www.balboapress.com
1 (877) 407-4847

ISBN: 978-1-4525-2488-7 (sc)
ISBN: 978-1-4525-2489-4 (e)

Printed in the United States of America.

Balboa Press rev. date: 08/18/2014

BALBOA.
PRESS
A DIVISION OF HAY HOUSE

In the late 1970s, China once called the Middle Kingdom; poked it's head over the so called bamboo wall and realised that it needed to modernise. The technology of the so called western world was driving their economies at a frightening rate, China was lagging far behind; it's flirtation with Russia had proved unsuccessful. China and its billion inhabitants were still in the 1940s. The great Chairman Mao (this said with all reverence and respect) had in his fading years suffered; as many past leaders have, present leaders do and future leaders will; megalomania. Look at Mugabe in Zimbabwe. China removed itself from Mao's yoke after the failures of the "Great Leap Forward" and the "Cultural Revolution", the so called "Gang of Four" also removed; then its new leaders decided it is now a game of technical catch up.

China was becoming a potential market of some 1 billion people; so industrialists in a country like Sweden with 8 million population; saw large marketing opportunities, coupled with Sweden's neutrality regime, it would not pose a threat to a China joint venture type business enterprise, in fact it appeared to be an ideal union. After many, many months of meetings and negotiations there eventually came into being a new Chinese law proscribed for Joint Venture Agreements. The bureaucrats in Jiangsu Province and its capital Nanjing were very forward thinking, in fact they had already opened its negotiation doors to a number of western countries, and in fact had already allowed those with a Chinese background mainly Hong Kong residents to utilize some of the underemployed locals in JV's (Joint Ventures), now they saw a golden opportunity for other nationalities to have access to their work force and above all import modern technologies.

After 18 years as Director of Finance and Administration for the Australian subsidiary of a Swedish pharmaceutical company Ann my wife and I had accepted the appointment as Finance Director South East Asia, a new position to be located in Singapore. In the early 1980s my employer had joined with three other organisations in European. Two were non competing pharmaceutical companies the other a government foreign aid organisation formed to provide technical training to developing countries.

Wuxi, a small city of about 1 million people situated on the railway line from Shanghai to Nanjing was suggested to the Swedish negotiators as a city ideal for the setting up of the new JV. Many, many months had elapsed since these negotiations had began, here at last was a positive step; the Western side agreed and joined with 4 Chinese state organisations to form a company constituted under the new Chinese JV laws. The contract allocated a parcel of land near a small village called Mashan; the site was presently farmed rice, wheat and fish; as a collective and located on an area of land reclaimed from Lake Tai by the educated masses (doctors teachers etc) during the Cultural Revolution. Some housing for the factory workers would be built nearby and more housing would be constructed for technical and management staff in Wuxi city proper about 10 k from the new factory/office site.

By November 1985 the 5 story, (no lifts), grey cinder cement brick buildings (a landscape feature of so many communist countries), had been finished as the city housing for the technical staff. A considerable number of suitable qualified people had been employed; a significant number of these technical and factory supervisory staff had already returned from Sweden; here they were trained in the modern operations of a tablet factory and a hygiene class 3, large volume parental infusion filling and packaging operation. Similarly staff had been trained in Sweden in all aspects of raw and finished goods warehousing and distribution operations in particular the complex batch tracking paperwork involved in pharmaceutical operations.

Training had also been given in marketing and medical information requirements. It was however envisaged that western professionals would be used for some years to ensure quality control. Chinese assistant managers were all trained at the three joint venture partners factories in Sweden to slowly take over the operations. This training had taken a considerable number of months, all costs borne by the Western partners. These costs were considerable, the costs alone of housing a large group in a Nordic country, travel etc plus all employees were on full pay. Consequently in 1985 there was a large investment already incurred as well as ongoing expatriate employment wages, travel and in country housing costs. Still any return was some 12 months away. A Sweden president; two production managers and two marketing advisors had already been employed and were resident in Wuxi; all foreign personnel were seconded from the Western JV partners on two year contracts, they all lived at the Hubin Hotel in nearby Wuxi.; a Western construction manager with his wife together with a short stay logistics manager made up the expat group, the three latter people were living at another hotel called Tai Hu on the outskirts of the city. My company had appointed a Finance Manager as the JV co-ordinator in Europe. Each in country expatriate was allocated a specific local assistant manager and a Chinese Vice President was appointed. So the investment amount was ever increasing without any income. The building complex was being constructed using local labour very low hourly costs coupled with well below average (to our modern way of thinking) efficiency added to the growing frustration of the Swedish side as it appeared to need a money tree to complete the project.

Ann and I were to leave Sydney at the end of May 1986 to take up the new position in Singapore. This was just one month after celebrating my 51st birthday. Part of this new role was to be the Secretary to the European JV partners and an advisor on Finance Systems and Procedures to the Chinese organisation. I took over this role as the previous incumbent a Swedish national was suffering ill health.

A Board meeting was scheduled for November 1985; so my presence was required for at least 10 days, firstly to prepare a progress report for the meeting, up to date financials and meeting agendas and finally meeting minutes. My new boss in London was looking for me to give him a clear assessment of the state of the project. To me this was an exciting leading edge opportunity, which I embraced with gusto. As the CFO of Astra Australia I had already spent considerable time in South East Asia, including Hong Kong, with the majority of our employees in these countries of Chinese extraction I felt suitable prepared for working with the mainland Chinese.

How wrong conceptions can be; the mainland Chinese at that time were totally different in understanding, social mores or even educated ways from those I had dealt with in SEA. The local residents had existed under Communistic control since 1949, a thoroughly controlling regime. I still believe that their harsh methods were necessary to unite the Chinese masses and to give them a liveable existence. But the harshness resulted in the total subjugation of the ordinary people.

My new appointment was "Foreign Advisor Administration" and Secretary to the European members of the Consortium. In 1985 mass communication was just starting, the new wonder fax machine brilliant as a communication tool but painfully slow taking 8 minutes to send an A4 page, never the less it was replacing the telex machines as a way to send not just messages but also pictures anywhere in the world where there was a telephone line. The technology was slowly evolving and it soon became possible to send an A4 page of type with pictures in less than 4 minutes; overseas telephone calls were becoming more commonplace, but expensive. One did not just pick up the phone to make an international call this became common from the early 90s when ISD (International Subscriber Dialling) became a reality. The only briefing I was given prior to arriving in Shanghai was short and direct. Your role is the foreign Secretary, provide an agenda then prepare the minutes, now remember China is a cash only society and for visa purposes it is necessary to get a letter of invitation from the company in China specifically requesting your presence and detailing the purpose of the visit.

The only way into China was via Hong Kong; this necessitated an over night stay, due to flight time schedules. At that time Singapore Airline were developing a flight schedule from Singapore but it was still some months away, There was no other choice but fly with the Chinese Hong Kong Shanghai ; the one and only national air line CAAC (Chinese Aviation Administration Commission) had a daily flight from Hong Kong to Shanghai; some 125 k from Wuxi. .

As this trip was being funded by Sweden I was introduced to one of their very important travelling tax features which covered overseas daily travel allowance. This was an amount that an employee was allowed to claim from the company for being away from home for over 12 hours; it was paid in Swedish Kroner and was tax free in your hands. Astra A used a different system where receipted expenses were reimbursement however the CEO of Astra A; a spend thrift himself; was very hard on others and often disallowed what he deemed to be exorbitant expenses. This was one of the very minor complaints that I had had against him, which had lead me to the request for an overseas transfer.

Reference to the Sweden travel manual showed that eating in China would be very inexpensive; hotel accommodation at the Hubin hotel would be arranged; but with the usual lack of small detail information suffered over the years there was no indication as to who would pay, Sweden Consortium, my Swedish Company or the local Chinese operation; credit cards were not acceptable in China so traveller's cheques or cash was the way to proceed. China situated in the northern latitude meant that November would be cold, an overcoat and warm clothes needed to be packed. Having already travelled a few times to European in all seasons my wardrobe contained extreme weather clothes although in the my early Astra days there was a company overcoat that one borrowed if you were going to Europe in winter.

I did not realise it in November 1985 but this was the start of what was to become the most interesting but also the most taxing time of my working life. Hong Kong and I were old friends after many visits; a night at the Sheraton on Nathan Road; a nice sumptuous dinner alone at the nearby Shanghai restaurant was in my mind a way to prepare me for the next 10 days; how wrong could one be; the difference became obvious immediately on boarding the CAAC aircraft. It was an old Boeing 707; my last experience of one of these planes was in 1969 and this was 1985, in the West 16 years had seen the 707, replaced with the Jumbo 747 V2, V3 but not yet for CAAC. The cabin crew were anything but helpful; the luxury of business class not yet developed, so I was travelling 2nd class as it was known at the time. The 6 seats across were rather tired and the décor showing signs of considerable use with a minimum of maintenance. Scary; yes.

Approaching Shanghai landing the usual customs/immigration documents were handed out so that they could be completed before landing. Something strange both migration and customs documents were in triplicate; this was unusual; duplicate was the norm but triplicate why? As always the process of time would reveal the answer. There was also another document; a health form and it asked a number very pointed questions. HIV Aids was not yet a problem but in later years it was necessary to have a certificate declaring you HIV free. At that time international travellers were required to carry a yellow health book that showed the inoculation status of a number of virulent diseases, a 6 monthly typhoid and 3 yearly small pox inoculations were required, these were all in order; however; to date in my considerable overseas travels there had never been a requirement to answer a list of questions as to my health in general. Another difference; the customs form required a list of all currencies and their value that you were carrying as well as an inventory of all jewellery and electronics; all in triplicate on rather flimsy paper; there was also a requirement to list the number of your pieces of luggage; this different.

Landing was in wet and miserable conditions; the walk from the plane to the terminal was an indication of the state of infrastructure in China, air bridges at major international airports were almost commonplace, but here a walk across the tarmac showed weeds growing out of the multiplicity of cracks that was present in the concrete tarmac, puddles of water needed to be dodged or walked through; then up the well walked metal stairs with green uniformed military guards stationed strategically on every second step; entering into the drab terminal building to line up to go through three sets of gate ways one in front of the other.

As is usual in international travel in due process of time I arrived at the first set of booths; the health form was scrutinised; my yellow health book flipped through, then allowed to proceed to the next queue. It was a long wait; in all booths there were two people; both studied minutely my visa and passport, peering at the photograph and then at my face; their visage was grim as if they dared me not to be me. They stamped (later to find out the correct terminology; chopped) the passport and visa then after another look returned the document together with two copies of the entry form; another difference.

Even after such a long delay the baggage had just arrived and I looked around for a trolley none; then a notice on the wall advised that trolleys cost 1 FEC. Prior homework had shown that the local currency was Yuan or Reminbi so what was an FEC? Over my time working for a Swedish Company I had found that they are often short on small but important detail. Customs was a repeat of immigration; the passport and stamped copy of the entry visa scrutinised, my face inspected closely and then the luggage was put through an x-ray machine. Since security now had become a feature of international travelling my luggage had seen the inside of a large number of these devices at airport check in counters but never had this been the case for incoming customs. Then, a broken English (Chinglish) request asked me to show all of my jewellery; at the time I always wore my rings and gold cross so that was no big deal; cuff links an integral part of the wardrobe were carried in the over the shoulder bag; out they came and were carefully inspected. The same with electronic items cameras etc. they had to be seen and inspected. All of the time without any word being spoken just hand gestures. A brief wave signalled that they had finished their inspection so with briefcase and suitcase in hand walked towards a swinging door; it was not self opening so needed a big push with the shoulder to go through.

Wow; confronting me was a solid wall of people; no matter how many times travelling in and out of China; this wall of people was always there, both on arrival and departure. In later times non travellers were not allowed inside the building but this solid wall of humanity then only moved outside to the footpath. It was a cold November day and the mass before me were clad in a range of what looked like old clothes; padded jackets of all types; not one could be called in any way decent, the jacket was worn over padded pants and then old shoes.

Everybody looked over weight not as I expected; lean; my information was that although food was ample it was not in abundance; how could all of the people look quite; well yes fat; also my experience was that the Chinese were a slim race particularly the young women; not so here and now. Later I discovered that what I thought to be obesity was in fact many layers of clothing. The colder the day the fatter the people became in those 1980 years. Cotton was the common clothing denominator and cotton does not keep out the cold.

There was an expectation that someone would meet me; there at the back of this wall of people, was a person with a sign; my name incorrectly spelt but still recognisable. As westerners we respect a person's "space"; however the majority of Asian races do not have the physical room for this luxury. This fact was noted on other Asian trips especially Hong Kong but this was the first time that this togetherness became a physical reality. I was very hesitant in just walking into the wall of people and pushing my way through; but that was what was expected. It was a procedure that never became easy but was indeed the only way forward. The 10 deep sea of people was negotiated without losing a grip on the luggage as I made my way to the notice. It was being held by a lovely lady; a native of

Cambodia and the wife of the Swedish Construction Manager. A Chinese was introduced as the driver and we forced our way outside.

Now with eyes agog; I surveyed another sea of humanity; all similarly dressed and all hurrying about their business in the airport surrounds. Next I was hustled to a big black car called a Zil; the Chinese equivalent of the Russian version of the US Cadillac. There was another person in the car, a visiting European Board member, introductions were made and then I was told in Swinglish (a Swedish version of English] that we were going into the city proper to have lunch before going to Wuxi. Another Swedish group had arrived previously and we would meet them at the 7 storey high Shanghai Hotel; so with eyes every where I experienced the sights and sounds of my first Chinese city; still very much as it was in the days of Chairman Mao. The people; warmly clad in what appeared to be old clothes, most with dilapidated footwear, all hurried on foot or bicycle through the city streets, the road to and from the airport was white concrete with many walled; well kept large houses along its borders, the majority of these I later found out were hotels for the top 5 cadre groups, a very interesting development for a people; who, so it is said, are all equal.

At the end of this street was a large round about; a landmark soon to be well known to me; straight through the round about and across a level crossing and we were in the city proper; now the streets became narrow and congested with bicycles, mostly with one rider but occasionally with a passenger or even two. At a slow moving pace with a cacophony of sound we made the confines of the Shanghai Hotel; which at that time was one of only two top (3 star) tourist hotels in the city the other was the Peace Hotel. Here we joined the other arrivals and partook of the first real mainland Chinese meal.

Now another quaint Chinese custom regarding hotel bookings was discovered; the other arrivals were only staying for a few days and had a mid morning departure flight, they therefore needed to arrange accommodation for the evening prior to the flight, the Chinese way then being; that you had to pay in advance for booked accommodation; this appeared momentarily quaint but the mind was too full of wonder at this strange land to pay much attention to what seemed minor details. Ho hum how this quaint custom affected all my future comings and goings up to 1987 and the advent of western hotels with their booking systems as we know them.

After an interesting meal, we prepared to leave for Wuxi some 125k from Shanghai, to me just a short trip and wondered why it was suggested that we all use the toilet before leaving. It was almost child like to be told to go to the toilet; the drivers arrived with the cars and the journey commenced.

How does one describe the road and the traffic and the country side after leaving the confines of the city; over the four years in China the road travel conditions improved dramatically, before we left in 1989; an expressway linking Nanjing to Shanghai passing through Wuxi was completed; but in November 1985 it was a rutted excuse for a road; used by all manner of conveyances.

There were very few cars, old buses and trucks with heavy loads were the predominant 4 wheeled vehicles but then there were all manner of other conveyances being driven by black smoke belching motors of all types. Firstly the so called open mini tractors that looked just like a large rotary hoe with the driver sitting on a bench attached to the trailer these had 5 forward and 5 reverse gears driven by a very basic water cooled diesel engine they were everywhere; dodging in and out of the flow of traffic. Then bicycles of all shapes and sizes, all mostly the two wheeled variety with one, two or even three people perching precariously on the frame; they also seemed everywhere, then a bicycle with a trailer carrying all manner of goods, then, any spare space was taken up by pedestrians walking with their backs to the traffic.

With one of the three Nissan sedans then owned by the joint venture following behind, we travelled this nightmare of a road; how did the drivers of our cars cope. The cacophony of noise indescribable; this, the road and the driving I would come to curse over the forthcoming 4 years. But to day was my first, it was one of those trouble free traffic days and we managed to complete the 125 k journey in some 4 plus hours to arrive at a hotel that soon would be called home; The Hubin.

The Hubin Hotel also called home to the in country Swedish Management team; another less salubrious hotel called the Tai Hu housed the technical people. During the trip it was realised why the toilet stop; before leaving the hotel was suggested. There are no service stations to ease your natural requirements and the way side toilets attached to small villages were used only in extreme emergencies. Later in 1986; a Swedish lady; tall blonde and leggy was being ferried to Wuxi and failed to heed the toilet time maxim. Mid way into the trip she had an urgent nature call and ventured into one of these toilets and soon became an instant draw card, the toilet block being besieged by local women wanting to see for themselves, a true blonde.

At the Hubin Hotel a further introduction into the Chinese way, firstly registration; this was a tourist hotel so English (Chinglish) was spoken; it was usual practice checking into a hotel in other countries you showed your passport; reception staff then make a note and checked you against the photo and it is returned; but not in 1985 China. Your pass port was taken to be returned some 3 /

4 days later. You were also required to produce your Custom's document; I assumed that this was to prove you could pay your bill as it was cash only economy. Within 18 months it would become a vibrant plastic card economy for foreigners however the locals were only introduced to debit cards some time after this; this timing was linked to the growth of the new rich. .

Up until the early 1990s; there were 2 currencies being used; FEC (Foreign Exchange Certificates) and the local Yuan. Most hotels and so called Friendship stores were set up to sell local goods to the tourist but they also stocked overseas spirits and cigarettes; they were only allowed to trade in FEC's. Foreign manufactured products could only be purchased with FEC; the locals had no access to this currency so they could only look at these wonderful imported products, the exchange rate was officially one to one however the black market rate was more like 1.5 to 1.

The dreary registration process over and room key in hand, no bell boy service so carrying my luggage I entered into a rather filthy lift to find the room. It was a small room by Asian standards but was slightly larger than what in local Swedish hotels would class as a single room. It was only a 10 days stay and the room had been arranged by the Company so it was accepted. Usual practice; unpack and then a walk around the grounds of the hotel before meeting the Swedish group for dinner. Cleanliness was not something fully understood, this room was clean, but later living in the hotel I did an experiment, a piece of biscuit left on the window sill in plain view was still there after I had been away for 2 weeks.

The Hubin Hotel is situated some 6 k from Wuxi City centre and was a bland 7 story hotel built beside Lake Tai the 4th largest lake in China. This area was known as the land of fish and rice; rice and wheat in opposing seasons together with rape (canola) are the major crops together with large ponds used to breed fresh water fish. Adjacent to the hotel was a Chinese Garden; a must have feature for any large town in China; across from the garden entrance was a bicycle park where garden visitors and commuters would leave their bikes and catch a bus into the city proper. This was my first view of a bicycle park. There was even a parking attendant to collect the daily fee; this park would have held over 500 bicycles; how the owners could differentiate I do not know as they all seemed to be the same heavy make, model and colour.

It was common practice in those early days of the drawing of the bamboo curtain that two hotels would be constructed side by side. One hotel usually the larger; would be by current Chinese standards; well appointed (ha) and the other smaller hotel for locals, just very basic. The large hotel catered for tourists and top Chinese cadres and the other smaller one for the few travelling locals. There was also a wide disparity between prices. The average monthly wage paid to our employees at that time was US$50 or ¥ 400; the Hubin tariff was from ¥ 75 per night while the other hotel ranged from ¥20; meals were also of a different standard and value as I later discovered.

A barbershop and a ladies hairdresser were also in a separate building, as my walk through the hotel garden discovered. This garden like any other Chinese garden are amazingly structured; although the grounds were quite small and there were a number of separate building for special groups; it was possible to spend some 15 minutes following the paths that meandered around the area; some times almost meeting; various garden forms and features including water ways provided interest as you wandered along. There was a small three bedroom cottage attached to the hotel and the Consortium had rented it for three of the Swedish experts who were based in Wuxi waiting for their villas to be built; once again I am racing ahead. This small cottage was reputed to have been built for the Nationalist President Chang Kai-shek who was ousted by Chairman Mao in 1949; escaping to Taiwan with his predominately southern Chinese followers plus a large portion of very valuable ancient Chinese relics and antiques, now on show in a special museum in Taiwan (formerly Formosa).

At dinner I met again with the other visitors and introduced to the "in country" team, they were all Swedish and my knowledge of that language not yet honed enough to grasp what was being said; I thought here is a rather lonely week coming up; all of the group were passable in Swinglish but using their mother tongue was much easier to converse so it was used all of the time. With 12 people seated at the usual Chinese round table with its small rotating inner table the first of a great many Hubin meals was enjoyed, the use of the chop sticks not an issue although not as expert as I later became. Table service; and over all etiquette was not on the waiting staffs list of priorities and the use of clean bowls for each course was outside of any of their training.

Next morning driven to the temporary offices and became familiar with the local management group; now it was discovered that I too should have booked a room in Shanghai to ensure being in time for my return flight in 10 days. Another feature of air travel at the time was the necessity to reconfirm your flights no less than 3 days prior to departure; this practice was not necessary in Europe or America as they had a more sophisticated travelling public but it was mandatory every where else in the world. If you were using any other carrier than a European or US carrier it was considered mandatory; on a later visit the consortium travel officer failed to do this and I was not allowed onto the flight being forced to wait two days until a spare seat was available.

So another lesson learnt on my first day; a simple edict; as soon as you arrive at the office in China the very first thing that you do even before a cup of tea, is arrange your departure travel details through the Administration Manager. This person was a very difficult, supercilious party member who displayed all of the absolute control characteristics of most of his fellow card carriers. He spoke very good English which to me was his only redeeming feature; as this my first visit the contact with him was only slight, but I later found how difficult he could be; over time; unfortunately I met many of his ilk; some even worse; as my stay in China progressed.

The head of the accounting department, a much older man but with passable Chinglish was introduced; he enquired if I had reconfirmed my return air booking and had accommodation in Shanghai been arranged. Naturally the response was "No", off we went straightaway to the Administration Manager. In what was in future to become a private war with this gentleman; he literally demanded my pass port; we had only just been introduced and now he was in the demand stage. Naturally, politely he was informed that it was in the hands of the hotel and it would be returned in two days; his retort; "come back then". I asked the Chinese CFO what his problem was; he advised that to reconfirm my flight and to book accommodation a driver would need to be sent to Shanghai. The driver would need my pass port and of course money for the hotel room; my question "can't this be done by phone"; no was the response; the telephone is very unreliable and money must be paid to book a room. Welcome to the reality of China in November 1985.

At this time the factory complex was far from finished and so the admin office was a number of the company residential units in Wuxi City; my time was fully devoted to the meeting and it passed quickly. Interesting; being a heavy smoker at the time foreign cigarettes were almost a currency in themselves to the locals; so I was very much accepted amongst the heavily smoking Chinese. The contracted, in country expats, were devoting their time training staff and preparing for the day when the factory complex would be ready. Marketing strategies were being developed and the future looked bright. On day one of the meeting, sitting behind the Expat Swedish CEO the proceedings did not make a lot of sense; it was a 2 day meeting and the first day was fully devoted to approve the minutes of the previous meeting; to me this process seemed very strange however as I was new to this situation I made no comment so the true significance of this fact at that time passed me by.

As visitors we were taken on a tour of the country side, in particular to some very ordinary to me but special to the Chinese, river caves some few kilometres from Wuxi; another opportunity to see the country side. The group were treated to a lunch at a small restaurant but knowing it would be a dull rather boring affair I preferred to walk around the small village and soak up the sites and sounds. During this time I talked to one of the Chinese interpreters, he spoke exceedingly good English, and it transpired that he was a farmer by birth but wanted more; he had taught himself German as well as English and now was translating some of the machinery instruction books for the complex pharmaceutical plant that was to be installed. With the building delayed, a lot of equipment was sitting in a warehouse, so he was translating the German instructions into Chinese. This young man became a very good source of information not only about life in China but also about ambition and wanting to succeed.

At that time there was uncertainty regarding the extent of my involvement in China but I soon realised that I wanted to be part of its future. The majority of the people that I could converse with in a Halting form of English, although briefly were enthusiastic in wanting to bring modern technology to China, there was almost a naivety about them, yet they were deep down devious and cunning. I came to love and hate this country and its people with an intensity that I did not feel was possible.

The plan was for me to return in January so an office was allotted to me, as I said previously; the offices were spare rooms in one of the grey cinder block building erected for the Chinese technical staff, executives and office workers. These buildings were 5 storeys high without lifts; each apartment comprised 2 rooms and a bathroom; each about 12 sqm all had a small balcony and were accessed from the open passage way through an ill fitting door. The bathroom was equipped with a bath and toilet (throne type); no toilet paper but equipped with a box of tissues so no worry; a note was made to bring some toilet paper with me in January. A single power point in each room and a single bare globe was the extent of the fittings. My office had a large sloping desk similar to the one used in my 1951 banking days naturally it came with a large padded wooden stool.

On receiving my pass port back from the hotel I revisited the travel office and delivered it and FEC's to prepay the accommodation in Shanghai; the next day the passport was returned and I was told that the seat was confirmed but the only accommodation they could arrange was very expensive at a senior cadres hotel. The Chinese CFO would be my companion on the trip to Shanghai and we would depart next day at 12.00 noon. No question or answer this was what was going to happen.

Previous experience in South East Asia did not equip one for the sullen rudeness that this man displayed towards a visiting exec. A similar 4 plus hour trip back to Shanghai; this time with the full attention of the Chief Finance officer; he was a man in his late 50s and had received a catholic education in Shanghai; as he spoke passable Chinglish there was an opportunity to increase my basic knowledge of this country. Yes; he still slept on the floor with a wooden pillow; it is more comfortable than the western fluffy blankets and pillows; he is not a party member and yes as an educated Chinese he was badly vilified during the Cultural Revolution. He believed strongly in the modernisation of China mainly to take the drudgery out of the people's lives; no; he did not see how mechanisation would reduce the number of jobs available to people, as far as he was concerned those people forced out of work would return to the fields or mines thereby increasing productivity to fuel the growing need for energy and food.

Over the next few years I heard many life stories and was told many versions of China; the overwhelming feeling each time was that each person was a survivor. For the most part they were only interest in themselves and used every trick and devious means they could to survive, hopefully develop; but above all prosper under the regime that had become evil and corrupt. There were some 20 million members of the communist party and they held the power of almost life and death over the remaining; in 1985' some 980 million people. This was not a first visit discovery but the understanding reached after many months of trying to bring Western business practices to almost totally agricultural China.

Today after the long torturously slow 4.5 hour trip over we arrived at the hotel in Shanghai, both of us were amazed to be introduced to the old worldly opulence that was accorded to the senior 5 cadres levels. Mr. Ciao the CFO was to accompany me to the airport the next day so he shared the accommodation; it was in fact an apartment with the main room being at least 25 m2 furnished with huge arm chairs, these oversized chairs were to become a feature in every future meeting with any important Chinese over the next 4 years. But this night I was just amazed by their size; together we sat and continued our discussion into the night before literally climbed into the huge bed, while

Ciao settled down in an adjoining small room meant for a servant. I learnt some of the stylised China formalities. I was to address Mr Ciao as Ciao Lu, as he was older than me he was he was entitled to this suffix; during the time in China I was known either as Mc Leod Lu or as Hector Lu by all of the younger staff.

The airport next day was a repeat scene of my arrival; people everywhere, the locals were still allowed to enter the departure lounge; this practice ceased within the next 18 months but the overflow still crowded around the entrance doors; a human wall that needed to be breeched before starting the officious departure procedures necessary for leaving China. Ciao and driver saw me through the sea of humanity, again the people were clothed in what one would consider; in most cases; to be well mended but unpressed tatters. The many layers of clothing were in the main patched, darned but clean, all of a padded cotton material so much bulk necessary to keep the body warm.

I am not a tall person but on average the Shanghai Chinese are smaller than me so it was enjoyable to have the feeling of towering over the locals; once more forcing a way with brief case and suitcase to the door and inside. Here I was greeted by a row of steely faced cotton green uniform clad male and female officials processing the documents of departing passengers. Firstly, there were two; always two officials; the customs officials to check how much money I was taking out of the country compared to the amount I declared on arrival; electronic devices and jewellery with me must tally against the list presented on arrival, my visa and passport rigorously examined and then; and only then; to the airline check in counter to be processed through the semi manual system.

I walked into the rather austere departure lounge which contained a number of counters with a large range of local handicrafts, jade artefacts, local and imported spirits as well as locally manufactured electronics and watches. These were of no interest to me; as yet no airline departure lounges had found there way into this seriously dilapidated building so wandered around waiting for the departure call. How grim and foreboding the atmosphere, an upper floor restaurant and bar was operating but again of no interest to me in 1985.

The flight was called in barely understandable Chinglish; once again on board for take off with the usual sullen cabin crew on the way to Hong Kong. The usual second rate plane then a 2 hour transit at Kia Tak, this airport almost seemed a second home over the ensuing years, both Ann and I used it for many transits but today it only served the purpose for travel, transit in Singapore, then Sydney and home. For some reason I recommenced my work in Australia with a strange feeling; I had never visited a communist country where people lived in a sort of controlled poverty; so different to The Philippines; there the slums are almost right beside the opulence of the Peninsula Hotel; yet the faces of the people young and old were happy faces even in their pitiful surroundings that so many people live with in the world; not the faces in China the sour dour faces of the children in Wuxi; sitting on a small seat that was affixed to the front bar of a bike, father pedalling and mother sitting astride or side saddle on the carry frame attached to the back, going about their business no smiles no laughter glum glum glum. How many times was this scene before my eyes and how many times did I have the thought "what will be their life?" Of course 28 years later we now have an idea.

Another happy Christmas with all the family around, Christmas day with Ann's family and Boxing Day all of our 5 children and now with grandchildren making a special feature of this day.. Every one knew that we were moving overseas, the arrangement being that Melissa and Karen would look after the house; as it was some 5+ years since we had blended two sets of furniture we would start our new overseas life with a new house and new furniture. It was decided that I would actually resign my position at Astra Australia as it was not fair to my successor if this was to be only a temporary posting. This temporary posting was in fact offered by the CEO of Astra A but he was becoming more and more difficult to work with; other functional managers were either contemplating leaving or actively seeking positions overseas through head office.

In fact Astra A was proving a training ground for other local and overseas companies; the parent company in Sweden valued our experience and business acumen. Although It was an established fact that the person to whom I reported in Singapore was a extremely difficult man to work for however it had been said by my boss in the UK that this executive would shortly be departing the scene so this should not be a long term problem.

After the visit in November 85 I realised how cold Wuxi China could be; so began a hunt in our very warm summer for clothes that would protect me against the cold during my next visit of 4 weeks in January/February 1986; During the November 1985 visit the Swedish CEO of China had asked me for a quick return and a longer visit to look at the accounting/administration procedures and to assist him in formulating appropriate systems applicable when the company became operational; this was work I enjoyed so I was now looking forward for a return visit. Indeed I jumped at the chance. My duties at Astra A were being taken over by my successor and the end of 1985 financial reporting procedures were firmly in his hands.

Singapore Airlines were now flying directly into Shanghai so I arranged to use this route to China keeping me safe away from CAAC; this trip Ann would meet me in Singapore on my way home and we would begin our search for a new home; this move was more exciting for me than Ann; I think.

China February 1986 once again before the same grim faced health, emigration and customs officials all in the same green cotton uniforms; all looking very fat due to the number of layers of clothing needed to keep them warm as they sat in their unheated small boxes processing the incoming passenger's paper work. A man in front of me in the queue did not posses a visa; apparently being told that he could obtain one on entry; armed guards stood by his side until the cabin crew of the incoming flight arrived, he was escorted by them and the guards back to the plane. It could be a frightening country.

The wall of bodies on exit from customs was no different from that in November last year; the wet windblown bicycle riders were all caped in a particular Chinese weather proof garment that looked almost like the potato bag rain coat used by my dad in early memory but instead of hessian it was made of rubberised cloth. Once again facing traffic jams of bicycles in the city which the driver had to manoeuvre his way before finding the road to Wuxi.

I was the only person arriving at this time so uscd the 4 plus hours time to take in the scenery; the driver very intent on his task. Steering the vehicle around the multiplicity of motorised vehicles that made up the traffic as well as dodging the broken down buses and trucks that littered the road; simultaneously he was dodging pot holes, evading the onslaught of bicycle riders and watching for pedestrians who could step in front of the car without warning.

I thought how good a driver they were, not at that time realising than within 2 years I would be following his example as we were allocated cars and tested for a local licence, more of that later. It was wet windy and cold, but I now snuggled up in a sheep skin coat which needed to be removed after some minutes as the driver had the heater on full blast; the road travelled for some time beside a river; on the river were concrete barges some with the same model diesel that powered the mini tractors; others sculled along with one oar but all loaded so that there was only about 10cm freeboard; they carried all manner of cargo.

The country side was veined with canals; small villages and large towns clinging to the side of these waterways each with there own harbour for the movement of goods. This area is part of the grand-canal system and it enabled a vessel to travel all of the way from Canton (Gaunzghou) far in the South to Beijing; There is approximately 10,000 k of these waterways, and they are alive day and night with barge traffic. Occasionally one would see a tug towing a line of barges, predominately made of concrete and occasionally one would see a line of metal vessels slowly making their way; mostly; however; they were single vessels crewed by a man and a woman who with their one child lived their whole life on board; the living space only some 6 m2; as they; under some controlling direction loaded and delivered and then unloaded before loading and delivering again.

The accommodation on board was a small walled in space in front of the motor and behind the cargo, the stove used by the majority of the people; was a small earthen ware device about 30cms tall, a small door covered an aperture near the bottom; this aperture was used to control the flow of air and thus the intensity of the heat coming from the fuel which was round moulds of clay impregnated with coal dust through which holes had been made, making these fuel blocks were common in all markets. These fuel blocks were lit by kindling and although crude were very effective. A large wok placed over the top was all that was required to cook a meal. Some families had two of these devices and in the high rise cinder brick apartment buildings the stairwell was used by the residents as their kitchen using this type of stove. Hence at cooking time the buildings smelled of all manner of spices and food as well a smoke.

The majority of the material used in the construction of the new factory complex came in these concrete vessels crew by a man & woman usually with a small child. China had at that time the so called one child policy for those of the Han group which makes up 95% of the Chinese population. To facilitate this shipping the first thing built by consortium was a boat harbour some 750 meters from the now slowly growing factory complex. To begin with the nearby canal was widened so that boats could tie up without blocking other vessels and a wharf, sheds, crane and mobile gangways was installed to facilitate the delivery of 95% of the materials used in the factory construction.

All of this was later knowledge but as a boating person I was intrigued at the life lived by these boat people; they knew where they were going, there were small harbours constructed for shelter of a night or in bad storms, loading was carried out with bamboo baskets, some times there would be a crew of people to do this work other times just the man and his wife or offsider would complete the task. Walking to and fro like ants; crossing the space between wharf and boat on narrow wooden planks. In all kinds of weather this traffic went on; who controlled it? where were the control points? there was no two way radio, no telephone even; it was and still is a mystery to me.

Sitting in the car I was amazed at our car drivers ability, the ability to pilot the vehicles through this almost heaving mass of road users. Also I had had little experience driving on the right hand side of the road which in Australia is the wrong side; but their powers of concentration needed to be very high. Later will be a description of a trip between Wuxi and Shanghai during one of Ann's early visits but this day I was just happy to once again soak up the sights, sounds and smell of this country which for so long had been hidden behind the bamboo curtain.

Hubin Hotel; this time my home for 4 weeks; had a particularly good kitchen and a large range of dishes all numbered in the Chinese way thus making it easy to order. Over time they were tasted and enjoyed. Wuxi cuisine is slightly different to that of Shanghai and totally different to the hot spicy Sichuan or the rather bland Cantonese dishes. The dining room at the Hubin was very large; hence it required many waiters and waitresses, the Swedish group were now adept at choosing a table that was not serviced by certain of these individuals. These table servers; waiters would be a supreme insult to those of that profession. These table servers were in the main so extraordinary bad, that even with this table selection the service was still appalling. Our ordering system was clear; those present chose a dish from the very large menu and then in by rotation by night one of the group selected another, a large dish for each person was heaped with rice; even with our attention to detail; it was extremely problematical that the dishes would be served in the order that were requested; if we were unfortunate to be shown to a table serviced by one of the bad group the dishes could be cold, often forgotten or served to someone else. For example on Fridays it was almost mandatory that some one would order white fish with chips, white fish were not the small fish served in English pubs but almost like a small prawn, they were battered and deep fried. Very very tasty.

The mandatory serving of rice would almost always arrive first and then could come the chips and they would forget the fish. Or they may bring the fish without the chips, the beer might arrive but not the glasses, hot dishes sometime steaming hot but maybe stone cold. A tourist group would be there with 100 plus people, all of them would be served and we who lived there could wait for half an hour for our orders to be taken longer for them to be served. All of this became more evident after my permanent relocation to China, so on this trip it was still an interesting experience. After dinner we would all retire to the bar, to discuss the day; it was a friendly group but as the only non Swede it was some what lonely as they tended to speak only Swedish.

The weather in January was freezing; the aerators in the fish ponds, large propeller like devices would have frozen spray festooning the float they were located upon. The shopping for warm clothes had provided a lamb skin coat, long johns and thermal singlets; a par of knee high, lambskin, fleece inside boots and long socks made by a lovely lady at Astra A provided warmth for the feet; whilst leather gloves protected the hands. The makeshift offices were not heated; it was against the law to heat houses south of the Yangtze river due to the shortage of coal. As we were in that region we were not allowed house heating. As described before; the local populace wore many layers of cotton clothing to keep out the bitter cold. My role as decided by my Swedish boss who lived in London would be to act as Chief Finance Officer for the South East Asian region this involved devoting 30% of my time in China. In China we worked a 6 day week and the basic task was to design and document a complete set of business operational systems from the ground up. As well, act as secretary to the Swedish consortium members attending meetings, preparing reports; agendas minutes etc. Having 2 accounting certificates and then spent 12 months in 1962 studying by correspondence to become a Fellow of the Chartered Institute of Secretaries and Administrators my CV was more than adequate.

The company drivers were supposed to pick us up at 8.00 am, two cars were necessary to pick up the group of 5 expats for the 6 k journey to the city where we worked in our make shift offices. The time of travel could be anything from 10 minutes to 30 minutes depending on traffic. Now I had the first real experience of the reliability of the Chinese drivers; they were all party members and had learnt their skill in the army driving trucks. Having this special skill meant they were paid more than doctors and were an absolute law unto themselves.

Their function was to provide transport for the Chinese Vice President, all of the expats and incoming visitors; the company had been issued with 3 Nissan 6 cylinder 6 passenger sedans. Overseas visitors were becoming very numerous, China was becoming more open to the outside world so it was an interesting place to visit, particularly if it could be arranged as a business trip. The drivers also provided transport for the Administration staff to arrange travel confirmations and accommodation for the expats and visitors of all varieties. However it was also known that they hired themselves and vehicles to fare paying cadres and any local dignitaries that would make a friendship payment.

Most of them considered themselves well above the average person and treated us as things to be tolerated; in the morning, the cars could be there on time or they could arrive any time later, no amount of words would make any difference. On the first day at the offices I looked for the usual equipment that one expects to find in an office, imagine the surprise when it was discovered that it comprised two abacus; one the property of Ciao; the Chinese CFO, the other for general use ; a telex machine, an ancient thermo fax paper copier and a Chinese typewriter.

This was an interesting device; it comprised a large box containing Chinese characters raised on small metal blocks. Reminiscent of the lead letters used in the old type setting for news papers. A device allowed each of these blocks with the required character to be picked up and hit against a piece of carbon paper that covered the paper on which the document was being typed. The typiste had to know the location of some 1000 characters to type a letter and as 1000 characters is only 25% of the number of characters read by a person literate in Chinese the documents would only have a broad meaning. This lack of characters went some way to explain why so often our documents had different meanings to the Chinese documents. This contributed in no small way to making the job of approving meeting minutes such a long process.

A quick evaluation and as in November last, I hastily realised that my hand written skills with fountain pen and ink bottle plus good old fashioned carbon paper would once again be called into play; there was no computer, although I rectified this very quickly; I had no Dale, my very capable PA in Australia, she would down load my rough drafts from the forerunner in Australia of a PC; In 1980 we called them an intelligent terminal as they had to be connected to a main frame computer. She would correct my spelling (no spell check then) or English then print and bring it to me for signing. There was no strip lister to assist with calculations; the only difference between now and 1951; 35 years ago when I started at the bank; was a supply of carbon paper to make copies as an original was prepared, also a telex machine for faster communication. There were telephones but these were so unreliable that they just decorated a few favoured desks.

Now like my 1951 banking days, I sat on a tall stool at a large sloping desk, removed the gloves, yikes, it was cold, the sheepskin coat had been discarded so was wearing just suit coat over shirt (with customary tie); underneath there was a light long sleeved woollen singlet, under that was the ordinary "chesty bond" to stop the itch from the wool, silk long johns over underpants with woollen suit pants covering long woollen socks up to my knees and ordinary shoes, the office person's working clothes. After 15 minutes it was so cold that the sheepskin coat was replaced as were the sheep skin knee high boots. This attire became my daily uniform for the next 4 weeks.

Day 1; unpacked my trusty travelling office, this comprised; a note book, pens, pencils, rubber, stapler and 2 hole punch, then went looking for the books and records presently being maintained. As per protocol for any system change; first know what is being done then using as much of this as possible at the beginning start to design and write new company policy and procedures. Wait; I had already almost overlooked the golden rule ensure all arrangements are put in order to ensure return Singapore, this eventually became second nature on day 1 of arrival in country, failure to take this step even with 4 weeks in country could and did result in major travel inconveniences.

Now to visit to the accounting office one floor below, where from my first visit Mr. Ciao who had Chinglish together with a young man who could also make himself understood in Chinglish were working. The other staff; all female had been taking English lessons so with difficulty and a lot of mime it was possible to hold a conversation. For myself, having been involved in a number of overseas presentations to groups of many languages had learned to speak a brand of English in a slow and controlled fashion; this was helpful to both sides in conversations with other nationalities. This controlled speak was to become a natural tongue until I ultimately returned to Australia full time in 1999, even then I only returned to bad English whilst in Australia, reverting to slow controlled speech as I travelled the world.

To see how the present records were maintained I asked to see the general ledger (naturally hand written) it was found to be only in Chinese, the numbers themselves even appeared to be of a strange make up. The by now well studied Joint Venture (JV) agreement stipulated that all records had to be in both English and Chinese, naturally I asked the obvious question of Ciao Lu and received an answer "oh yes but". These words were very often the first words spoken in answer to many of my initial questions. The JV had been in operation since 1982; my predecessor had been visiting on a 6 monthly basis for some 3 years, financial reports were derived from this very large general ledger and to date no one had requested that the terms of the JV in regard to financial records be adhered too. The first glimpse into the way the JV agreement was being controlled.

The JV was now almost 4 years old; the full time staff count included all management, technical, office and logistics personnel all being paid just as if the company was operating, money was flowing out at a furious rate, the factory completion was now many months behind construction deadlines; what else would I find on closer examination into this business venture. In many ways I should have stopped my involvement at that point but now there was a growing interest in this country and its people; here was a challenge not to be foregone. How much of a challenge? Well; that was still to be revealed.

Eventually I drove home the point that all company records must be in both English and Chinese so commenced a full translation of all account names in the general ledger as well as ensuring the present strange Chinese way of writing amounts would cease and the more internationally recognised format be used. At a hastily called meeting with the Swedish CEO the Chinese CFO agreed that all of the accounting records would be expressed in the usual international manner; the method they were using was an old method; apparently still commonly used in China and the old CFO preferred his way. Two hours into my new appointment as foreign advisor Finance and Administration and I am starting to upset the natives; however this step was established and agreed upon. Returning to my stool in my so called office, took of my gloves which were put on during the latter discussions to keep some warmth into my hands.

Firstly it was necessary to discover what was the agreed upon organisation chart; so back downstairs to the CEO again, no intercom phones here; he provided a very crude organisational chart of the local management, and the overall Swedish Joint Venture and the Chinese counterparts. This was just a rough sketch on a piece of note paper I could see immediately that the task of bringing modern technology as used in Australia to not only the Chinese organisation but the Swedish one as well; was going to be a large task.

The rough diagram given to me showed; locally a Swedish President, a Chinese Vice President, a Swedish wet products production manager, a Swedish Dry Products production manager a Swedish Laboratory Manager and a Swedish Logistics manager, the Construction manager was also Swedish. Each of these had a Chinese assistant Manager in training. The Finance and Administration was totally Chinese controlled, my Swedish predecessor had recommended that there was no need for the appointment of an expat Finance person. Many years before, I had been the catalyst in having this man losing his position of CFO of a small in house group by an amalgamation of two finance functions and even over time his management skills and international understanding had not improved.

Day one and it was now close to 11.00, legs were losing their feeling and the cold was creeping into the lower body. The many layers of clothes on my upper body were keeping me warm but it was the cold coming up from the concrete floor that was doing the damage. I returned to the finance office to see how they were progressing with my request and noted one of the ladies putting her hands inside the draws of her desk and after a time taking them out; a question and she produced a wool covered devise about 10cm square that was warm. Each person in the room had one of these which they used to keep their hands warm enough to continue writing. The cinder brick building, with the ill fitted windows and doors easily allowed the strong wind that was blowing to come through all of the cracks; without any heating it was like being inside a butcher's cold room. The temperature inside was equal to the temperature outside and that was minus 2; with slow progress on my request and the 11.30 lunch break approaching the question in my mind now centred upon "how to keep warm".

On first entering my office at 09.00 I noted a large pump type vacuum flask in the corner: these were also in all offices in the building; the finance area had a number of these flasks. In the general office there was also a variety of utensils that resembled mugs with a lids and mug sized decorated bottles. In fact each desk had one sitting close to the person; the vacuum flasks all contained boiled water; the mugs and bottles contained green tea.

The pennies dropped; the locals like their green tea, in Astra A the staff drank copious quantities of coffee, in China it was green tea. Could this be the way to keep the inner man warm, so resolved to purchase a mug with a lid; I had seen them in the Friendship store at the hotel.. At 11.30 the CEO knocked and we joined the other expats for the trip back to the hotel for lunch. The first comment from each person was how cold they felt and how it affected their functioning; all following on with the statement that it will get colder. Swedish people complaining about the cold! Complaints from people who live in a country where they almost pray for a white Christmas, for me from milder climes it was perishing.

During this stay, for the 6 days a week that we spent in the office all my warm clothes were worn including the sheep skin knee high ugg boots; after about 3 hours the body became so cold that thoughts were more concentrated on the cold than on work; by 11.00 and in the afternoon around

15.30 hours, you were so cold that a vow was made that for the next winter visit heavy woollen underwear would be packed to supplement the present light underclothes. The Swedish guys coming from their climate were fully equipped with the right gear but even then; they complained of the cold. Working in these cold conditions was difficult, the redeeming promise was however once we get into our own offices at Mashan, heated by our own boilers; working conditions would normalise; how wrong would that prove to be.

One can still feel the welcome warmth of the dining room at the Hubin for lunch; one favourite dish at lunch time was minced pork and chicken with chilli and bean curd (tofu). The meats were minced and then mixed into the bean curd with a liberal sprinkling of chilli; together with large helpings of boiled rice really warmed the inner person; later found that drinking copious quantities of hot green tea; sitting on the high stool and keeping the feet as far off the cold concrete as possible; then and only then could the frozen body syndrome be delayed a little longer.

This 4 week period living at the Hubin Hotel; working in the temporary offices in winter was particularly hard on both body and mind, the lack of office equipment; the requirement for the first time to bring together an actual financial report in both English and Chinese; hopefully based on a confirmable history and then to try to extrapolate that into the mid term future for the next meeting was considered by me to be nothing short of blue eyed dreaming, what a challenge. Ciao lu the CFO was of the old school; his Trading account as a prelude to a Profit and Loss account; the first line was production: why; because under the centralist system in China all production was sold. For the non accountants Western traditional way of starting was with a revenue line Sales.

Trying to prepare a set of estimates that would give the Board an idea on such things as break even points, profitability and cash flow was nothing short of guesswork. The production guys knew their equipment capacity and output, the one marketing guy knew the market was huge (compared to European), Ciao the CFO had no idea about cash flows; payment terms etc. as far as he was concerned what was produced was sold.

The JV strictly stated that the business must be foreign currency neutral, therefore sufficient export dollars were necessary to meet the cost of imports; the production team were not sure what was the possibility of local materials that would meet the stringent pharmaceutical standards, least of all their costs. All they had was an undertaking from the Chinese that they had local factories that could produce materials, chemicals and packaging to the narrow specifications required by overseas

31

health authorities and as well as to meet the fine tolerances required by the imported manufacturing equipment. It was indeed ho hum.

So many unknowns; yet this project was the much vaunted apple in the eye of the Swedish JV partners; a set of estimates were prepared and the Board met over 3 days; once again the first day was devoted to the last meetings minutes. The problem; over and over again; the Chinese members; each from a different bureaucracy needed the Chinese version of the Minutes to reflect them in a good light. A direct translation of the Minutes in English would contain words that translated by a Chinese interpreter when one of the Chinse spoke; apparently this did not always convey the real meaning that the speaker had intended at the time. It could be that the person who did the translation of the Minutes (afterwards my Minutes) into Chinese could not find a suitable Chinese character on the Chinese typewriter to convey the meaning. Resolutions passed at the meeting; could; after the Chinese Board members returned and spoke to their superiors be unacceptable to that bureaucrat or his superior. It was frustrating in the extreme.

It was also very obvious that the Chinese played the wait; and we will prevail game; the Swedish Board Members all had other jobs to attend too, they would come into China for a specific number of days usually 4, day one was travelling to Wuxi. Greetings; inspection tour and banquet. Day 2 and 3 meetings; day 4 finish the meeting and depart to Shanghai; the Chinese knew that if they procrastinated long enough the Swedish group would give in to their demand just to be able to move along in the spirit of so called consensus; how I came to hate that word as years went by; the leader of the Swedish JV was an ex Astra person and although an extremely nice guy he was totally inept in dealing with the Chinese and they ran rings around him.

It is interesting here to make an observation; this was my first contact with this "consensus" phenomena. During the next 14 years working under Swedish Management this consensus style of management became more and more evident; and to me somewhat disliked. The Australian management style is totally different; the CEO is the boss he will listen to all sides of the equation and then make a decision; in European it was not only necessary to listen too all sides of the equation but it was also necessary to let every one who could be mildly affected have an input and discuss their points of view; the decision was more often than not the decision of the group not of the decision maker. This style of management is one that is perhaps more widely used today but it can be very frustrating, and in many cases leads to long delays in achieving an outcome. This was particularly true of the China project as well as another project that I ultimately was appointed to head, working in the head office in Sweden. That was some time after this project.

China at this time was still very much under central control, all production of any kind was for the state, farms, small business all owned by the state, the central economy decided what was to be produced and in what numbers. There was no such thing as fashion, clothes were what were available in the store the day you needed a replacement. Shoes were serviceable, not fashionable. Watching the pedestrians on the streets you would see strange colour mixtures, although at this time in winter there was a predominance of green padded army great coats. The Swedish guys found a source of supply for these coats at $2.00 each; they were very serviceable and warm so eventually all wore them during the winter months going to and from the office.

The other modes of cartage, other than by boat on the canals, was by old trucks, mini tractors, three wheeled bicycles or man pulled or pedalled carts. I have seen funerals using pedal power, even a funeral mini tractor. The body wrapped in white was laid along the tray of the vehicle, the mourners also in white sitting along the sides of the tray. In the case of the pedal power one man was pedalling while the body lay and 4 people sat in the trailer like conveyance. Similarly very ill people were also transported to hospital in these vehicles. It was wet it was cold, what was life like to them?

As arranged, Ann and I met in Singapore to find our new home, the appointment as CFO Asia meant domiciling on that small island. There was a considerable down turn in the world wide economy in 1986 and expat living in Singapore seemed very attractive. We met the CEO of the Asia Region; a person not liked by the people reporting to him; but as my new appointment set out that although my day by day activities were controlled by him I reported fully to the Head of the International Head Office in the UK. The local Manager set out his requirements as far as the choice of accommodation was concerned, it did not fully correspond with what we had been told in our contract, however we commenced the search.

The economic down turn had severely affected the expat rental market in Singapore; a lot of places were inspected although time was limited. Astra conditions did not allow for the house that was our first choice, then we missed out on another place very close to Orchard Road the main tourist area in Singapore; we did however manage to settle on an apartment that was to us luxurious to the extreme. 396 m2 on the 25th floor of Fontana Heights at Ulu Pandan, 4 bedrooms all with ensuite, maids quarters, a sunken lounge room leading down from a large dining area. In the complex; two tennis courts, a swimming pool, gymnasium, squash court, coffee shop, the required security guard centre and of course your own car space. This apartment was to cost Sing $5,000 per month and at that time Aust $1 was equal to Sing $2. After some demurring necessitating a phone call to the boss in the UK, the local CEO agreed to commence all of the necessary procedures for both Ann and I to become Singapore residents and after the 4 day stay we returned to Australia.

An interesting point, throughout the next 4 years this apartment was home. We did not continually live there for any great length of time but yet it was still classed as home. The economic position both world wide and in Singapore improved substantially over these 4 years; Singapore moving; thanks to increasing use of the Island as an Area Office for many trans-national companies; into a very strong economic position; a recommendation would be to read the economic miracle and history of this small island. When the lease was renewed for an additional 6 months in mid 1989 3.5 years after the signing of our original lease the monthly rental was Sing $9000 per month now Aust $ 1 brought only Sing $ 1.25. We could have (money permitting) purchased this apartment in 1986 for Sing $ 500,000 and in 1989 it was still for sale; now at a price of Sing $ 1,000,000. If one looks at those comparative figures in our dollars Rent was $2,500 per month in 1986, in 1989 it was $7,200, the purchase price $250,000 in 1986 and in 1989 $800,000. Yes if only we had raised the money in 1986.

Feeling very pleased with our selection of a new home; we returned to the peace and comfort of the family home at Dural. During the next 9 years we lived in a variety of accommodation, from 5 star hotels to considerable less than one star those of course Chinese hotels; but no where else did we find the serenity and peace of the 1011 ONR Dural.

In the early days of Astra Australia; at my suggestion a social club had been formed, once a year we would close production plus the offices after lunch and all of the company personnel would come together for an International afternoon. All employees were asked to bring one of their special national dishes, just before leaving Astra A at one such afternoon there were counted 93 different nationalities. At that time our total employees throughout Australia was about 300+ people; some cheated of course by claiming the so called country of their forebears but it still showed how multi cultural Australia had become in the 40 years after WW11.

One lunch time I gave a small presentation to whomever wanted to hear about mainland China; even though the bamboo wall had been slowly coming down for some years China was still an enigma to the majority of people, so many wanted to hear of my short experiences, this presentation concluded by saying that Chairman Mao must always be counted in history as a man who saved the Chinese people from their own history. Even after living there for 4 years and subsequent return visits this belief is still strong. Communism, as bad as it became in the later years as Moa deteriorated it was the only way forward for such a large body of people after the Sino-Nippon war.

If one reads the fascinating history of this the worlds most populous nation it is evident that over 4000 years China has seen countless strong rulers challenge the present status quo and formed there own dynasty only over time to revert to the subjugation of the people for their own or forebears wishes until another strong person steps up and once again starts afresh. The prolongation of the non democratic regime as the best way forward for the largest nation on the planet is a question that only my great grandchildren will be able to answer.

In June 1986 the month after my 51st birthday I left Astra A after 18 years as their CFO and with Ann moved to Singapore; there to assume the role as CFO Asia; strategically based in Singapore. How short this permanent appointment was will soon be seen by the reader.

Just after settling into the new position, new office, new home, a telex was received from the UK based boss asking that I go to China as soon as possible for at least 4 weeks; a new set of financial estimates were required and the CEO in China wanted me to become more familiar with the total project. Realising that the job would be so much easier if there were better tools; particularly after being used to a computer assisted environment at Astra A. It is worthy of note in 1986 Astra A was considered the leader in the whole Astra group in the use of electronic data processing (EDP as it was called, "IT" as it is today).

Knowing that ultimately the new electronic tools would take over a lot of the drudgery of clerical effort and this would need to happen in China as well; I approached my boss in the UK for approval to purchase a transportable computer (now lap top), the only one then available was a "Sharp"; the Japanese had started the miniaturisation process well before any of the major US companies had even thought of the word.

The Sharp had a five and a quarter inch floppy disk drive, it was necessary to carry a number of floppy disks one of which contained the "boot" (start up segment) others were needed for any application software such as Lotus and Word Perfect; then there were spare floppies for your data. Lotus 123 and Word Perfect; were the most commonly used applications in 1986. The computer also came with a sensitised paper printer, all together a box some 40cm long 30cmwide and 30cm tall needing 240 volts for power. The all up weight was about 10 k; to me a luggable computer. It's cost Aus $12,000 and at the time was worth every cent. How these cumbersome devices have developed into the light powerful lap tops of today.

Those of my age will know that in 1986 to the ordinary person a computer was some magical device consider then how this device was received by the customs officers in Shanghai, naturally the word was understood but could this small box be such a device, was I bringing in a banned item, 3 hours in front of a group of angry faced green cotton uniformed Chinese customs officers and they were convinced it was real and admonishing me very strongly that it had to leave the country with me, then I could leave and proceed to Wuxi.

Now into the office carrying the magic box. By today's standards this box was so archaic as well as so terribly slow; however in 1986; it was a source of wonder in the office, there was now so many hours devoted to demonstrating its power and flexibility to the company at large. Once the CEO realised how easy it was to prepare correspondence and reports and I was the only person with the skills base; all of this became my function. This was not part of the job description however he was hand writing all reports and correspondence, if a Chinese version was required then he relied upon his secretary to transcribe it on the one and only Chinese type writer. This as you can imagine was a slow, time consuming process; now he found that I could compose his letters and reports; he could change them as necessary, these changes could be quickly made on the computer and a nicely printed document produced. He saw how much more efficient he could become and immediately asked the Swedish JV to look at the procurement of some Personal Computers. From my point of view this was very necessary as it appeared that part of my role was now very much like that of my secretary in Australia.

All of a sudden the role in China changed, instead of being an advisor on Finance and Administration matters it changed to being an integral part of the expat team; the in country CEO recognised this and demanded that more of my time be allocated to him; going from the present 30% to at least 75% in country. The Singapore President complained that he was not getting enough time devoted to his needs. A stale mate; then the in country CEO requested the appointment of a foreign Advisor Administration/Accounting. The position was offered to me after consideration and getting approval to maintain the apartment in Singapore during the initial 2 year posting ; I became The Foreign Advisor Finance and Administration in China. Ann not at all positive about this move; however the contract conditions looked appealing.

The offer included a rise in salary, a travel allowance to be used to rotate out of China every 12 weeks for 1 weeks RR, accommodation in China to be provided in one of the 3 villas that were being constructed for the projected 5 permanent expats allowed under the JV; as well the full maintenance (all utilities were paid by the Company) of the condominium in Singapore plus a car whenever Ann or I or both of us were in Singapore. The small accommodation in China was really only for a single person although we both stayed there for some time when Ann came in country to be with me.

The villas being constructed were an interesting amalgam of so called east and west. Constructed using Chinese materials and labour from a design by a Swedish architect. They were intended to house a family as well a self contained apartment for a single person. The laundry area would be shared as is quite often the position in European as we would later discover. The accommodation down stairs consisted of a large lounge/dining room opening onto an outside patio, the kitchen area was large enough for a good sized kitchen table; a separate laundry area situated in the back entry; a guests toilet and a good sized study. Up stairs was the master bedroom with ensuite; the small self contained flat had a small bedroom, lounge, kitchen and bathroom with large balcony. All white goods were Swedish; the furniture also of good quality from a Swedish supplier. The floors were all parquet.

So my short term position as CFO Asia over and saying my goodbyes to the Singapore office staff we packed our clothes for China it was August 1986 and Ann's first visit. As the gods would have it; on arrival it was drizzling rain; Ann was not convinced that she really wanted to be here in another new country but with my enthusiasm she also became a little excited to experience the sights, sounds and smells of China. A dark drear day making the entry into Shanghai airport and subsequent processing even more foreboding then customs declarations then with me in the vanguard we forced our way through the usual wall of humanity. As a red head she created more than a good a deal of interest when she emerged in front of this solid wall of dark haired, rather plainly clothed people. Like all of us from less populated countries where we have been nurtured to accept our own personal space, Ann had been warned about how lacking this was in Eastern countries but even with this warning she still had difficulties with this invasion to her personal space to her it was a strange new phenomena.

In fact throughout the next 4 years this lack of personal space and even public touching came to her to signify some of the bad things about China and the Chinese.

The journey to Wuxi passed without undue incident although the frequent sight of men urinating beside the road was a little disturbing. Otherwise the usual 4 hours for the 125 k passed without real incident; as an old China hand by now; a steady flow of chatter kept her informed as to what was happening. Also provided details of our in country accommodation which would be a suite at the Hubin. Maybe an explanation of the what was involved in this hotel living should be expanded as it was quite a feature of living in country in those days. Details of some small events will be expanded; these small events really served to make life colourful, often frustrating but with never a dull moment.

One of the simple facts of life, living in a hotel; paid for laundry functions were necessary; the majority of hotels world wide offer guests a laundry/dry cleaning service, the Hubin Hotel was different; it only offered laundry; dry cleaning at this time had not arrived in Wuxi. Chinese laundry with a 24 hour turnaround was very hard on clothes, a pair of underpants had a life of about 6 weeks, at the end of that time they would be threadbare and ragged. Shirts could arrive back either stiff as a board or wilted and limp. Missing articles which were never found were a constant hazard; and many long frustrating hours were spent in discussing with the room staff that a certain number of articles had been placed in the cloth draw string bag but less had been returned all to no avail.

The date for the activation of the extremely unsatisfactory air quality (conditioned too good a word) systems were fixed; heating activated on the 1st of November, and turned off on the 1st of March; cooling activated on the 1st of May and turned off on the 1st of October. Unfortunately the weather does not follow these strict rules, one could be very cold in the hotel before and after they turned on the heating and very hot before and after they turned on the cooling. Bath or showering was an event that depended on luck. The water could be very hot or very cold, it could be clear, or it could be liquid mud; one never knew until the taps were operated. There was a correlation between the tourist season and the availability of hot water for a bath; after a while you learnt whether it was best to shower on your return from the office or wait until the morning it all depended on the number of tourists buses parked in the car park.

Once we moved into our own villas and started to use Chinese products in our daily lives there was gained an understanding of the quick demise of our clothes. Laundry detergent was called "White cat" it was not hard to imagine a black cat placed in a reasonable light solution for a few minutes would be white. Boiled water in a pump type vacuum flask was delivered to the hotel room twice a day and this was used for washing your teeth, or even washing your smalls; during all of our time in China we had to use boiled water for drinking; ice making and even cleaning your teeth. These pump vacuum flasks were a feature of China; every where you went; every office you visited at whatever level there sat one or more of these dispensers of boiled water.

The cleanliness of the rooms at Hubin was good compared to many other local hotels that we stayed in; but still left a lot to be desired; one evening a piece of biscuit dropped beside the leg of the desk in the suite; this piece of biscuit stayed there during those 6 weeks and was still there on return to the same room after two weeks at home in Singapore; are our standard too high.

Shortly after our arrival one of the Swedish expat's two year contract expired and he was replaced, this change gave us the opportunity to move into the (so called by us) "small villa" attached to the hotel, in earlier days it had been the summer house for some official visitors to China before communism as well it was rumoured Moa stayed there when in this region. This gave us a change from hotel living, The villa had 3 bedrooms a common room and a small kitchen and a refrigerator, we were not allowed to cook there but when one wanted a break from the hotel food or when there were too many tourists, the rule was broken.

That reminds of another strange event at the hotel, mostly during the heavy tourist season. They would advise our group (usually we were 6 people but sometimes more) at breakfast although it could be lunch that we as permanent residents could not use the dining room for dinner; there were too many tourists to accommodate so we were excluded. Now we had a choice use the dining room attached to the Chinese hotel next door or go hungry. Similarly we could arrive for breakfast and be told to go over to the Chinese Hotel; strange but true. The hotel for locals attached to the Hubin had an inferior food quality but was much cheaper than the Hubin. Other amenities were attached to this local's hotel; you could get a very good haircut for Aus$1.00 and the ladies could get a styling for Aus$ 3.00; unfortunately you could not read the magazines while you waited.

The food at the Hubin, was recognised as the best food in the Wuxi area; the other large hotel The Tai Hu had a reasonable dining room but still inferior to the Hubin; Tai Hu was still considerable better than the one next too us. Occasionally; of an evening during the tourist season we would wander over to the locals hotel disco bar, we could not enter if there were any locals having a function but if it was empty it was a change from the same room with the same bar staff asking the same questions every night; and of course in season tourists and their guides. How often did we blow apart the tourist guide's painted picture of an open and expansive China.

The construction project was moving very slowly, the JV time frame estimated that the factory, office and villas would be finished and certified in early 1986; however when on the first visit in November 1985, the interior fitting in the office were close; the factory a long way off and the 3 villas were still just shells. This first, and subsequent visits enabled an examination first hand of the Chinese construction methods and materials. The lack of safety concern was appalling; my thoughts are that in Australia we have gone overboard with our OH & S regulations which is petty bureaucracy gone mad; but 1986 China was far below our still lax 1986 standards. Power cords were draped all over the site, inside and outside, there was no effort made to water proof where the two plugs connected; even there were cords running through water puddles across muddy paths. There were workmen toiling on the top of bamboo ladders that at best could be described as poorly constructed; there was no effort made to warn people of the existence of a person above either for their safety or yours; there was no hard hat area and hard hats if worn were made of bamboo.

Tools used were basic, hand tools were of the 1900 design; in fact we purchased a number of new wood working planes and a saw that would have been on my great grandfather's bench. The handles in the four digging implements, namely a shovel, mattock, hoe and rake were literally cut off tree branches. Large metal wheel barrows with metal wheels provided 50% of the load carrying, the remainder was in bamboo wicker baskets, carried on the shoulder using the two pole yoke system employed by my grandfather on his farm in the early 1940s. The procedure for the placement of steel girders; was that used to build the pyramids and all materials for the various building levels was hand carried up ladders; and the task was to construct a hygiene class 3 sterile factory for the manufacture of human infusions and tablets using these tools; will it happen?

Eventually Ann and I took up our residence in the small villa at the Hubin, our fellow lodgers were two Swedish men who each had a bedroom on the first floor; we had a large bedroom on the ground floor and shared the bathroom, kitchen and common room. This arrangement was not ideal but it was better than living in the hotel. There was an old Chinese man who's job it was to clean the villa, the three of us men would leave for the office at 08.15 (drivers permitting) and return for lunch at 11.30, we would then go back to the office at 12.30 returning home at 17.00 traffic and drivers permitting.

The big trouble for Ann was to fill in this time. For all of those in country to fill in between 17.00 and 07.30 the next morning and of course what to do on our 1 day a week off.

Ann would come in country for two or three weeks and then return to Singapore, a lonely existence for us both. More so for Ann as I had work and work mates, she alone in Singapore; in Singapore one would usually join an expat group and they become your entertainment and free time friends; this was difficult for Ann as I was no longer associated with a local group of expats. Our original decision was based on our belief that we would not return to live in Australia until my retirement, our understanding was clearly that in 1988 we would return to Singapore and I would re-assume the role as Chief Finance Officer Asia. We had brought very little with us as we wanted to start a new life with new house and furniture, we had left our pet dogs Australia.

One day sitting on one of the large balconies of our 25th floor condo, watching the black threatening clouds, and realizing that these would soon convert into the usual tropical thunderstorm with great lighting show it was decided, that for company during my absences Ann should have a pet. The condominium rules allowed either a large dog; two small ones or two cats. During the next day the address of a pet shop was found and we made a visit, it was not known what exact pet was needed just we must have a pet as company for Ann during my many weeks absences. In the car and visiting the shop; there sitting in the corner looking all forlorn (a look that dogs of this breed don't have to practice) we saw; or should I say we fell in love with a pug; yes a very much Chinese breed. He became our Foo; unfortunately looking far ahead it was to take some 6 months in quarantine and AU$6,000 to take him home to Sydney so when we left Singapore in 1990 he was given away; a heart breaking very emotional moment.

Back to China and the Hubin; it had a bar that served all manner of western drinks, as told above; the neighbouring Chinese Hotel also had a disco bar as did the Tai Hu Hotel; however these bars were only available to us on certain nights, or if their were no locals in attendance then we could visit. At that time, discoing had not started amongst locals so most evenings we were welcome in to spend our money; however the presence of 1 local traveller or a couple having a quiet drink meant we were excluded for the night. The Hubin bar which catered only for westerners and too expensive for locals was freely available every night. During 1986 and a significant part of 1987 there were few long stay westerner's in Wuxi.

This changed after the long awaited completion of the factory office complex. Now the installation of the complex equipment sitting waiting in storage for us some 12 months could be installed by the supplier's technicians. Hence in late 1987 there was a surge in the number of expats of all nationalities for both our JV and others that had also started in the mid 80s. So for some 12 months of 12 weeks in and one week out living at the Hubin our nights were spent as a small group usually 5 or 6 ; we would meet for dinner and then either go to one of the disco bars or sit in the bar at the Hubin, a few drinks later, partaking either of the local very cheap very nasty whisky or brandy or expensive but nice; imported scotch; we would then retire to our respective rooms to do whatever to fill in the time until breakfast time came around. It was free time boring, work time utter frustration time.

Now there were many visitors from Sweden; technical experts, product specialists, marketing gurus, top divisional managers of any one of the 3 Swedish JV companies pharmaceutical companies or Swede Fund the other member of the JV; all were looking at or contributing to the Chinese quest for modern technology. If the guest was of sufficient importance then the 4 local board members and their off siders would have to be advised. This would result in the inevitable 24 or later in 1987 by law 12 course banquets to attend and survive. Naturally scenic and construction site tours coupled with local and Shanghai stays needed to be arranged. To appease the thirst for foreign currency we were obliged to arrange visits to the various local factories thereby enabling the visitors to see the local Chinese at work, naturally it was expected that all would put their hands deep into pockets to buy the handcrafted articles, mostly of high quality, that were in plentiful supply; as the locals could not afford the prices. To us they were a steal, hand made silk ties for the equivalent of $A2.00.

Wuxi had a large number of industries that produced truly first class handicrafts, it was a centre for the silk trade, fine china ware a speciality, cloisonné and lacquer ware among the best in China; all of this was available at the Friendship Store. My interest however was to see how these items were truly individually hand crafted. There were also a number of worsted mills that were buying quality merino wool from Australia and converting into world quality material. The Chinese Admin manager would arrange these visits, it was expected that the top foreign advisors would attend the banquets as well as go on the tours, meeting with the big names and explain our roles in furthering the Sino Swedish aims of technology exchange. The majority of the visitors were Swedish so as a non Swedish speaker I was initially excluded from some of these activities but as time went on my role developed into a significant member of the welcoming group; particularly after my appointment as the Expat advisor to the Local Wuxi Government.

The large number of these visits resulted in them becoming rather mundane but through them a number of interesting Chinese factors emerged. The banquets were of particular interest; often if local dignitaries were involved there would be two banquets held on consecutive nights, one hosted by the local government officials and the other hosted by the visitors. The one hosted by the locals could be at one of the down town restaurants, Wuxi boasting one of the best Peking duck restaurants outside of Beijing; these events became common place to the in country people, some enjoying the opportunity as a welcome break from the daily grind and to others a boring round of speeches, and replies.

One interesting thing about them was that they would commence usually at 18.30 and end no later than 21.30. The Hubin Hotel had a theatre and during tourist season a show would be performed for our travellers or arriving tourists. Chinese opera was the main feature and after attending a few of these with the in coming guests they were something that had to be endured. I mean endured, it maybe music eastern style but to the western ear it is totally non melodic.

Living in a tourist hotel there was a lot of contact with these; eyes wide open, rubber necking, touring people some were downright strange to both me and the Swedish group. At Hubin they were mostly from the US of A but occasionally a mixed group that may contain some Aussies would arrive; to me these were special occasions. A number of instances come to mind; one evening while sitting waiting for our dinner to be served, the tourist groups naturally being the first to be waited upon and served; a lady approached the table and asked what tour we were on; learning that we were local residents she asked could we arrange her immediate return home; she was on day three of her 10 day tour, the local guide had refused to assist her to go home immediately, she could not abide the Chinese food, so had not eaten anything for three days; her last meal was a so called western breakfast; toast and coffee at the hotel in Shanghai.

As in country people we maintained a small personal (sometimes very personal) supply of western foodstuffs; smuggled through customs using various means. My supply was ample also Ann was arriving with new stock within a few weeks; so the group invited her to my suite after our dinner. This was the one and only time while I lived at the hotel that any in country person visited another in country expats suite, at the small villa we entertained regularly but never in the hotel rooms. In coming visitors who also brought in western food always invited us to partake of some of the much longed for western tucker but always in their room.

The lady enjoyed the food but it did not solve the overall problem; she had another 7 days to go on this trip and would soon be very hungry if she did not eat, the suggestion was made that she visit the Friendship store where they sold a range of biscuits and sweets of Chinese manufacture but of an acceptable western standard; she could also buy western potato crisps and an orange juice concentrate which we used when the smuggled orange juice ran out; if she could exist on those items then our recommendation was for her to continue the tour. We could not assist her to desert the tour; we had been vigorously warned about negative comments to tourists so the local tourist association would take our interference in a very, very negative way. She decided to continue her tour; on her return home she sent a thank you note saying that she did go on to enjoy the experience but not the food.

A traffic story; that encompasses all of the things that one came to hate while being driven and later driving in China, also centred around a visit of dignitaries. All of us were now working in the just, almost completed office building; travelling daily to and from the Hubin every day, now the in the Swedish CEO's car; a Volvo had been delivered and he was granted special permission to drive his car without having to get a local driving license as we did in 1998. His car which had a special registration # 1 eventually mine was # 5. A visiting delegation from Sweden was of such stature that a banquet including the JV Chinese Chairlady was arranged at the Tia Hu Hotel, this hotel was only some 10 kilometres from the factory location. The arrangement was that 4 of us all resident at the Hubin were going to return to the hotel as usual; departing at the 16.30 the same time as the company buses that ferried the employees to and from the city. We would change into our best suits as befitted the occasion collect Ann who was in country at that time and then drive the 5 k to the Tai Hu arriving as scheduled at 18.30.

We left the office behind the bus at about 16.35 but due to traffic conditions we were forced to go straight to the Tai Hu Hotel arriving at 18.40, yes 10k in 2 hours and 5 minutes; Ann was still at the Hubin. There was no way to contact her, we had just sat in the endless procession of cars on a dirt track road; the reason; a bus had broken down; not unusual; on a stretch of road that was under construction there was no way past the bus until it could be moved. The buses two front wheel were at odd angles so it could not be steered, the driver did the only thing possible he commandeered all nearby road users and they literally picked the bus up and carried it the 100+ m out of the way. Ann sat at the Hubin very worried at our non appearance, eventually on arrival at the Tai Hu one our drivers was sent to collect her; she declined as it would have meant a very late arrival at a very important official's dinner.

Road travel during our 4 years was problematic at all times ; in September 1989 just before our permanent departure in November of the same year; a new expressway was opened between Shanghai and Wuxi this we travelled twice before we left; until that time we used various routes; the way changing as we became more familiar with road signs, also to evade lengthy delays caused by road reconstruction work. One of the new group of expats for a chewing gum joint venture, had in late 1988 a new Audi motor vehicle delivered from Germany; on his second trip to Shanghai using a local driver; (he was not yet licensed). The car lost both front wheels ripped off as the driver ran into a large ditch across the road concealed by rain water. Hazards of this type were commonplace.

During 1986 and 1987 we were forced to rely upon drivers to take us anywhere, the original road from Shanghai meandered beside the river and then passed beside Soochow before cutting back into Wuxi; there were originally two level crossings on this road, trains were frequent and very long; all pulled by steam engines. The traffic on the badly maintained road would need to come to a halt as the trains passed; motors were turned off to conserve fuel, it was then a very common occurrence for one or more vehicles; old trucks or buses that were well passed the use by date to refuse to start. There was no way past these vehicles, the road was higher than the surrounding country and lined with trees, spaced at such intervals that precluded any way around the broken down vehicles.

Once this happened the road would become chaotic; it was every man for himself; pedestrians there were many, hundreds of bicycles and the ubiquitous min-tractors would all combine to move through any narrow passages available; other vehicles would also try to force there way through the traffic snarl, some dignitaries would have their drivers put a blue flashing light on the roof to get through, until in the end everything came to a dead stop until the broken down vehicles in some manner moved; the traffic mess would become less chaotic and eventually the slow moving lines of traffic would recommence going forward. These hold ups were a daily occurrence on the Shanghai; Wuxi Road' 4 hours for the 125k trip was the norm, one trip with driver took 7 hours due to an accident with a bike; another 13 hours the subject of a later story in this book.

The basic maintenance of local roads was interesting; one day on the way to the office it was noted that a 2k section of the road just outside of the hotel was covered with large almost fist sized blue metal. This covering over the next few days stretched to where a new road was being constructed, a distance of some 7 k. This surface was murder on the Volvos tyres, but even more so for the multitude of bike riders going wherever they went, some with one, others with two or more passengers; human or animal; clustered aboard. The size of the gravel made it almost impossible to ride over. After some

4 weeks; a 4cm thick covering of smaller size gravel was added together with a white powder that appeared to be lime. Once again we travelled over this surface for some weeks when another 4cm thick covering of much smaller gravel and lime was added. Some weeks after this; a layer of hot tar was added and the road now some 10cm higher had been maintained.

This road maintenance method over the many years had gradually raised the level of the road over the surrounding country in some places by up to 1.5 metres. Old houses in Shanghai were in some cases 2 or 3 steps below the surface of the city street so this was an old and much practiced method. The steep slope created from the fields and villages to the road was a problem for heavily loaded mini tractors. The drivers sitting precariously, some times on an inflated tyre tube to make the ride more comfortable as they did not possess springs or shock absorbers of any kind; they needed a lot of momentum to reach the road level. Their headlong flight and often the unheralded swift arrival onto what was called a road; often caused untold havoc with other road users.

Now living in the small villa attached to the hotel gave a reason to do some food shopping; the fun now really started. At this time there were 3 types of market, the government one; a so called free market where farmers were allowed to sell portion of their produce and the free free market where local people would bribe the local officials and sell some of the produce they grew on their own small plots. Moving; firstly from the hotel to the small villa; then to the small apartment in the new villas on site and to eventually taking over one of the villas this shopping became increasingly important. At first the only interested was in buying some local fruit and vegetables but of course once we moved away from the hotel, serious day by day shopping requirements needs needed to be addressed, we all know what manner of other goods that a house holder requires over time. More of this later.

During the hotel days we became used to a good standard of food from Hubin; the service was appalling, but the menu extensive much of which was very excellent eating; a few were never ordered but in truth they were few. The in country group usually numbered 6 including Ann; the Chinese practice of ordering one dish per person plus one for the table with the unending supply of boiled rice became our norm also. A table of 6 could order any of the 50 odd dishes that were available; two in particular; "beggars chicken" and "chicken in lotus leaves", were full bird dishes; and very very enjoyable; these two dishes have been tried in other restaurants but no where have they reached the culinary level of the Hubin. Wuxi spare ribs a much ordered favourite have never been duplicated and some of the hot sizzling preparations still make the taste buds drool.

During the time living either at the hotel in the suite or small villa; Ann would only come and stay for one or two weeks, life was too boring, after we left for the office she would use the only bathroom and then had the whole boring morning in front of her, a wander through the Hubin garden; read a book in one of it's many small nooks was the only pastime; when she left I was faced with the company of my Swedish colleagues; who tended to use only their mother tongue; although English was a compulsory subject in Swedish primary schools and the level of spoken Swinglish with people the age of my friends was very good.

In the most part this high English skill level was due to the predominance of US movies shown on the then one Swedish TV channel none of these shows were dubbed. In the more populous European countries these movies were dubbed but it was not considered necessary in Sweden. One evening sitting and left well and truly out of the conversation I interrupted, excuse me gentlemen; I have a choice; sit here quietly like a dummy, learn Swedish or Chinese; as Swedish is spoken by only 8 million people and local Mandarin by some 1 billion people the time would be better served learning Chinese and talking to the locals; they got the message and from then on English was spoken whenever I was with the group.

When ever Ann came in country we would try to meet at the airport in Shanghai; these brief sojourns to Shanghai were welcome breaks from the day by day drudge at Wuxi, even though the 9 + hours of the to and from trip were hair raising, to say the least. It was my practice to always accompany Ann on her way home as far as Shanghai. One day we sat as usual back seat driving; while discussing minor matters as one does in a car; we had reached a spot that was now well known on the trip; it was about half way to Shanghai the road was straight visibility good for some 1 k, when a man on a bicycle was noticed riding in the middle of the road; this was not a usual occurrence; single riders tended to ride as close as possible to the edge of the roadside, a group may spread across the road but single riders no. Just as this was noted by the brain cells; the rider decided to turn into a village that was close by on the left so did a hard left turn immediately in front of our car.

The driver tried his utmost to stop but it was just impossible; a collision; the rider was thrown across the bonnet of the car and onto the left hand road way. Ann as usual sitting behind the driver; the safest seat in the car; me sitting beside her, the man came to rest right beside my door. Quick thoughts; will he be lying in a pool of blood, slowly dying, will our driver be carted off by the police; leaving us stuck half way between Wuxi and Shanghai. Thank goodness we were over-nighting in the new Hau Ting Sheraton hotel; Ann would hopefully be aboard her flight out tomorrow. The bicycles in China are built tough, the riders even tougher; the bike had been struck at the front forks the man airborne over the bonnet and onto the road; with by now the usual congregation of pedestrians and other road users swarming around the car and the injured man, our driver jumped out and ran around, I opened the door and the rider sat up, rubbed his arm and leg, his much mended trousers had another gash in them but there was little blood and no gore.

A quick comforting word to a horrified Ann, and then assisted the man to his feet; the bicycle would need a new set of front forks or maybe a weld job by the local bicycle mender; there was one of these every 10 or so klick's beside the roadside; maybe just a heat and then straighten them. Now their were other question flooding through our minds; would the police arrive and cart off our driver; should we give the man some money for his trouble; Ann thought that this would be a good move; the crowd around were very volatile; there were some for and some against our driver. This idea was put away; there were a lot of people crowded around (we were now sitting in the car) one never knew who could be in the crowd; we only had FEC paying this and we may be accused of trafficking in foreign money.

Using all of the then available sign language vocabulary the position was discussed with the driver; he made me understand that the majority of the crowd were against the rider; some of them had seen his actions and knew it was his fault; people from the nearby village were now drifting across from the fields and the rider; obviously known, was being assisted by some concerned locals apparently friends; the thought was that he could be in shock but he seemed to be coping, although still sadly inspecting his battered front forks. The driver talked at length to some one assumed to be the village chief as he had some control over the 50 or so people who were minutely inspecting this strangely coloured lady in the car. After about an hour of discussions the trip was resumed, we extremely thankful that it ended as it did. A pleasant night at the Sheraton; morning saw us both to the airport; Ann to fight the sea of humanity and officialdom at the airport, while I made my lonely way back to Wuxi and work. The driver had some chores in Shanghai so it was arranged that he would pick me up at the airport after seeing Ann into the building. Officially non passengers were not allowed into the small departure check in area although a "friendship" payment would enable me to be her vanguard pushing through the crowd and then safely to the first customs check before the airline check in counter.

This accident showed up a particularly bad hearing situation for a large number of residents in China, the level of noise in a factory was not controlled; working 10 hours a day 6 days a week in an environment where the decibel level was at best just painful to the ears; created a multitude of people who suffered some kind of hearing problem. The road rules at the time in China contained a provision that when passing another vehicle on the road the horn must be activated; bicycles of course were not counted; if they had been the horn would quickly wear out; our driver had hit his horn as we were approaching the rider, the rider did not hear the blast, neither did he look to see if any traffic was approaching, once again a not unusual occurrence; he was just going about his ordinary business in his ordinary way. Cars were not a road feature but an occasional happening, loud noised trucks and buses could be heard but the quiet engine of a car not audible.

There was a prior mention that during the early days in China whenever a visiting delegation arrived then we would accompany them on factory tours; this way the in country people could spend time with the visitors; it also allowed us to get some idea of the various manufacturing concerns that were in Wuxi; it was naturally expected that some FEC would be spent in these factories; therefore every factory had a small shop created to part the visitor from their FEC; a worrying sign of private enterprise to come. Silk production was a big industry in Wuxi; many hundred of moue (a Chinese land measurement of about 800m2) was devoted to the cultivation of the mulberry tree; for those interested there are many ancient stories and beliefs about the mulberry tree, it is considered that every part of it gives a benefit to mankind.

Untold billions of silkworms feed on a diet of rich mulberry leaves and then weave their magical thread into cocoons; some are kept to breed next years crop but the majority are collected; after soaking in hot water the end of the thread is located; the fine golden thread is then unravelled onto spools. The silk spools are collected and woven into the most sensuous of all materials. Night wear, lingerie, ties; jackets are made from this silk fabric. Magical embroidery conjured up on garments to evidence that the wearer is a person of substance; sounds magical does it not, the result may be but the labour conditions to bring this into being is horrendous.

A visit to one of these big industrial undertakings was revealing; this factory complex employed many hundreds of workers; wages were US$ 30.00 per month, plus all allowances, more of that later. A visit to the silk worm operation was not allowed; but the resultant crop of billions of cocoons all in large cloth bags. Sitting in a long row each person had one of these large bags on the left side. Each operator sat on a high stool before a gently sloping open drain about 10cm wide; the water gently flowing by gravity to the end of the line where it was reheated and started its cycle gain. The operators were spaced an arms length apart and about 20 to a line. The water was above 50degrees C; the operators all women, picked a handful of cocoons up and placed them in the slowly flowing water; she then proceeded to locate the single thread on each cocoon and attached it to one of the 10 or so spindles that were spinning at eye height; once the thread was attached she then had to ensure that the unravelling cocoons dangled in front of her until all of the thread was removed, she did this for 10 hours a day 6 days a week, her fingers due to the continual immersion in water that we would find far to hot to bath; were red and crinkly like a well soaked prune, all this activity accompanied by the noise of the belt driven spindles snapping and rattling on the big driving wheels. The noise far above our acceptable level.

As each cocoon was unravelled the small spindle containing the silk was removed and dropped in to a near by basket; periodically these baskets were collected and taken to the spinning room; here the spindles were placed onto another machine and each fine golden thread spun together on to a larger spool, the eye sight of these operators was amazing; they could pick the oh so fine thread off the small spindle and attach it to the spinning machine so quickly and unerringly, all of them appeared to be young ladies, the resultant large spools of silk thread was finally taken to the weaving rooms. Large cavernous rooms with big machines all driven by belts, the plain fabric rooms each with 100 or so looms were noisy but not nearly as noisy as the rooms that contained the embroidered cloth looms.

In the embroidered cloth area the huge looms; each with a separate pattern controlled by a series of holes on hard cardboard sheets (like a pianola roll); these cards were joined together with hard string and then a belt driven wheel slowly placed one card after the other on the device which read both the weft and the shuttle requirement for that particular thread; once selected the shuttle rocketed across the material width with a loud bang; another card; another selection; another almighty bang. The noise was incredible; it hurt just to stand at the door, further inside the noise escalated until it felt as if you were walking through a wall of impenetrable noise. Even on leaving the room ordinary conversation was impossible as the ears were still ringing with the incessant clatter and bang, rattle and bang; of 100s of shuttles as they shot across between the cross fibres.

We had occasion to visit many different types of factories and none of them provided any protection against the most obvious health affecting operations. On our many trips to Shanghai we passed beside a factory that had large piles of sulphur visible in the yard, I don't know what it produced by at certain times you would see a work shift leaving the factory and their clothes were covered with a yellow residue. Red rimmed eyes looked at you as you passed them by in your air-conditioned car, the acrid smell of the factory permeating the vehicle as you slowed to a walk, a manoeuvre necessary to negotiate a hard right hand and then left hand bend that led onto a narrow bridge filled with bicycles and pedestrians making their way home.

No wonder that people on bikes failed to hear the strident noise of the horn; the mini tractors had no silencer attached to the exhaust so they also contributed to the noise level on the roads, this coupled with a road rule that specified that you had to signify your passing intention by blowing your horn before passing a motorised vehicle; all in all driving in China is incessant loud noise. Until you came near a hospital or some special place where there would be a sign indicating "no horning".

A mention above of "Allowances" being paid on top of the monthly salary; there were a number of allowances that were added to a person's wages, these could be money or they could be food stuffs. There was a bicycle allowance; anyone who was required to travel more than a certain distance from their home either to work or to the nearest bus station that would take them to work was entitled to a bicycle allowance. This enabled them to purchase a bike and then pay to have it parked at the bus station. Each person was allowed a certain quantity of rice per day according to the type of work they did; an office worker received only half of the rice that a manual worker would receive. There was a cooking oil allowance, and if you were well up in the hierarchy and had a gas ring allocated to you then you could also get a gas allowance. It was a strange system; however it meant that all had enough staple food to live, it eliminated beggars and followed the communistic dream; all people have an equal share. Ho Hum.

Returning to the factory construction project; adjacent to the now useable (note useable not finished) office block was the staff dining room; this was to be fully equipped with state of the art Swedish equipment as well as the necessary Chinese rice cookers and the most necessary of all utensils; woks. The kitchen staff had already been employed, they were operating in a make shift kitchen attached to the bicycle garage; a feature of all of the large grey cinderblock apartment houses that had to be built for our workers. In these makeshift kitchens the staff prepared meals for those employees still not required to go on the bus to the factory; they also prepared dinner at a small price for those who did not want to cook. One thing that communism did was to spawn millions of these drab featureless grey cinder brick apartment houses of many floors and often built right along the length of a street without gardens or trees. They are synonymous with all the old communist controlled countries, which I later visited, street after street of these buildings littering the landscape in places like Warsaw, Budapest and the outskirts of Prague, and surely every other like city; Wuxi was no different.

With some 40 workers now at the factory site on a daily basis some of the cooks were now required to earn the pay that they had been drawing for over 12 months and prepare meals for those at Mashan; the factory location. A small building attached to what later became one of our local food supply shops was rented and a makeshift fireplace built that would heat 2 large woks. The reader must realize that the majority of our workers were the product of the so called "Cultural Revolution"; that period between 1966 and 1976 that the masses in China; spurred on by an old megalomaniac Mao wrought havoc on the cultural history of China. All learning institutions were closed, ancient relics destroyed, scholars, professional people all vilified with many dying during these purging sessions; old historical building razed to the ground, every one you talked to had stories to tell of this time, and I shall recount some of these stories as they arise in our travels.

The 200 plus people now employed, and paid while they waited for the factory to be completed were of three groups, those who had recently finished university studies, an older group of those who had survived the cultural revolution although their life had been affected by it and those whose education had been disrupted when all schools and universities were closed. The drivers and cooks were all military trained; having been an army cook I knew the quality of training but these army cooks were beyond comprehension. The food prepared for the staff albeit in rather rough conditions was almost non recognisable. The expats would walk the 300 metres to this make shift dining room; where a special table would be set up and a number of dishes containing barely recognisable vegetables and meats (predominately chicken and pork) swimming in grease and some kind of sauce were placed on the table. Each was given a small bowl containing rice; these were constantly refilled if required and using our own chopsticks we served ourselves from these dishes. These lunches were endured as these were our cooks preparing the meals for our staff. Our staff appeared to be enjoying lunch why should we complain. Once we took up residence in the villas; all expats living on site would return home for lunch those still living at the hotel were often invited to the villas for lunch. Even supplying proper facilities and equipment did little to improve the culinary expertise of the so called trained cooks.

During the first visit in 1985 a lack of specific serving utensils for the ordered dishes in the Hubin dining room was noted, this was the norm; every one used their own chopsticks or eating irons to serve themselves from the central dish, it took us a long time to convince the dining room staff that a separate spoon or another set of nimble sticks (chopsticks) should be available to serve from the food dishes. Over time we managed to create this habit of the staff providing separate chops sticks or spoons set beside each dish with a spare set of chops sticks beside the nominal host. This spare set of chopsticks was necessary as the host would always serve the guest of honour small titbits from the dishes and using your own chopsticks for this went against our normal hygiene habits. Over time the practice of the dining room staff of actually serving the guests at formal banquets became the norm but in the early days it was serve yourself with your chop sticks or your spoon if it was soup. These were small improvements and as one travelled and western culinary habits were introduced to hotels catering for tourists; it took a long process of time but this lack of personal eating hygiene sat heavily on those thrown into the chaos that was mainland China in the early and mid 80s.

The factory site at Mashan was on an area of land that had been reclaimed from Lake Tai by the so called educated professional classes during the Cultural Revolution, one medical professor who became a confidant called it the great chaos. These educated professional people and even their spouses were forced to repent their combined cultural sins by hard labour; usually with little food. This site for the factory and three villas was below the level of the water in Lake Tai, the water held back by a large wall on which a concrete road leading to the local water treatment plant had been constructed. This plant as well as supplying the local populace was to be the source of water for our production facility. Being below the surface of the lake; water drainage canals had been dug behind the villas and factory area. These canals now a feature of the landscape; however, it was necessary to build special pump houses for both the villa and factory areas to lift the ground water to the level of the adjacent lake. Heavy rain would bring outside construction to a standstill; the operational part of the factory was constructed on the first floor level; some utilities were installed above the lake water level, but the large ground floor open space partly used to house the main utilities supply pipes; but in the main was vacant wasted space, this design did however make the factory look a lot bigger than what it really and was, however the design was very necessary in the event of flooding due to a break down of the ground water pumps.

To paint a picture; the factory land was secured by a large 2m + white plastered brick fence topped with broken glass, bounded by the canal at the rear with farm fields in the front; it stood about 300 metres from the main road; two concrete roads accessed the front and rear of the site, a block of the usual grey cinder brick houses fronted onto the front access road and the once again grey cinder brick toilet for the houses was across this factory road. The houses were occupied by the peasants who farmed the land in front of the factory; next to them and fronting the access road was a farm building and large concrete slab where the rice and wheat harvest was threshed and winnowed, all by hand and a large electric fan. During the wheat harvesting season the hand reaped wheat would be laid on the road; vehicles running over the sheaves would dislodge the grain and periodically the peasants would remove the sheaves and sweep up the grain from the road. I don't know how they removed the dirt and pebbles form the swept up grain but I am sure there was a system.

At the front and back of the factory where the two roads entered; were 24/7 manned guard houses that monitored all access; the back road led from the harbour; built behind a number of small factory buildings which fronted the main road, one factory which made shoes, and another (the old kitchen) now sold staple supplies. Adjacent to the factory and protected on three sides by a 2m white high plastered brick wall topped with broken glass was the villa area. This area comprised the three expat villas, designed to hold a family and a single fully contained apartment. A canal ran along the back of the villas and was unfenced until an incident involving one of the many boats. The crew seeing a nice grassed lawn felt it made nice relaxation area; so a bamboo fence was erected with locked gates prevented further incidents of this nature. To access the villa area one passed through two large iron gates that the residents were supposed to keep locked. A pump house was situated both at the front and rear of the villa area; these were also kept locked to stop itinerant workers lodging there.

A number of very rough sheds had been hastily assembled as work huts, one of these eventually became the home of 4 of our manual workers, it was only about 12 m2 and the walls were made out of many small pieces of scrap timber; beside this shed was a well constructed open shed containing a large concrete mixer with attendant sand and metal dumps, this shed was luxurious compared to the one used as house. The grey cinder brick farm workers houses were a feature of the landscape all around Jiangsu Province; where ever one travelled these houses abounded; usually 3 stories high; therein each family had two rooms; piped water was provided but not usually to each unit; there being centralised water pick up points; a toilet block was constructed usually some distance from the residential buildings as they were well known to reek very heavily. The output from the toilets usually was piped into storage pits and then used to fertilize the surrounding farmlands. As toilet blocks were some distance from the housing buildings wooden buckets (so called honey pots) were used by the residents and emptied during the day time into the pits.

The toilet for the village on our access road was actually diagonally across the road itself; the effluent flowed into drains that led to the fields; inside a bucket kept under a usually leaking tap served to flush the toilet and perform personal ablutions. The toilets were of the squat variety, two concrete slabs about 15cms apart were placed over a large drain, this drain led to the fields outside. Those using the toilet crouched one behind the other or if they wanted to talk facing each other. This system certainly did not pander to modesty and to our mind with "bowl toilet spray" plus a multiplicity of blue loos" was dreadfully crude but that was the moderninity of China in this period, they probably still exist in parts of Wuxi even today.

All housing units had a "honey pot"; a wooden bucket with a wooden lid and rope handle used for in house toilet purposes. In the cities these honey pots were collected every morning usually by older women who pulled a two wheeled large barrow moving from house to house. These honey pots would be delivered to a nearby depot; the depot would usually be beside a canal where barges were moored. The pots would be emptied and washed with water from the canal, the washed pots used as replacement pots the next day. The barges would take the effluent to a farm area where it was emptied into large tanks for distribution onto the farm land. This collection process was not needed in the country side as each village had either its own collection tank or like the village near us; a drain leading directly onto the field. In some instances individual houses or large set of units would have their own tank and the gas emanating there from was used as a cooking fuel. This use often led to explosions as the leaking gas was ignited by accident. The toilet block fronting our access road always provided the visitor with a whiff of country toilet perfume if they did not have the air conditioning functioning in the vehicle.

All water had to be boiled before personal use the same purification was necessary for any farm produce; the rule was if you could not boil it or peel it you did not eat it. In season, grapes and strawberries were in abundant supply but could not be boiled simple washing was not good enough; on a visit to Australia we obtained a supply of water purifying tablets; now these fruits could be soaked in a solution for some time before enjoying them. The constant state of awareness regarding this health problem could be almost nightmarish; however failure to follow the simple rules would have dire consequences. This situation was not just China specific; other popular destinations in Asia were the same. We had an R&R period and decided to go to Puket a holiday island not yet famous in Thailand. Arriving first in Bangkok; naturally staying at one of their opulent hotels; Ann inadvertently forgot to use the specially provided water to clean her teeth, for the next few days her tummy a constant reminder of the error.

Before leaving China for the 1986 Christmas break; all in country people had a big party; looking forward to returning home and in 1987 moving into the villas; this was a constant question asked of the CEO "when will we move from the hotel?". Winter again, and although there was now a boiler working at the factory to provide office heating the office staff, preferred to turn them off and open the windows, their body shape had bulked out as they now wore many layers of clothes, the preference was to leave these clothes on; so the heaters were kept off. This meant that whenever a need to visit the accounts office arose it was necessary to don padded jacket before walking down stairs; alas to keep a room warm it was necessary to tape up the gaps that were around the window and door opening, the biting wind would whistle through any small crack that was not taped.

We returned to Singapore and then to Sydney; the usual wonderful family Christmas celebration at Dural. It was a welcome relief from both hotel and apartment living. To walk around the garden in the peace of Dural, to breath the clean air that surrounded you, to drink the water direct from a tap, eat a tomato without soaking it in purifying solution, munch on an apple without peeling it, simple ordinary every day pleasures enjoyed by Australians without thought; and oh so missed in China and to a certain extent in Singapore.

Christmas 1986 and the infliction of a bad cold; at this time my smoking habit was consuming up to 40 cigarettes a day; the duty free allowance on entering China was 4 bottles of alcohol and 400 cigarettes; during the tourist season western cigarettes were available at the Friendship Stores so it was no big problem, only once was it necessary to resort Chinese cigarettes but that was an excuse to quit. In China, cigarettes, particularly western brands were the common "friendship" medium. With this cold persisting identified by a persistent cough usually started by a cigarette; so one day at a time; making no promises I refrained from smoking; ultimately it was recognised that there was no need for them and on return to China some 4 weeks later; carried them only for the use of others and of course the ubiquitous "friendship" payments.

Train travel still pulled by the mighty steam engine was the way to travel between cities in China, there were three classes, soft seats, hard seats and no seats. In the early days we quite often caught the train between Shanghai and Wuxi, on one occasion even travelled to Nanjing using this means. In many ways it was far preferable, reliable and comfortable than travelling by road and plane travel was precarious at best. Our use of train transport for short journeys ceased once the three expats took delivery of their promised Volvos. We would always try to travel soft seat class for obvious reasons; a separate waiting room and young ladies would walk the soft seat carriages selling fruit, cakes, lollies and green tea; all of the seats had a lace covering on the head rest and they were relatively clean.

A one off experience in hard seat class was a very trying experience, firstly there was no seat and so stood for the 2 hour journey, secondly the travelling companions had all manner of luggage in all types of containers, food was being consumed; there were even chickens in a bag. Personal space had no meaning and there was a constant movement of passengers along the aisles. It reminded me of a flight from Bangkok once, a welcome first class upgrade then a wander down the aisle of economy class. The plane was full of Muslims on pilgrimage to Mecca, the next stop was Bahrain; they were carrying all manner of cooking utensils, food was being eaten from cloth bags and the whole area was cluttered with their belongings. Thai airways certainly looked the other way on this pilgrim flight.

As the only westerner on the train I was the source of some wonder; it seemed that people would want to walk past just for a close up look, within the confines of the rocking train it sometimes was a very close look. The lack of personal space in public and Chinese inquisitiveness is something that you never get accustomed too; for Ann with her red colouring it became a source of constant annoyance when ever we ventured out into the public arena. There were many instances when children would walk up and touch her, men and women would stare as we walked past and it was not unknown in a shop to have a crowd around us when we were standing at the counter to purchase an item.

In China at the time the political climate was very volatile; one never knew if the openness was going to continue or if the bamboo curtain would once again be closed. At a meeting late in 1986 most of the Chinese directors and their assistants (they were like nuns they always travelled in pairs), were dressed in what we would call western clothes, suits (very rough cut) with shirt and tie for men and women in skirt and blouse, half stockings were the go, panty hose not yet available. That night on the BBC there was a news report that spoke of some unrest in the Chinese politburo, the next day all Chinese members arrived in Mao jackets and caps.

The only source of outside news was a small multi band short wave radio; this was occasionally blocked out by we assumed local interference; Radio Australia was our favourite although the Swedish group listened avidly to the BBC. There was an English edition of the China Daily; also any incoming person was asked to bring in Hong Kong news papers. It was interesting that Astra International's rules of engagement for overseas postings provided that a daily edition of a Stockholm newspaper was mailed to the expat. The HR people mostly forgot about this rule for non Swedish expats until the person found out about this benefit; then that person had to fight rather hard to be treated equally. It was interesting to see how work would stop when one of the Swedish guys received a bundle of papers; mundane news from home was consumed, such was the loneliness of being behind a possible lowering bamboo curtain.

On the return from Australia in January 1987 the timing of the move from the hotel to the villas was a daily topic, every one wanted to get away from the hotel and the daily journey between the hotel and the office, you never knew how long this trip would take. On one occasion taking a trip to Wuxi to visit the local bank manager, accompanied by an interpreter we departed Mashan; on the way into Wuxi there was a large army base. The road was under construction so the driver decided to drive through this base as a way around the traffic block that maybe could take hours to negotiate. As we drove through this army area a large truck filled with men standing up passed by. Each man had a cardboard sign around his neck with their hands manacled to a pole that was at waist height; soldiers stood in the truck facing the men their backs leaning on the truck cabin; guns at the ready. When questioned, the interpreter explained that the signs displayed each man's crime; they would be driven round the base and then executed; their family would be charged with the cost of the bullet; to the interpreter this was a common occurrence and not even worthy of comment.

The beginning of 1987 saw the arrival of a number of other JV groups; also we had a considerable increase in the number of technicians sent to install the complex equipment needed to manufacture pharmaceutical products. All of these technicians and many of the new JV start up people lived at the Tai Hu Hotel. At one time there were over 30 installation technicians from 5 different European nations located at the hotel together with other JV groups from an Italian printing JV and a chewing gum manufacturer JV from Finland. There was nothing for them to do after they returned from work in the afternoon which depending on traffic was usually about 17.30; although the working week was 6 days; the loneliness; the absence of women and drinking to dispel this isolation; caused trouble to develop among our group as well as the other groups.

Our company ethos forced by the local bosses stipulated no fraternization with the locals; this was also the rule clearly defined to the hotel by the local authorities; with little to occupy this large group of men; every second night they would gather in the sparsely furnished but garishly lit disco bar; no locals allowed, no ladies except for the occasional visit of one of the men's wives or partners; only alcohol to ease the loneliness. With alcohol came arguments and with arguments came dissention among the varying groups. There was even a situation where an engineer arrived accompanied by his girl friend; during his 6 weeks stay the girl friend decided another man from another JV was more impressive than her original partner, this almost caused a riot. Administering these problems became a source of annoyance for the CEO and it also involved me as his Administration Manager.

This CEO had one of the most positive attitudes I have ever seen; however over time one could see him wilting, he was constantly fighting battles on four fronts; the Chinese VP was very supportive but an old man who had suffered badly during the cultural revolution; his wife was an invalid; all he wanted a quiet life before retirement. To accomplish this in the Chinese political environment required a "bamboo bend with the wind approach". The local authorities were becoming demanding; this national manufacturing show piece was not yet in production; the Swedish JV were under pressure to make this project work; they too wanted to bask in the limelight; so they were pushing for quicker progress; the expats were becoming disenchanted with the slow progress coupled with the extreme physical and mental conditions that they were continually being asked to face; the local company Chinese managers were under pressure from their party bosses to assume greater control to evidence that Chinese could run highly technical factories. On top of all of this the sometimes physical fights amongst the technicians was the last straw; black eyes, facial bruises and highly emotive behaviour in the work place all were evidence of a night at the Tai Hu.

An example of the drinking capacity of one of these groups, every second night 4 of them would gather at a small table in the disco bar, drinking cans of Chinese beer (very inexpensive) until each man's stack of cans reached the ceiling, it was not a single tower of cans but built on a base so that it was free standing. I never counted them but one would imagine each man would need to drink at least a dozen cans to reach their targeted bi-nightly height. Two litres of duty free alcohol does not last very long in an average six to 8 week in country project so recourse was often to the local liquor, these inexpensive; 50c a bottle rough spirits caused the most horrific hangovers; many an argument would occur as these men; trying to install, test run and then train local engineers in the maintenance of this complex equipment while battling substantial hangovers.

Eventually the CEO was advised that his villa was available however there was no heating (it was winter) nor was there any power for the air conditioning system, cooking or light. In desperation and to make a point he decided to move in and spent a number of freezing weeks living in the sub zero temperature villa. He would have dinner at the hotel and then drive back to his lantern lit, lonely and far from cosy villa. Eventually all of the villas were ready; my home became the very small self contained own entry apartment on the first floor of villa #2. it did however have a huge balcony; and so made ready for Ann to arrive. Hotel living does not imply shopping, cooking, washing and cleaning, this was the new challenge. At the time fresh local produce was very seasonal; there was no inter province trading in foodstuffs; in fact food for sale at the free market only comprised goods locally produced. This somewhat harshly policed regulation was left over from the Great Leap Forward movement where every village was supposed to be self sufficient in all things. This national regulation was enforced up till the winter of 1988 when movement of produce between provinces was finally allowed.

At one time this particular regulation saw the death of some 1.5 million people in a province that was suffering from drought while the adjacent province had food aplenty; this event coupled with the Cultural Revolution and the gang of four short era; signalled the end of the Moa Dynasty. Another effect of this rule saw the northern cities in autumn stock up with the local favourite green vegetable; cabbage. It is said that the average Chinese eats some 94k of cabbage per year, like rice it is a staple, the country side around the northern cities like Beijing are too cold to produce cabbages in winter so they were stockpiled in the streets during autumn, making them available during the non growing months. In 1988 this practice was no longer necessary so winter in Beijing saw the streets reclaimed from their cabbage piles.

Working 6 days, usually Sunday was the day of rest and shopping, my Swedish landlord and I accompanied by our next door Swedish neighbour did our first real shopping to stock our pantry and laundry cupboards. There were no supermarkets, all shops were government owned; non of the three of us could read Chinese, all products locally made; we could only rely upon the pictures, if any, on the packets or bottles to determine the contents. There were three small general stores near the new villas so we stopped there on our way to the city, just an exploratory venture.

This initial stocking was real time hit ands miss; as an example; what we thought was vinegar was soy sauce, what we took for plain cooking oil was chilli oil, if possible we tried to get behind the counter where bulk stock was in open containers, this enabled identification but this was often stopped by the shop assistants; sugar was discovered by this method; once you found what was needed it was easy as you would take a sample or an empty container to the shop and the mostly helpful shop assistant would quickly find your replacement stock. On the first foray we purchased 4 bottles of unknown product however at 20c cents a bottle it was not a big investment in mistakes. The amazing thing about shopping was how it was passed across the counter to you. The modern plastic bag usage had not yet invaded China, we watched patiently as the shop assistant bound these four bottles together with string then deftly made a carrying handle at the top; other purchases were put onto brown paper and a nice parcel was constructed. Here I was again back in the 1940s shopping in Ballina in far northern NSW my home town. This shop lady became one of our friends as we used this local shop for our basics. However chocolate, biscuits, flour, beer, even Chinese wine was purchased in the city.

As for payment we had to rely upon the honesty of the shop keeper; in the early days this was not a problem but as time proceeded and the locals realised that money could be grafted from the rich foreigners then we would be charged considerably more than the locals. However after many days of shopping one could tell if you were being gouged or just ripped off and pass back the produce when usually a more reasonable price was obtained. At this time we were not allowed to use the local currency so all our purchases had to be FEC, the shop keepers had to be quick as quite often the usual crowd of inquisitive locals would contain a smarty who grabbed the FEC from your hand as you passed it across and replaced it with local money. They knew that they could buy imported cigarettes from the Friendship store or even trade the FEC for twice the local money. By price and quality comparison it was far below the standard and cost associated with Sydney; so one did not mind paying the money; eventually however it became a blatant rip off; in the early days some honest locals would remonstrate with the stall holder over a high charge unfortunately this honesty changed for the worse over time.

1987 the building and equipment installation was now almost complete; to us just as significant the opening of a western hotel (the first) in Shanghai, it as custom dictated also had an attached Chinese hotel. This hotel was a joint venture between the Shanghai local government and Sheraton Hotels, a number of the top management were from Australia including the head chef. Things changed considerable with this opening; to remain competitive (a word not yet in the Chinese vernacular) the past cash on booking, three day notice; no credit cards procedures; disappeared overnight. Of course prices for a room also increased astronomically particularly in the old former glory days hotels; like the "Peace".

This opening the first of many with the Hilton opening within a few months had a big impact upon our lives, we could; drivers permitting travel freely to Shanghai knowing that a room would be available, a good western meal could be enjoyed, there would be service and cleanliness, a friendly smile as you checked in and a clear English, "Can I help you". An added benefit the hotel was on the edge of town and we could buy (expensive) steak which was impossible to get in Wuxi.

The factory was not yet in operation thus we would go shopping on Sundays, this always an experience; first a wander around the government operated market to check the quality and availability of food basics. The government market; adjoined the so called free market and then on the footpaths leading into both of these markets were the free; free market vendors. Rarely did we buy from the government market, preferring the freshness of the free or free; free market stalls. Like any well organised market there were stalls set up in rough baskets with stall holders who vied for your business, putting their produce in front of you if they saw you inspecting a neighbours goods, it was always an experience not always fun.

Produce was brought by weight, even eggs, they used the old style counterbalance scales, a stick or pole the length dependent on the amount to be weighed; had gradients marked along it's length, a basket hung from one end, a piece of string was attached to the top near the basket and a weight also on a piece of string was moved along the gradients until the basket and weight balanced; the gradient was then consulted and the price quoted. They even had this type of scale for weighing very heavy articles when the pole was suspended from the roof. Our weights and measure inspectors would have been in for a field day as the possibility for error was considerable.

The stall holder did not provide bags for your purchases you always ensured that you had a supply of containers usually plastic bags brought in from Singapore, and used many times after washing and hanging to dry. Buying meat was an interesting experience, it was only pork and of a good quality; if you were early enough you would see the butchers; as many as 10 on any given day; arriving with one or two uncovered carcasses in his bicycle trailer, the carcasses would remain lying uncovered in the trailer until it was needed on the trestle table, here the butchering was done and the various meat cuts displayed. The trestle tables were out in the open although it had a roof over the top; there was no refrigeration; usually the butchers would have a cigarette hanging from the side of their mouth as they used their large broad knives to prepare the various meat cuts.

Customers would walk along the tables inspecting the meat, if a closer inspection of a particular cut was required then the piece would be picked up and either purchased or returned to the table. After the choice was made the butcher of that particular carcass weighed it on his pole scales and passed you the meat. It was up to you to provide the necessary post purchase container; we used plastic bags but most of the local women would have an open basket. The shopper would select her vegies, eggs or what ever, all uncovered would be placed in the basket and she would walk or ride home. Chicken (actually chooks) were available live, as well as live fish, snakes, eel, ducks and quail. People shopped every day; there was no refrigerator or even ice boxes to keep food from perishing it was like living in a suburban bush pre 1940s. This need to shop daily meant that when free enterprise started its gallop, local markets sprung up all over the city; farmers taking the opportunity to reap the benefit of their own labours. These local markets were open at about 06.30 and closed at 09.00 in Wuxi the main market centre was open all day.

The meat we purchased would require a slim outer layer to be cut away before use, this removed any external contamination from other hands and cigarette butts. During the 4 years the markets became more organised but the butchers made no change to their habits; chickens were purchased live; one did their own killing and dressing; as a country boy this did not pose a problem but too many expats it did; as free enterprise galloped along from its start in 1987 with a brief shut down and then with renewed vigour; a man and his wife set up a stall and there they would butcher and dress live chickens at a cost of about 20c. Food shopping was never dull, particularly the free, free market, regularly there was a stall holder; an older man with bicycle and trailer; on his trailer he would have live quail or young chickens and a basket of quail eggs. If you purchased his chicken or quail he would; if asked slaughter them before your eyes and pass the still warm bloody bodies for you to put in your plastic bag or basket. Similarly live fish, eels and snakes were all available and at a price that was to us ridiculously cheap.

In mid 1987, construction was just about finished, the local government contractor sent a final account for settlement; according to the joint venture agreement it was a fixed price turnkey contract; at least that was the English translated version; the Chinese version however apparently allowed for any over run to be reimbursed. It was in this type of conflict situation that the Swedish side were very gullible; they believed the words from the mouths about mutual co-operation friendship and harmony; consequently they were ripped off by the Chinese at every turn. No amount of hard evidence would lead them to think that the Chinese were above reproach. This as we called the blue eyed approach shall be mentioned again; in this instance there was an extra construction cost amounting to 3 million Reminbi (Yuan) due and payable. This additional payment request was passed to me; after discussion it was decided to do a complete rehash of all building costs paid over the 3 plus years of construction.

Using a Lotus 123 spreadsheet; a translator to interpret the words on the invoices, a 3 month long task all day every day was commenced; literally hundreds of pieces of paper ranging in size from bus tickets to A3 size were perused translated and entered into the spreadsheet grappling with this 3 million yuan question. The task was daunting, frustrating and infuriating; if you have ever worked with interpreters or translators two specifically different people, you will appreciate part of the problems. My translator; who was never my interpreter in official meetings and who eventually because of this allocated task became my secretary was a young very pushy lady. At this time her use of English was limited to translating any in coming Chinese correspondence. For that task and for the new task in hand she used a Chinese English Dictionary; searching for a Chinese character then using the English possible equivalent; note the word "possible" as it is the operative word. Naturally this task considerable increased her translating skills.

The process went this way; a bundle of payment documents would be retrieved from the archives; the papers/documents making up the payments for a specific period would on initial processing been two hole punched and filed in hard cover binders. These binders were in short supply so after 6 months filing in these easy access files, a piece of string was passed down and up the holes and the documents lifted from the binder. A cover was placed on the top and the string passed through the holes at least once more and pulled very tight. Before the analysis process could commence each bundle had to be returned once more to the hard cover before the stringing process could be undone.

Each piece of paper was handed to the translator, she would refer to her Chinese English dictionary and hopefully find the English description of the article; hopefully; building terms were total foreign as far as she was concerned it was in itself another language; a good example one of hundreds of similar situations; the invoice read "the supply of 100 units goose neck bends" she had no idea what a goose neck bend was; the character did not even exist in her dictionary. Oh the complete and utter frustration. After 3 months working 6 days a week excluding a week of RR in Singapore plus a considerable amount of angst between me; the Chinese Vice President and Purchasing Manager, my report showed that we were being overcharged by some 1.5m Reminbi, the outcome of the final negotiations was a closely guarded secret although the effort was lauded by the Swedish side.

One of the difficult aspects in the process was trying to come up with real figures on the major building components like sand, cement, steel, copper, timber and metal roofing. This difficulty arose from the process of how materials were allocated and paid for under the centralist system. It is not rocket science there are different types of the above components required in a construction job. One example, many types of steel are required in a plant construction; plate steel, reinforcing steel, steel to build the water tanks, sheet steel for the roof, plus many other steel components. On the first visit to the site I wondered why there was such a large fenced area containing building materials, yet beside the road leading to the construction site was a number of large plates of steel about 5m by 3m and about 50m thick. Firstly they would be too heavy to steal hence outside the secure area; the truck carrying them could not enter the muddy secure area site so unloaded them beside the path, but there was even a better reason.

During construction the steel that was your allocation for a period was delivered in the type of steel available from the government agency supplier on the day of its allocation. It was then up to the constructor (builder) to swap this steel (in this case plate steel) for the same tonnage of the type of steel, required during the various building stages. The logistics of this was frightening, 2 old trucks, 3 old buses and 3 new Nissan sedans had been allocated; the trucks and buses; well past their prime; to operate these vehicles 8 drivers had been allocated to the JV.

Briefly this is how the system worked, the construction at this stage required reinforcing steel; the local government bureaucrat; there was one in charge of every project would contact one of his number who had available the type of steel our site needed; if they did not at this time require our type of allocated steel then another construction site who needed our material needed to be found. The game went on until the type of steel needed was found. Our ancient trucks with drivers; loaded with the plate steel would then go to all the intermediate organisations swapping steel until they eventually returned with our reinforcing rods; the circle complete; concreting could commence. In this process; at every point; some type of "friendship" payment was needed to ensure that everything ran smoothly. This friendship payment mostly money occurred at every level of the transfers it even included the guys (usually local farmers) who would load the trucks, their payment would probably be in local cigarettes.

Wood was of a different problem; the builder did not go to the local timber merchant or now Bunnings and select the timber required in the size and lengths that would suit the project or construction. Wood was delivered as trees; the construction work shop had a large circular saw, about 1m in diameter without any safety devices; just the saw mounted in a wooden bed with a belt driven electric motor underneath. From this saw hut came all of the timber that was used to construct the whole complex. Even the balustrades of the circular stairways in the villas were made from timber cut in this shed. Considering the tools used by the builders, carpenters, plumbers, electricians etc were still of the early 1900s design it was a marvel that the overall construction standard was as good as it was; although very basic. The majority of the workmen were local farmers who learnt their skills working on government farms, or had been taught by the army; possibly there was an apprentice system but it was not evident.

The same went for employees, originally our JV was allocated 8 drivers; as time passed it often happened that a driver was required elsewhere the head driver would advise that as of yesterday there was only 7 one had been re-allocated; it could be that there are now 10; 2 more allocated for some reason. A person sent for training in European at the expense of the JV Swedish partners failed to arrive for work; the answer they have been re-allocated. It is also the other way around; a visit to the dining room at lunch time, there to see a group of people sitting around a table outside of the allocated lunch time , a question would elicit the answer; "these are newly allocated workers, another question "what will they do"? Then answer; "oh you will need them when production starts". They could possibly be trainees from another factory just come to spend three training months with us. The Chinese management did not seem to have any control and certainly the Swedish side were only informed after the event.

Time in China would not be complete without an explanation of the 'friendship" system. European like the US of A subscribed to the premise that corruption in China did not exist if it did they were not involved. Having worked a number of years with our South East Asian organisations it was realized early that one must recognise that there is corruption but the trick is to try to determine what is the acceptable level ? In all SEA countries except Singapore there was is an acknowledged level of back hand payment for all activities, just as tipping is acknowledged in developed countries. In my mind tipping is just another name for a Chinese "friendship" payment. The Swedish construction manager had been in charge of a number of projects in South East Asia (he married a girl from Cambodia); one of our pastimes was to discuss the need and levels of these "friendship payments" eventually we reached the conclusion that the levels being paid were far in excess of what one would consider the norm. Our Swedish masters buried their heads in the sand and continued with the line that the Chinese would not do that; so they continued in their naivety to be ripped off. This construction manager who tried to reign in the exorbitant friendship levels was eventually sacked by the Swedes on the strong advice of the Chinese even though the local Swedish CEO strongly advised against it. The construction manager was replaced with a local who ensured that the exorbitant payments continued.

It is indeed bribery and corruption nothing more and nothing less. The phrase so often used "power corrupts, absolute power corrupts absolutely": One sees much evidence of this but no where greater than in my China, it cannot be remembered without thinking of the necessity to forever pay for free services. It begins at the lowest level and reaches into the very top of the powerful party machine. It took many and varied forms, all of us who have lived and worked during this time ensured they always had a supply of "Parker" pens, (must be "Parker"); solid metal cigarette lighters with some insignia that evidenced its western origin, cartons of western cigarettes, Japanese wrist watches (Citizen or Seiko), really any item of western origin that during a meeting could be inadvertently left on the table, or maybe passed across to be used and then pocketed by the official.

During the first examination of the books in 1986 after the account names had been translated there was a special account named the same as the JV. Over the 4 year tenure nobody would tell me where the income came from or where the expenses went. This subject was raised at Board level on a number of occasions but it was denied by the Chinese and ignored by the Swedish members. A lot of money went through this account and as far as I am aware it was never accounted for; even the Auditors from Hong Kong left it alone. My theory is that this was the clearing account for corrupt receipts and payments.

One could see the results of these types of dealings; our Purchasing Manager after 5 years on US $100 per month saved sufficient money to move to the US. The purchasing manager's position was very lucrative; a supplier to a Joint Venture operation had to show "friendship" so that their organisation could be selected to supply product, then always supplied at a price well in excess of the cost of the articles to a local factory. Even if the supplier was an allocated supplier by the local government, a "friendship" payment was necessary so that he could prove his friendship with the bureaucrat who did the allocation. This subject could be discussed many times over, it was endemic. Today China is trying to clean up the system and some high profile bureaucrats have been sentenced to death but however there is saying "a little grease oils the rails" which makes the decision easier to arrive at in a way beneficial to the donor.

Here is a small example; early in 1988 as the senior Swedish representative of the JV I received a message that Time magazine were researching in China and their Nanjing office wanted an interview for an article on "Doing business in China". It was arranged to meet this person at Wuxi railway Station. At the time of the arranged interview my appointment as Vice President had been approved, with a car now allocated to me I could drive to the station and as dictated by the parking attendant, park the car and pay the parking fee, next a visit to the ticket window to buy a platform ticket. After some time and pantomime it was understood why there were so many people sleeping on the pavement outside of the station proper, the government had banned the sale of platform tickets. Remember

Chinese is not my language, the ticket seller spoke only Chinese, it took a lot of hand signals and pointing before the penny dropped.

Firstly why had this happened; it was on the eve of the only national public holiday; the one and only three day weekend in a year, it was called Spring Festival and celebrated on the usually termed Chinese new year, Moa had however done away with all past tradition so it was no longer Chinese New Year in China but Spring Festival. At this time people who had been allocated jobs away from their home, a practise very prevalent; were allowed to visit their home town; this meant train travel. How would they get a ticket, buy it from the ticket seller, or buy a platform ticket and then bribe the individual carriage attendant to get on the train a very very common practice and naturally it was cheaper to do the latter, so it was decreed at this time that no more platform tickets would be sold. My need was legitimate; having stopped smoking in 1986 however western cigarettes were still carried for this express purpose; two cigarettes was the friendship cost to provide a 1c platform ticket so that I could meet the "Time" rep. This young lady was actually staying with people from the American Legation in Nanjing; she told me that the lower echelon employees there sold FEC currency at the black rate, thus doubling their spending/saving power; it was not just the Chinese making a fast buck.

When we moved into the office building and later the villas it was necessary to clean up the rubbish left by the construction crew, we all know how builders tend to leave their mess behind even in Australia; in China it was 100 times worse; parquet floors were all the rage in new offices and up market villas; ceramic tiles also were used: in the offices the floors were parquet with tiles in the large admin building foyer. Tiles naturally on the stairs and toilets; however before the cleaning process began the actual surface was unknown. All surfaces were literally covered with every conceivable dollop of material that make up a construction site. Cement, paint, grout, mud, in ground glue all had to be removed. The wooden floors were easy they could be sanded and polished but the tile floors everywhere had to be cleaned of this mess. A group of people were made available reporting to me; these were women peasants from the surrounding farms, here their houses had either dirt or brick floors and were without running water, their idea of clean was far removed from mine. The Chinese laboratory manager having good English was approached and a list of necessary materials in Chinese was prepared, this list given to a person in Administration to buy the supplies. A week or so later (a request from a foreigner so it was last on the to do list) the supplies were placed on the floor of my office; at last the appointed cleaners could start work, during the delay they were either sleeping in

68

the large lounge chairs on the upper floor reception area or sleeping with their heads on their hands in the canteen area, yes this group of 8 people were catching up on their sleep in a quiet comfortable environment.

Using my translator secretary as interpreter the job was explained, First the toilets; these were throne type but even the bowls and seats were covered with builders mess. The usual toilet gender differentials were evident and one person was despatched to each toilet on both floors. Every one was issued with the materials necessary to do the job; some time later I returned to check on progress and found no one in the toilet that I visited. I then went to the other toilets and found that all 8 were now in the one toilet with 2 in each of the two cubicles and the other 2 in the wash basin area. This need to work closely together stems I suppose from the lack of personal space available to the Chinese people, many examples of this personal closeness during working are spoken about. At this time in Shanghai the average living space per person was 2 m2. The goal was to double this by the year 2000 I am sure that this goal was over achieved.

Stories abound about this lack of personal space, Chinese migrating not able to sleep in a room by themselves, gangs of workmen digging a trench for a gas line, so close together that it was amazing they did not injure each other with their digging tools. We employed a group of local farmers men and women to mow the lawn of our villas; each given a large pair of shears to cut the grass. Now sitting on their little wooden blocks each right next to each other as they slowly moved forward in a line mowing the grass. Again watch the peasants in the field or washing in the local pond or canal see how close each one is to their neighbour. Another interesting fact; as these peasant ladies did their washing in a local pond or in the canal, why not use the clean water in the toilet bowl, it was there and it was clean, yes I saw it done and did little to stop it.

Eventually; after many tries an acceptable standard of cleanliness was achieved, considering the circumstances this was very far below an acceptable standard in our terms, but compromise was a key word developing in my lexicon. While on the subject of cleaners, one lady aged in her late 20s was particularly helpful and picked up very quickly on what was needed; although we had no common communication language; there developed an understanding of requirements. She became the backbone of the cleaning squad, one day months later she asked me to change some local money for FEC; at this time we were licensed to use local money, the going black market exchange rate was offered but refused and did a one for one swap. This transaction took place a number of times; one day she disappeared; the Administration manager said she was ill. Next day a real smarmy answer, "she has gone." This was the only explanation available; the immediate supposition was that she is now a well trained cleaner, most likely reallocated to another JV; after the appropriate friendship payment or maybe she was dismissed because of our currency trading, her fate was never discovered although in early 1989 I was accused of currency fraud; another story.

One of the frustrating things that so often occurred, was the almost in bred ability of the local staff at every level to look you squarely in the eye; tell you something that they knew was untrue and even they knew that you knew was definitely untrue. How many times would one try to ascertain the true reason behind a specific happening; every one you discussed it with would have a different version of events, finding two versions with some similarity then maybe a ring of truth about the event, a rerun of subtle questioning could lead you closer to reality but how frustrating it was, when all you wanted was information that would assist you to make worthwhile decisions based on facts.

It is was very necessary to understand, that everyone you spoke to was a personal survivor; those old enough had survived the Cultural Revolution; those who were children during this time had some relative who was persecuted and maybe even killed; some younger managers had been red guards the very perpetrators of vilification trials; one of the laboratory heads a well educated man had been such a person, he was very fluent in Chinglish; one night at a function he told some stories; as a red guard he could travel all over the country with his red guard group usually from the same university; following the trail of the large crowd gatherings that were a feature of the vilification campaigns; waged against the cultural professional educated classes, ranging from clerical assistants, kindergarten teachers to those in high managerial positions.

The young accountant who grew in considerable professional stature during my time and eventually travelled on a fact finding education missions out of China; in fact he eventually joined Astra in Shanghai as their CFO; he told of his father; a purchasing manager for a Shanghai shipping company; this young man's father also at that time a young man was persecuted and died during his vilification process. Now this young man was blacklisted by his work "danwei" and twice had pay increases rejected by the powers that ruled these things.

An explanation of "danwei"; each person in China at this time belonged to two danweis, the controlling group where he lived and the controlling group where he worked. These controlling groups were made up of party card carrying members and were appointed apparently by the next higher level. Once again competency was not a reason for an appointment but so called friendship;

how often this word appears when talking to the ordinary person these danwei (control groups) had absolute power over individuals, most will know of the one child one family regulation in China, as a matter of interest it is not that clear cut; and in truth it was an economic necessity. However; every body's actions, comments, even asides were monitored and reported back to either their work danwei or their residential danwei.

If any of these incidents were considered by the danwei to be anti establishment then retribution was swift; retribution could take many forms, maybe the withholding of gas for a much coveted gas ring, or maybe like that of a senior manager (one of ours) who failed to be aware of an affair between a male westerner and a Chinese girl that led to marriage (our first but not the last interracial liaison); this man requested approval to attend his daughter's wedding some 100k from his home this was refused, no travel permit was issued.

Women could be forced to have abortions; a wage rise could be stopped. A written vilification report may be required; our Chinese VP had transgressed by allowing some building disruption he was required to write a report setting out his wrong doings, this report was then publicly discussed at a special gathering of all of the Chinese employees; for a short time he was referred to as the vilified VP. All manner of so called benefits could be withdrawn for infringements against the establishment order. It is worthwhile to realise that these rules or regulations could be at the personal whim of the local controllers; they could use their absolute power for what ever reason they thought fit. Favours of all kinds were given and received to ensure survival. Sounds harsh; it was obscene; in many ways it was like to the powerful church regimes or the feudal farming systems in the 17th and 18th century. Priests and Lords had absolute power over their flock.

During 1985, to 1989, there was a slow transition from the tyranny of these powerful groups; some things happened fast others very slowly. Since 1989 there has been a tremendous move forward; near the Sheraton Hotel in 1987 there was a boarded up building in a grave state of disrepair, it looked like it could have been a cathedral. The last visit to Shanghai in 1993 it had regained its former glory; a cathedral it was. The blossoming of religions in China was just starting in 1988; during one business trip to another region a Roman Catholic Church was visited; you may not be aware that this church to survive from 1949 until the present had to disassociate itself from the Vatican and elect their own titular head. At this small church the priest told us that he had 34 novitiates who he was sure would take their vows. In Wuxi itself a Protestant Church came into the open after years of underground worshipping, and now slowly gaining a large following to their Sunday services.

Many things defied description or even good sense; the central Government had decreed that the economy could afford a pay rise; a particular percentage of the payroll was advised to each establishment. The work danwei would calculated the amount of additional funds that would be available for distribution, everyone in that work danwei would then vote to determine who would received a proportion of these additional funds; those receiving the most votes would then receive a pay rise. Our young accountant because of his father's back ground was twice unsuccessful in the voting process and this black marked him to be an unworthy person; he was performing well above standard so management were approached to increase his remuneration package; this black mark was written into his personal records maintained centrally for every person in the country, this was brought forward as a reason that he should not receive the increase; a true story and one that took a lot of inventiveness and compromise to ensure that he was not lost to another enterprise. The "big brother" concept had arrived in China in the early 1950's.

Due to my pressure in 1987; we were allocated 4 IBM PC's; these were considered at the time to contain technology that could only be exported to China under strict conditions; to get approval it was necessary to go through a rigorous US of A checking regime. Those of us in China thought this rather strange; the complex, state of the art manufacturing and filling equipment manufactured in Europe and now being installed in the factory contained a plethora of mini computer controls. Our reasoning was this tight procedure had more to do with the fear by IBM that if a PC got into the wrong Chinese hands they would using the old retrofitting procedures, develop and manufacture their own brand of IBM PCs. As one might recall such clones were a feature in the Asian market at much reduced prices but because of strict Intellectual property restrictions IBM received a royalty for the use of their DOS operating system. China would have no such restrictions.

This delay in allowing us access to the IBM PCs was creating problems; the Sharp luggable was the only piece of modern equipment available, much time was devoted to secretarial work, not the Company Secretarial work but mundane typing work. Most of the company's correspondence in English was being produced by me; Board reports, financial reports of all kinds were of my design and production. We did have one electric, plus a number of manual typewriters also one Chinese typewriter, all used carbon paper to make copies; all reports and presentations for meetings required at least 10 copies, the old model sensitized paper copier was continually breaking down, to increase efficiency something had to be done.

The possibility of bringing in some so called IBM clones from Singapore was discussed at the lunch table; to do this they would have to be smuggled; with of course the appropriate friendship payments made to our Chinese Management once they discovered what we had done; a possibility that this may also be necessary at Customs should we be discovered. Modus operandi would be; a goodly supply of FEC in your wallet, a number of cartons of cigarettes; special metal cigarette lighters with logos and of course some Parker pens; a small short wave radio was also good to have in your luggage. Customs examination when entering the country was strict, as was a similar examination when you departed; as set out previously; on departure you had to produce the list of what you had declared on entry and then identify the same equipment as you departed. At that time I was carrying a letter from Sweden showing that my luggable was a tool of trade thus allowing entry into most countries customs without any trouble. Twice entering Bangkok it was confiscated and returned on departure, there was also a clearance from Australian Customs enabling me to come and go with this equipment. How things have changed.

After discussion with the Swedish CEO it was decided to bring in at least two PCs then wait until the IBM's arrived. We planned the smuggling operation to take place when I returned for the next 12 weeks in country tour. A reason was manufactured to return to Singapore after just 6 weeks in country. We were now in the habit of bring from Singapore various items we considered necessary requirements; some examples; toilet paper; it was available in China but was square individual sheets of brown rough (yes rough) paper if you used it on your nose it would scratch, there was to a piece of string in one corner of the bundle this had two purposes one was to keep the bundle together the other to hook over a nail on the toilet wall; to me it was reminiscent of my country dunny days when newspaper on a hook was the luxury. Aluminium foil, plastic wrap, not yet available in China so both lovingly washed and re used wherever possible. Coffee, orange concentrate to make up brekkie juice, butter, margarine, condensed milk, bacon, ham, and always a kilo or two of frozen meat were things we took into China to make our life more bearable. This was only made possible because the incoming x-ray machines were no longer being used...

This time it was my intention to pack the luggable computer into this supply suitcase and have the IBM clone as extra luggage. PCs were now becoming more powerful, the clones purchased were known as a Series 2 and had a 10 meg hard disk, two 5 and quarter inch floppy disk drives, these disks held 3.5k, the ram was 256k, all loaded into the usual large CPU box; the usual green resolution screen was another large box, a dot matrix printer and key board in separate boxes with cables completed the set up. At this time Ann and I travelled through HK and as a business class passengers was allowed extra luggage, although the carrying of this much luggage could impose a heavy penalty; for some reason this time the over allowance was waived both in Singapore and Hong Kong. On arrival at Shanghai faced with the usual long slow health and immigration processing before the luggage claims retrieval area; now equipped with local money for two trolleys fully loaded, forward to the customs inspector. The declaration showed one computer, it also listed the currency, jewellery and cameras both a still and movie. It also showed that we had 3 suitcases, 2 briefcases, 2 over the shoulder bags and 4 boxes.

With heart pumping and clammy palms the two officers were approached; their sign language asked "what is in those 4 boxes"? Open them up, sure enough he recognised the screen, and the key board, the printer was strange; after a thorough examination he opened the box containing the CPU then summonsing a screw driver he opened that as well to peer into the back; no drugs or whatever he was looking for and they moved to the next passenger; leaving me to repack the boxes. Through the door into the seething mass of people, pushing two trolleys; divided the sea of faces and emerged into the street, the first attempt at smuggling was so far successful. Unusually my driver was there and into the car and off on our journey. I was now a criminal, but on arrival at the office I was a greeted almost as a hero; we had our first computer.

It was decided that this computer would be my tool and we started preparing for the next smuggling trip in 7 weeks. Both luggable and clone were set up in a room and training began ; at that time Word Perfect and Lotus 123 were the commonly used software; Microsoft DOS the operating platform, Bill Gates had not yet started Windows development. Now faced for the first time instructing people in computer use where the pupil had very little English and the teacher only spoke Australian with a smattering of computerees. During this time I developed skills that on taking up the International Consulting position in 1994 enabled me to bring the computer as an office tool into many of the Companies countries.

As a start there was the personal space problem, for those not experienced in this it can be disconcerting, pupils of both genders would drape themselves over you as you sat in the chair for a preliminary run through. Classes were arranged for both available applications; these pupils were in the main from the accounting and secretarial areas. To get a good picture you need to turn the mind back to PCs in 1986 they were still a relatively new tool. Today of course you switch on the PC and the hard drive whirrs away and the windows screen appears with all of your application icons;

in 1986 this was a concept only in the boffin's minds. Let us look at the PCs in 1986 and how they have developed.

This PC was an IBM Series 2 clone, it had a 10 meg hard disk, two 5 and quarter inch floppy disk drives, each with a write capacity holding up to 520k, and the ram was 256k. It was normal to have the DOS initiating procedure (boot) on the hard drive but as a precaution you carried a floppy boot disk. You normally had the application software on the hard drive but once again you always had an application floppy, my practise was to use the hard drive for day to day working; always backing up the data on a floppy.

Remember it was plain DOS (disc operating system) operation not Windows; when you started a class (no one had seen a computer before although some were computer theory trained without any practice), a boot disk was inserted in Drive A the power activated and eventually came a nice screen with green writing and all it said was C:/. Next you placed the disk with application soft ware into drive A: and using the key board typed "CD A", this instructed the computer to now read from drive A; Once A drive was activated you typed in your applications name ie Lotus 123 or Word Perfect and hit the enter key. Provided your disks were not corrupted a common occurrence the application soft ware would come onto the screen and you typed in the next execute command. There was no mouse; everything was key board activated so you had to know the sequence of instructions; as well as the words that needed to be typed.

All of this had to be taught before you started teaching the application. To become a proficient user of this modern tool it was necessary to familiarise yourself with the DOS operating system. For beginners the main interest was teaching the application so only as much DOS was taught for them to save their work using different drives and to read what they had on those drives. For those who wanted to get the most out of the tool they studied the DOS instruction book that came with each PC.

Once the application had been used to do your work it was now necessary to save this data it was not just a click and point, the correct DOS instructions had to be learnt; the class size was usually 4 people, they would gather around the chair and as the instruction proceeded I would literally be covered in bodies as they peered at the screen and watched the key board operations. Always using the principal that you learn more by doing than by hearing; so as soon as possible there was a student before the screen and key board, applying what they had heard, once more the bodies would huddle all around as the lesson was continued. This body contact was disconcerting and often discussed around the hotel dinner table or over the nightly sojourn at the bar.

Another disconcerting habit particularly by the female participants in any group undertaking was the way they sat. Many would tuck their crossed legs under their bottoms as they sat on a chair, with a short skirt this displayed plenty of thigh and crotch, most would have boxer shorts under these short skirts but those that did not; displayed an immodesty that was difficult to understand. The same display often occurred when they rode their bikes; there were very few girls' bikes in use. We purchased one for Ann but for some reason most women rode so called men's bikes.

Now to complete the smuggling exercise successfully it was necessary on leaving; to declare the luggable computer as the customs officers ticked off all of the items you carried on entry. In the space of some 6 months 3 more PCs were taken into China using this method without any problems, except on the final delivery. Both of us were entering China; now sufficiently confident in the procedure that discovery was not a fear. Ann usually only came in country for short periods not my 12 weeks stints; if there was to be a problem it would be on departure and she would be safe and secure in Singapore. As usual we came through Hong Kong, by now having a favourite bar in the transit lounge at the old Kai Tak airport, here many 2 to 3 hour transit delays were spent usually fortifying ourselves for the CAAC flight and the 4+ hours drive to Wuxi.

On arrival at Shanghai Airport it was to discover that another flight, delayed out of Hong Kong had landed just before we did; as a result no trolleys. Our luggage comprised 3 suitcases, (wheels on luggage had not yet been invented) all quite heavy as you carried everything you needed or even thought you may need, plus food supplies and of course the old computer in one suitcase, 2 brief cases, 2 duty free bags a personal over the shoulder bag each, a barely manageable load itself but this time as well we had the computer set comprising another 4 boxes, CPU, screen, key board and printer. How do 2 people with 2 arms apiece carry 14 pieces of luggage, even to this day we cannot recall how we managed but we did, struggling again through the sea of faces to our driver, then to find that even the Nissan had trouble accommodating all of this load.

There is an addendum to the tale of the 4 PCs clones; the IBM's were eventually delivered and installed; many people were taught the basics on these; what today would be considered archaic tools; a Canadian soft ware was discovered that would translate in a fashion English into Chinese characters, not fool proof but better than nothing and so the EDP department in the consortium was established.

Yours truly the instructor, the soft ware engineer, the hardware maintenance/installer as well as the help desk; call me if anything went wrong.

From a help desk point of view hardware maintenance was simple; if a computer malfunctioned you would firstly establish that it was not a monkey on the key board problem, next you would place another CPU beside the one out of service and interchange the circuit boards until you discovered which one was faulty, if it was a Singapore clone; on return to Singapore; buy another board and replace it; when the IBM computers failed it was a different story. One had to wait for a visiting IBM engineer and this could be a matter of weeks. The power supply in Mashan was dodgy to say the least, even though we had our own sub station on site; delicate production monitoring equipment was continually braking down because of power surges; so would be the computers, the power supply board would be blown by the spikes; even so the Singapore manufactured computer power boards was more resilient to the power spikes however they could still be affected but were easily fixed. They were readily available in Singapore, spares could also be kept on hand; the IBM were different with the extended down times it was not long before a decision was made to seek local Chinese units the IBM equipment had too much down time to be considered useful.

The time came for the official inauguration of the factory complex; one of my roles was to ensure that all of the grounds, offices and general service areas were up to the standard that was expected of a western pharmaceutical plant. A very tall order in China, one had learnt to accept a different standard than that considered normal in other parts of the world; compromise was the key word, visits to some other local pharmaceutical factories had shown the then Chinese standard; certainly our plant and its environs were very much superior to those visited, the overall building finish far superior, the internal fittings and plant; when it was overseas sourced far more advanced that any thing yet seen in China, most of the local equipment was of 40 year old design but of course newly constructed, so the challenge was to buff it up.

Landscaping Chinese style flourishing with great pressure to keep them well maintained; paint was only to be on the required painted surface, splashes over runs etc had to be removed, concrete and glue splashes; endemic all over the area must to be ground away; all surfaces cleaned to look as they were meant to look. Material to do these jobs was mostly in short supply, once again compromise, for example broken handmade bricks were used as rubbing stones; inventiveness was forced to surface. A business selling lawn mowers was found; they were the old rotary push type; the lawn was an unrecognised variety, the grass had a very fine leaf ; it did not grow fast but matted very quickly; the lawn mower broke even before even completing the first mowing of the Villa area; a new methodology needed to be developed. Very large scissors were ideal for cutting this type of grass; manpower was usually plentiful but unreliable, this temporary labour force comprised local farmers trying to earn some extra money however if the fields and crops needed attention the work force would disappear.

A few days before the arrival of the VIP group consisting of the Swedish Prime Minister; big names from the 4 Swedish companies; local top cadres as well as senior figures from Beijing; this was to be a very big affair. Timing they say is all important, this timing was the rainy season; the Swedish CEO ordered a large quantity of umbrellas to be used both as gifts and emergency covers if it should rain. A few days before the event, the heavens opened; floods are the norm in this part of the world, the factory was built on reclaimed ground below the level of the lake which was only 100 metres away. Returning from lunch at the villa it was almost necessary to swim to get to the front door; all of the internal roads were full to the top of the gutter; the water had risen over the top of this and formed a lake about 10cms deep all over the site; water was washing away the hours of attention that the garden detail had spent in preparing the raised flower beds and small hedges.

The spirits fell, how can we bring all of these important people who needed to walk along these roads to inspect the complex if it rained like this on the day. Why was the water not draining away through the guttering system? This needed to be investigated, no water appeared to be running away through the drain holes in the gutters; were the pumps that had been installed to take the water from the land into the canals and then into the lake not sufficient to handle these types of down pours. Were the canals properly graded to ensure the water drained from the site into the larger canals that led to the pumping station? All questions to exercise the mind.

Now we all know that my trade is accounting; I am not a hydraulics engineer nor do I have any skills in engineering or construction; but in China or any country where you don't have the language and where assistance in ordinary matters is not reliable; then one has to bend the mind to all manner of problems. In knee length rubber boots; the trusted bicycle waterproof cape over head and shoulders; the comfort of the office was left and ventured out onto the road that was now a river, First look for the drainage hole nearest the office door it was still plugged up with the white foam placed there when the gutter was formed; from drain hole to drain hole, all around the road at every place these holes still contained the foam material placed to form the hole where a drain pipe could be inserted. The drain pipes were installed and once the foam was removed the trouble was over. Oh if only all the problems that arose in China was that easy to solve.

The CEO had ordered a large number of umbrellas both as gifts and as safety measures; at a meeting of functional managers he made this announcement revealing nice golfing size umbrellas with the logo prominently displayed. The Chinese VP said that we could not use them; in China when you opened an umbrella it could signify that all of your luck would be falling out. A warning about too much initiative in another culture; the hunt was now on for new gifts that would be given to all attendees at the inauguration; now only 4 days away.

Arrangements for the day were now completed, the local school would provide the usual honour guard of flag waving well dressed children; the official party would be greeted by a line comprising the functional managers. A flag raising ceremony would commence the festivities and then the official opening with many speeches, an inspection and then of course a fireworks display. An official banquet was arranged for the evening. It was a grand affair and well covered in the media. All top level staff was presented with a leather Gladstone type bag, a consortium tie, with tie bar and a pen with logo; friendship gifts for all. Naturally the top officials would be blessed with much more elaborate and costly friendship tokens.

Fireworks are a big thing in China; they need no excuse for a fireworks display. While living at the hotel every time a new group of tourists arrived there would be an elaborate fireworks display. These were real fireworks any one could buy bungers that could double for a stick of dynamite, multi hued rockets that seemed to disappear in the sky before exploding and filling the night sky with their wondrous colours; during the 12 plus months as a resident of the hotel these fireworks displays were witnessed on many nights. Not as good as new year on the Sydney harbour but still spectacular. Ann wanted to bring some home but we dissuaded her in the interests of air line security.

The factory was now in production (sort of). The end of 1987 saw a major change. The Chinese VP retired through ill health, he was replaced by a much younger man whose wife was high up in the medical administration in Jiangsu province, the Swedish CEO had fallen out of favour with the Chinese Board, and the expats in charge of both wet and dry production did not want to renew their contracts. The hunt was on for new people to replace these key expats.

The JV was in some disarray, focused particularly on the subject of foreign exchange earnings the Chinese side were insisting that exports should equal imports in value; (exchange neutral) there was an influx of Chinese party faithful appointed to take up key positions in the organisation; these people had not received any training in European; knew nothing about the product portfolio but were given senior positions. The accounting procedures had been established, monthly reports designed and now being issued; Ann was asked to prepare a general instruction hand book for new and existing employees. This hand book was to cover a large number of things including: how curtains were to be arranged over windows, leave and sick pay reporting, expense reports with mandatory furnishing of receipts, behaviour in the bus to and from the city and even personal hygiene for non factory employees.

These were basic; very basic and when reviewed at the end of our contract, brought a lot of laughs but in 1987 these regulations filled a real need. While this booklet was in progress my time was partly filled in with writing a Company Governance and Procedures Manual; but every month the JV Board would require a new set of financial forecasts; this was time wasting to the extreme; the factory was not in production for the market yet; it required certification by both Chinese and more importantly Swedish inspectors; if production was to be exported then the factory must meet Swedish standards. The Swedish trained Chinese production employees were now at work full time; their 2+ plus years of drawing a salary with hardly any effort was over. The lesser qualified process factory workers were now allocated by the local government and training began. These people of peasant stock were housed in the building constructed for this purpose in a nearby village. Plant running and production now became not just a discussion point but a reality.

The whole place was chaotic. I remember vividly how on the first day that the various hygiene class production areas commenced training. The first lesson was what to wear then so called personal hygiene; followed by the correct procedure for entering these areas through airlocks and safety baths. Part of this procedure was the mandatory wearing by all factory staff of specially imported lint free uniforms with an imported one use disposable blue lint free head covering. That first afternoon and continuing for some days until a regulation was circulated concerning correct disposal; the factory people as they left the production area to the bus stop a large proportion of those; who that day had been issued with their daily disposable blue hat; wore them to the buses; they were telling the world and their work mates that they were the elite workers in the factory, they entered the holy ground of sterile work areas. For weeks the country side was littered with blue hats, disposed off into a pocket not a bin and then handed over to a friend as a memento, some of the near by farmers recovered them and wore them under their cane hats. Modern disposable technology had arrived in Mashan.

A common comment is that Asiatic people including Chinese are always calm and inscrutable; not wholly true. In our new workplace so many and varied new procedures were being introduced, ranging from ensuring no litter in the factory grounds, yes a new concept as the majority of local production units were littered with all kinds of material that had no recoverable value. When issuing new procedures; the best way forward is to first write the procedure then test it with the group who will be controlling the end result; adjustments are made to facilitate shortcomings of the draft procedure then the people involved in the steps along the way have to be consulted before the final written procedure is approved by management. This introduction of new procedures was not new to me. To bring Astra A into the modern computer environment a whole range of new procedures had to be introduced coinciding with the impact computers made on office and factory routines; also part of the Company Secretarial function; involved amending company governance policies and procedures as company behavioural standards altered; this is an enjoyable type of challenge; as it can and does lead to often heated discussions; necessitating on occasion to a hard sell of your ideas.

This implementation of new procedures took on a whole new meaning in China; a relatively simple procedure could take hours to explain using interpreters; the volatility of the people who would be charged with the implementing or working with new procedures was mind blowing; for example in Australia we had introduced a new creditors invoicing payments system when the new Wang Office was implemented; as standard practice each manager now had a certain "delegation of authority" to spend money according to his/her annual budget. This person was now responsible for costs within there functional area so was required to approve each individual expense as it occurred by signing the suppliers invoice. A simple procedure but different from many organisations where a signed company order was sufficient authority for an accounts person to approve the payment. This was to us in Astra a substantial improvement on past practice and naturally it would be good to have this procedure implemented in China.

In Australia each incoming invoice is registered by the accounts department; an authority slip is attached and the document forwarded to the Manager responsible for the expense. In Australia there had been discussion at management level whether to use an authority slip or have a rubber stamp impressed on the invoice itself; this discussion was over in 15 minutes and proceeded to more important features of the system. In China I arranged a meeting of department heads; decision to make; use a pre-printed authority slip or a rubber stamp? In China people always arrived late for meetings, sometimes I felt that they were proving they were superior to the expats, showing that they really only complied with our request by sufferance. So as usual the 9.00 am meeting did not start until 9.15; at 12.30 we stopped for lunch still without a decision, tempers flared at one stage a person even stood on a chair to be noticed. In mid afternoon it was decided that a rubber stamp (chop) would be used, and the meeting finally broke up at 15.00; one person who was a obviously a party member even wanted to re-open the discussion the next day; one thinks he had reported to his leader during the evening and had changed his mind. Yes I kid you not a paper slip or a rubber stamp demanded party attention.

Was this an unusual occurrence; no; in 1987 free enterprise or much better called a free economy was starting in China; this manifested itself in many obvious ways, an example, travelling daily from the hotel to Mashan we drove past passed an area that was often used as a tourist stop to look over the placid very picturesque Lake Tai; there was a fishing village near by and it was interesting to watch these large square bamboo slattern sail driven vessels; two to a team dragging a fishing net make their slow way across the lake. It was scenically rather unique; old style boats doing what they had done for many hundreds of years; I for one could sit at this large parking area for hours and watch this sight; many tourists as well as locals did just that.

One day a man selected a spot overlooking the view and set up a card table; on this table there was a range of soft drinks; in the trailer attached to his bicycle; were a few boxes of replacement stock. My first view of the new free economy; here was an entrepreneur on his way to be riches; his start selling soft drinks; in less than two months this area contained 2 roadside restaurants; a very makeshift truck driver sleeping building as well as other small stalls selling cakes and trinkets. It changed from a scenic viewing spot to an instant hovel. All of the buildings were constructed using whatever timber could be scrounged from the surrounding country side; cotton cloth formed the walls of the restaurants, and the truck stop sleeping establishment tar paper the external walls and roof.

To add insult to injury, the truck stop sleep over owner employed a young scantily clad lady beckoning to the truck drivers as they drove past. This employment of a scantily clad young lady only lasted a few days before the local authorities stopped the practice. But free enterprise had started in China. As I travelled out of China for Christmas 1987 all along the road were small road side eateries many with young ladies in full but sometimes revealing dresses beckoning to the travellers to sample the wares of the eating establishments. The party members could see the writing on the wall and were using every thing they could to keep their grip on the people; from now on it was interesting to watch the development of China and its people; I consider myself lucky to have been there on the cusp of their real great leap forward even though it was an extremely difficult personal life style.

Talking about food brings to mind a happening in the summer of 1987; living now in the small apartment. On returning to China from Singapore with the usual suitcase full of necessities; not available locally including a supply of beef both minced and steaks. In the small apartment there was a very small fridge; the freezer compartment commensurate with the over all smallness of fridge and apartment. As mentioned before the incoming customs x-ray of luggage had been abandoned, one regular piece of luggage was a very large canvas black bag, it concealed a mid sized Esky, within this would be any frozen or food needing to be protected against the elements; Ann had decided not to return on this occasion; it was summer, hot and sticky to the extreme.

For some reason or another; maybe becoming blasé about the customs practices; I did not conceal the esky in the black bag; on arrival at Shanghai airport the Customs officials seized the esky and declared it contained prohibited imports. Looking around I saw at the gate an official who had collected a whole group of customs officers including what appeared to be the top man at the airport; this evident by the look on his face and more importantly the fine cut of his clothes. Naturally I was prepared to play friendship money if I was going to goal; and let the officials have the goods. Looking at the large group of officials I realized that the cost would have used up all of my friendship gift supply also it would be have been a bartering process working my way up the authority chain with them calling the shots and price. Explained by sign language my ignorance of this import restriction on meat; I did note however that some of the group also seemed unaware of this regulation; however they would confiscate it; this decision, the group for now seeing a once in a life time, expensive steak dinners on their plates.

It is interesting that the Chinese authorities all wore the same uniforms at this time. This uniform was made out of a green cotton material with a green hat, green socks and then shoes according to the wearer's economic position; these ranged from worn out sandshoes with green rubber trim to smart polished leather brogues; there was no insignia to denote rank or the type of controlling body to which they belonged. They could be members of the so called People Army; a customs official, a local policeman, or a health inspector; all dressed the same, apparently they each had a badge which denoted the type of official but this was beyond my identification process.

Happy that I had once again not been expelled or put in jail but somewhat perturbed. It was summer thus for 8 weeks I would have no access to imported fresh meat. Summer; fresh pork was never purchased in summer; flies everywhere; outside summer temperatures melting the fat on the carcasses as they lay in the open on a trestle table. The meat hovered over by the butcher with his cigarette ash hanging over the meat; not particularly a good purchasing picture; dress your own live chicken the only alternative. Our contract allowed one free day a week; the factory in production mode and due to the irregular supply of electricity and water; one never knew what day it would be, The day off could be tomorrow or 10 days away, to maintain production the factory operated whenever electricity and water utilities were available. This uncertainty coupled with the requirement by the Administration manager that a trip to Shanghai required at least two days notice, to arrange a vehicle and driver for your trip; so there was no chance of buying meat from the Sheraton; the only alternative tins of Chinese luncheon pork.

For 8 weeks interspersed by the occasional chicken meal; many ways were found to make Chinese tinned luncheon pork as appetising as possible. Naturally there was a hunger for a large juicy steak, in fact after 8 long weeks; arriving home in Singapore at lunch time culminated in an immediate visit to the Cold Storage supermarket close to our condo to purchase some large Aussie T bones; heaven had indeed arrived. Oh such small pleasures missed in so much living in China.

Summer heat now slowly dissipating; Ann decided to come in for a couple of weeks; so we filled up the Esky and food suitcase. By now my travel was light; a supply of clothes in China, as well as another in Singapore; a list was kept of what was where so all that was needed to be carried was those clothes that were not duplicated, or which needed to be cleaned in Singapore; where there was expensive; by Australian standards; dry cleaning. The clothes kept in China consisted of a change of suits, as well as a pants and blazer coat ensemble. In summer coats were not needed so a good supply of business shirts and ties with well cut strides was the uniform. The purchase of tailor made clothes in Singapore were inexpensive so I could afford to travel light; thus the business class luggage allowance of 35 k could be utilized in importing our traditional western necessities.

With this good supply of western food and basics accompanied with the duty free allowance of 800 Alpine cigarettes and 4 litres of liquor we both felt equipped for another 12 weeks stay. Tourist season was starting so Dimple scotch and Bacardi rum our current tipple were available in the Friendship shops but why buy at those exorbitant prices if you could import them duty free. Imported wine was now also available at the Friendship stores, priced reasonably as was sweet Chinese wine and German brewed local beer. Life was becoming westernised; in a small way. Now we could catch a taxi (yes a taxi) to the hotel particularly if the hotel limo service had failed to materialise. Some taxis comprised a small China made van often with springs that had disintegrated many months before, or it could be the locally made Volkswagen all showing signs of hard use; deciding on the fare value was always interesting. As locals we knew the average price from previous usage but the game was played; both in sign language and a few common word vocabulary such as no ; too much; most drivers always being prepared to accept 50% below the original offer but still a small pittance compared to Oz prices. Into the small van we put our 7 pieces of luggage plus 2 duty free bags and scrambled onto the hard dirty seats behind the driver. You never ever sat beside the driver; this practice being far too dangerous; the safest seat was behind the driver as you know he would swerve to protect himself.

The Hau Ting Sheraton; a peaceful island in a sea of ill clothed; almost morose, citizens straining to go about the daily grind; washing of all types hanging out to dry on ropes or bamboo poles stretched between the trees that lined the streets; smog laden air sometimes acrid to the taste; over crowded ancient buses struggling sometimes to even keep up with the bicycles and certainly no match for the few cars that were on the streets, traffic policemen plying their trade some with cloth masks, less than 50 % of the residents with running water, a much less percentage with sewerage; a honey pot town; elderly women with large barrows plying their trade along the streets; 15 million people with 5 million bicycles; that was Shanghai in 1987.

As a frequent user of the Hau Ting Sheraton there was as usual an upgrade to a junior suite with a front window view; after calming the nerves with a good 2 fingers of Dimple, naturally with ice from the on floor ice maker we sat and watched the traffic at the large intersection that the Sheraton overlooked. Hand trucks, bicycles, mini tractors, old buses, old trucks; taxis and the occasional car converging from four roads into the intersection. A 3 storey police tower in the centre directing traffic, the sounds of a whistle being blown to signal a traffic infringement, or movement was the vista spread out before us. As the day moved to night the vehicles continued to add to the smog, parking lights the only illumination allowed, bicycles were devoid of any lights or even reflectors.

Our driver was to arrive at about 09.00, so a quiet night reading, this was before in-house tv with its multitude of channels; our minds focused on the next days, privately thinking of our somewhat perilous 4+ hours trip to Mashan; next morning a leisurely English buffet breakfast and after the usual toilet call; called a porter to bring the many bags to the waiting Nissan. The porter had hung our duty free bags on hooks provided for this purpose on the luggage cart; at the street he started to load our suitcases into the boot of the car, lifting the last quite heavy suitcase into the boot; now the weight of the duty free bags unbalances the trolley, all came crashing to the ground. Glass meeting concrete has a deleterious affect on the glass so now we had 2 plastic duty free bags, one filled with a mixture of Dimple and Bacardi nicely flavouring the 400 Alpine cigarettes and in the other bag the other 400 cigarettes flavoured by one bottle off Dimple, a bottle of Bacardi stayed intact. Other than cry what could we do? In retrospect we should have returned to our room and stayed overnight as this was just the start of a long; very long day.

The head concierge arrived and suggested that the porter pay for the damage, however these people were well known to us; they always treated us well (with a good tip of course) so waved this offer away and glumly sat ourselves in the back seat of the car; Ann as usual in the safe seat behind the driver. The usual hassle through the city bicycle traffic then onto the main road leading to Soochow and Wuxi.; we reached check point Charlie (our naming) where all traffic had to stop, report and be inspected for illegal travellers and merchandise moving between Shanghai and the surrounding countryside but we were as usual were waved through. Back on the road, Ann and I settling in for the remaining 3+ hour journey, losing ourselves as normal in the sights and sounds of the Jiangsu Province countryside. The boats on the river; some under power others being sculled along with one large oar, carrying all manner of cargo; the water chestnut vendors beside the road, and the continual stream of pedestrians and bike riders going; who knows where; all contributed to the ever changing scenery.

Although your eyes were taking in all of the sights, your mind or that part of it that which makes you a back seat driver was also conscious of the other traffic on the road; in fact considering the state of the road and its users probably more than half of your senses were intent on the road. Now travelling along a rather good stretch of road, approaching a looping bend when a large truck that we had been following for some time came to a complete stop; There was sufficient space at the speed we were travelling to stop in plenty of time unfortunately the driver took that moment to have a nano nap; a not unusual occurrence. He had travelled from Wuxi that morning an early start to be at the hotel at 09.00; he had already spent some 4.5 hours negotiating the traffic and roads, as we later found out this required all of your concentration; so we hit the rear of the truck with considerable force; luckily Ann had responded quickly to my shout of "look out" so we had time to brace ourselves for the impact.

A now; well awake driver and I immediately got out of the vehicle to inspect the damage, the truck it was undamaged; however our vehicle was going no where. The driver was now walking around somewhat dazed; then for whatever reason, he disappeared, leaving us sitting in the car which was right in the middle of the road. Now rain commenced, then a slight smell of petrol wafted. I got out of the car into the light rain and noted a small dribble of this volatile substance leaking from the front of the car; unable to lift the hood of the car to find the source of this leak but quickly noticed that the leakage was very small and was quickly dissipating in the rain water on the road so with some trepidation we sat in the back seat of the car for protection from the rain steadily gaining in intensity. Unfortunately up to this time we had not developed the emergency procedures needed in our type of environment such as carrying notes written in Chinese with various messages that could be used to communicate with those around us; so all we could do was sit back and await developments. We knew that we were only some 10k to a large town, and suspected that the driver had caught a lift into this town to seek the police and assistance for us, there was no telephone call boxes in this China and mobile phones were light years away, no NRMA to call if we could for assistance. An hour elapsed then the driver returned on the back of a police motorbike and side car.

With the passing of time there was an ever increasing crowd of onlookers; a vehicle accident always attracts a lot of attention in any country; here in China with so many people walking and riding bicycles, the crowd seems to be greater; particularly when there are foreigners in the car; added to this scenario was lady with red hair; almost a circus oddity in this sea of lustrous black hair. So you can imagine what an attraction this smashed vehicle was; bees around a honey pot comes to mind; every single person who passed by had to have a look at the red headed lady sitting in the back seat. It was raining so a clear view could only be achieved by first wiping the window glass clear of rain; this was accomplished using a variety of materials; a piece of rag; maybe a coat sleeve, part of a shirt or blouse, anything, then it was necessary to place ones face hard against the cleared portion of the glass. Even babies had to see this unique creature sitting with ever increasing disdain on her face; wishing she were anywhere but here. I tried standing outside the car window but all this accomplished was to move the crowd to the other side of the car. In the end efforts to block the view were abandoned and we tried to ignore both the danger we were in from another vehicle failing to stop and hitting us from behind and the ever increasing crowd of on lookers peering at us like we were fish in an aquarium.

The police failing in their efforts to obtain information about the accident from us; concentrated on taking measurements and walking around the accident scene; which now comprised solely an off white Nissan sedan with badly damaged front end sitting in the middle of the road surrounded by onlookers; the truck of course was long gone. Using an ever increasing sign language vocabulary I tried to get the driver to arrange a taxi for us; he however was busy with the police investigation, worrying about his fate, and not concerned for us at all.

Our immediate concern was to get away from this circus; sometime after midday, after sitting there for over two hours, a three wheeled vehicle arrived. Lo and behold it was a taxi from the nearby city; these vehicles which comprised a motor bike arrangement for the driver with a small car like body attached were used for a multiplicity of purposes, taxi, taxi truck, ambulance, hearse, public transport, meat wagon etc etc etc. There are no seats in the back of these small cumbersome looking vehicles; the hirers being content to either sit on their luggage or cargo or straight on their bottoms, always there was clear evidence of what was the last or second last load that had been transported. Both drivers assisted by the police placed our luggage in the back and we climbed up onto the suitcases and gingerly tried to make ourselves comfortable. The canvas cover over the back tray was dropped to protect us from the wind and rain, the driver mounted his motor cycle seat grabbed the handle bars, kicked started the motor and we putted away. To where; we knew not; in one way we were hoping it would be to Mashan but that was still some 80k away and on the these roads, sitting on our luggage in a vehicle with no shock absorbers moving as a boat would in very choppy water we changed our priorities. The wish then became; please let our destination be the nearest large hotel hoping that there would be one in the nearby city.

Bounce; bounce, bounce and sway; more sway; jog jiggedy jog, sway bounce and sway, the suitcases bruising our nether parts, enclosed in the black water proof covering affixed to the tray of the conveyance, not knowing where we were or where we were going, down the road towards where. Words cannot describe that period of time, there was anguish; there was anger, a feeling of escape from the crowds and upper most was a dim hope that soon we would be at Mashan. With a wheeling flourish that threw us off our perches the driver stopped; the back cover was lifted; and we beheld a group of people standing looking at us. Once again we felt like animals at a zoo; they patiently waited as we clambered down from our precarious perches to place our feet attached to trembling legs onto terra firma. Bodies still trembling from this ride yes we were ushered into the cities largest hotel. Now accompanied by a group of people we climbed the steps to our second floor room; in China this was the first floor, the ground floor is counted as floor one.

At last a semblance of peace; away from the gaping crowds; this peace was not to last, no sooner had we entered the room and closed the door, in walked unannounced two smiling house maids, each carrying an almost white towel. Chi Chi (thank you). We felt that a drink from our remaining bottle of Bacardi with coke would bring us some normality; at least in China as in the world everyone knew coca cola. Yes it was agreed we badly needed a Bacardi and coke to settle our nerves maybe two actually; a Dimple would have been nice but it was sloshing around with our cigarettes in Shanghai; thankfully as both smokers we had a couple of spare packets of cigarettes.

The usual pantomime would achieve the desired right results; the two ladies disappeared; the door had hardly closed when in walked unannounced two other ladies, carrying two small cakes of soap; smiling broadly they delivered their small parcels and backing out of the door closed it behind them; why did they bother, it was no sooner shut and in walked a bell boy with a pump vacuum flask filled with boiling water; the twice daily requirement in any hotel room at the time. During the next 30 minutes we surmised that every employee of the hotel found an excuse to visit our room, to look at the lady with the red hair; in the end we gave up, proceeding to rinsed two glasses with a small amount of our precious Bacardi before pouring a goodly dram of the precious spirit and topping them up with the ice and coke that had been deliver by two different people over the last 30 minutes; so we sat and mournfully surveyed the situation. It was now late afternoon; we surmised that by now our non arrival at Mashan would have been noticed by the expats hopefully they would send someone to find out what had happened. How wrong we were.

After a couple of stiff drinks coupled with the calming affects of a cigarette or two we sat on the bed, and calmly discussed the dilemma and contemplated on a number of scenarios. Known fact our driver had not accompanied us to the hotel; where was he? Had the police arrested him before he notified our people at Mashan; if so would they know where we were. We theorised on how long it would take for another car to drive from Wuxi; we had had nothing to eat since breakfast; the third Bacardi was fuming the brain; it was now 18.30; nine plus hours since we left Shanghai; time to eat; let's find the dining room. Down stairs; into the large dining area, it was completely empty. When we appeared a waitress materialised from what could have been the kitchen; when she saw us she beckoned to two other waitresses and the three of them proceeded to place about a dozen cans of cold drink on the table that they had led us too.

Using our local dialect which comprised a type of miming we made them understand that drink was not the prime need, food was our request. After some time a person, dressed in cooks garb delivered a large platter of the red coloured smoked pork so often used in Chinese cooking; it sat there on a large platter; nothing else not even rice. A gigantic assumption was made; the hotel was empty of guests, so the kitchen was not operational. Partaking a few pieces of this rather unpalatable meat; we decided to return to the room and await developments, rising to our feet a bill was presented; this bill was twice the value of a 6 course meal for 4 at the Hubin. Once again in pantomime mode explaining in broken sign language that we would only pay a fraction of the amount; as a sweetener this would be in FEC. The face before us was clearly shown that we would not argue; we climbed the stairs again and decided that the answer was another Bacardi.

At 20.00 a knock on the door and a well known face of another driver presented himself; once again we carried the luggage to the car and eventually arrived home, 13.5 hours after leaving Shanghai. The guy whose villa we shared was astounded to see us so late; no one had been advised of our predicament; they were concerned at our non arrival but by 16.30 every one had left the factory area and so there was nothing more they could do but assume we were held up and would eventually arrive.

Ann and I over a quiet dinner in our little apartment wondered what would have happened if we had of been injured; so decide from that day onward we would carry some notes in Chinese asking to use the phone or call an ambulance or contact this person please. When we eventually were licensed to drive and began more hair raising adventures these notes became extremely important, now such notes as "Which way to the destination where ever we were headed needed to be carried. This time was still in the future.

There were two Swedish production managers they lived in Villa 2 and 3, home to Ann and I was the small apartment in Villa 2. On our one day weekend the three of us would go shopping; at this time we were allowed to drive provided we had an international licence; in 1987 this regulation was changed forcing us to apply for a Chinese driving licence but more of that later. The two managers by this time each had their own Volvo; we would drive into the city with our shopping list and return some hours later with supplies, it was all very domesticated and the various stall holders came to know us, they would vie for our business because we would have to pay using FEC. The egg lady; was a classical example of a stall vendor, always a ready smile and was adamant to ensure that we passed her the FEC; it was not uncommon for one of the plain clothed authorities who patrolled the market to grab the FEC and replace it with local currency, but they never seemed to do that with her. Maybe she paid them off who knows.

The decision to buy a bike was made, on one of the shopping excursions we ventured into the department store which had a bike department; a simple enough decision; there was a choice you could have a black one or a blue one, these were very basic, extremely heavily built bikes, no gears; a bell and two hand brakes, the only equipment, there was no legal requirement for a light at night neither a need for a rear reflector. Once it was clear to the shop assistants that the intention was to

90

buy a bike, the three of us were totally surrounded by people; after about 15 minutes of discussion; really about nothing; the crowd had increased to fully fill the bike department all gathered to watch our show. Near the bike department was an open stair way leading to the (first) in China second floor, this stairway was crowded with people, curiously watching three westerners buy one bike. Many hands assisted us to carry the bike to the car, there to take off the wheels and put it into the boot. One never ceased to be amazed at the almost child like way local people reacted, even though we were now an accepted part of the landscape.

In the summer of 1987 Ann came in country from Australia; there was a need to improve the level of Chinglish spoken within the company; she was approached to provide English speaking classes to the factory operating staff, they were mainly young local peasant class school leavers, who had failed to be accepted into college or university. With a pre determined hourly remuneration rate to provide these instructions; she happily entered into the project ; it would give her an interest and a reason to stay with me in country; some English language instructional material had been purchased to assist in this work and was she was keen to progress. The summers in Mashan are hot and frightfully humid due to the nearby lake and canal drainage systems, no air conditioning was provided in the office or canteen area of the factory although there were heaters for winter; it took all of my insistence to have a small room unit placed in the window of my office after being appointed VP in 1988 however in 1987 it was expected that we would survive in the Chinese conditions.

The temperature now in the mid 30s with 100% humidity day in and day out; the smallest effort such as picking up a pen then writing resulted in being wringing wet with perspiration. Entering into this project with gusto but after a few days in the excessive heat with clothes sticking to the body the enthusiasm began to wain; the young people were more inclined to doze in the heat than attend to the well prepared exercises, it was apparent that they were not at all interested in improving their Chinglish; to her credit she managed to retain sufficient drive to continue the classes until a shortened depart date was arranged; after that these classes ceased.

In the last months of 1987; the position of Vice President Administration/Marketing was offered to me by the Swedish JV partners.; the factory was now starting to produce, the April inauguration ceremony with the attendant world wide publicity was now a memory; the Swedish CEO's contract was completed; he was returning to European; the Swedish Marketing Director as well as the Hong Kong native and based Marketing advisor also departed. A new American wet production Manager was arriving and so far they had not been able to find a new Swedish VP. A new Chinese CEO was appointed and it was expected that the new Swedish VP would be production oriented. To accept the position meant that my employer would be the Swedish Consortium not by Astra. The President of Astra AB a good friend had recently died of cancer; this brilliant man had taken Astra from a small Swedish Company into a dominant world player, the previous CEO of Astra Australia during the majority of my time there was also appointed as an advisor to the JV; I had a high opinion of this man considering him to be the best boss that I ever worked for; so was looking forward to working with him again, coupled with all of these changes was the big executives movements in the Astra Head office..

We knew that they were having trouble in Sweden finding suitable replacements for the outgoing expats; the Swedish consortium's Chinese employment conditions were well below those offered by US companies; the Consortium Finance guy, whom I had replaced in China was a typical envious Swedish accountant who did not like to see people paid more than was the norm in European; even though surviving in China was a rough call. This was the same guy I had replaced as Secretary in 1985 and who as the reader may recall lost his position as head accountant for the Astra International Group; being voted out by his peers (I was one of them) at an International Conference in Denmark some years ago; we did not see eye to eye on many matters.

Ann and I realised that we had a more than positive negotiating situation; we discussed what would be the price for us to commit to a further 2 years in China. Firstly we wanted to keep our home in Singapore; the outgoing CEO's villa was very well furnished so would be nice to live in; we did not want to share it with another single expat living in the small upstairs unit could it be ours without the need to sub let; both the Singapore Condo and the Villa in China should be fully maintained from a utilities and telephone position; the present salary level to be paid in Australian Dollars into an account in Singapore plus an additional 10% paid in US$ in China; this 10% would cover our in country costs. The present contract provided for travel Singapore China return every 12 weeks however we had heard that the Swedish in country expats were given a US $ 20,000 as an 12 monthly travel allowance, this should also be available; we then prepared a wish list of items that would make every day living in China easier in each of the three villas.

This wish list comprised a small freezer, so pork could be purchased in winter and stockpiled for the summer months when the heat and flies made buying melting pork a health hazard. A small dish washer, readily available in Singapore this would make the provision of lunches by the villas residents as well as western dinners for western food hungry; short stay visitors easier to clean up after. A local person to clean our villas; the experience of just living in the small unit on the top of villa 2 showed that after two weeks without dusting; all surfaces were covered with very oily dust scum. The results of the air being almost a solid mass of smog from a large aluminium smelter located some distance away.

An above ground swimming pool to be erected in the villa grounds for the use of expats; summers were unbearable hot and swimming in the lake was a health hazard from liver fluke; to complete the picture of outdoor living a gas barbeque to be provided. Additional small white goods like sandwich maker, hot water jug, toaster, mixer; a larger TV set with video recorder and satellite reception (A modern invention just put into the commercial sphere). A rental car for use while in Singapore plus my choice of a car in China coupled with a paid driver to be shared by the residents of the three villas. A definite in country period, with paid time off if this was exceeded; as we were working 6 days a week this additional work day per week to be added to the annual leave entitlement, plus some sort of paid employment on a casual basis for wives.

This was hard bargaining but agreement was reached on all matters except for the additional time off, added annual leave, employment for our wives and satellite reception; the JV accountant previously referred to was instrumental in not allowing all of these benefits; he felt we were overpaid as it was. My boss in the UK a frequent visitor now to China approved all; but he was overruled by the other consortium members; as a pacifier my boss said that my time out of country would not be monitored as he trusted me to do the job that was required.

After our usual 1987 family Christmas at Dural it was very much surprised at how fast the grandchildren were growing; we returned to Singapore and went shopping for all of the white goods; Astra A were instructed to purchase the largest above ground pool, with sand bed filter, a large gas BBQ and a large supply of a supply of chlorine; Singapore at that time was a shopping mecca; white and electronic goods were at least 50% cheaper than in Australia and certainly more than 60% cheaper than European, the cost estimates were based on Sydney prices so by shopping in Singapore we could ensure that a few extra pieces were added; walking into a retail establishment in Singapore with a purchase list comprising 3 of a lot of items immediately resulted in a clamour for the business, by shopping around some good deals resulted in a much underspent budget. Surprise, surprise, even the accountant in Sweden commented on the thrift.

Late January returned to China and moved into Villa 1, ours. Ann stayed in Singapore; it was winter, bitterly cold; so she had agreed to defer coming in country until arrival of the new purchases now to be airfreight to Shanghai. Now we were very friendly with the expat managers at the Hau Ting Sheraton; so when travelling in or out of China there would be an over night stay. This arrangement was good; it meant that we would not miss our departures flights due to bad traffic conditions, not just probable but a real concern which had happened to a number of short stay visitors; we could also buy milk and steak; yes at exorbitant prices compared to Oz; price did not matter, real milk after the powdered variety was heaven and the occasional steak was a big change from pork and chicken; particularly after the smuggled supplies had run out.

The fresh milk story goes along way in gaining an understanding about the gap between the Chinese and ourselves and how they seem to imagine that all our needs were satisfied. Almost at the end of our time in early 1989 it was discovered that there was a dairy quite close to our villas; not only that they delivered milk on a daily basis, sure it was in glass bottles with a piece of brown paper covering the top held on with a piece of twine, but it was real milk. All expats were excited when it became possible to buy real milk at the international hotels that were springing up in Shanghai in late 1988; each hotel had a shop where the ever increasing number of expats could buy so called western goods for their kitchens; usually in hotel owned serviced apartments; but this was a long way off to us in the beginning of 1986. My secretary told about this supply of local milk in early 1989; she was now more interested in going to Australia than being a secretary and used every available minute to practice her Australian, a chance question led to the discovery of the local milk supply.

Now with a very liveable residence in China; the arrival of a American couple and their young son together with the anticipated arrival of a new Swedish VP with his wife; Ann now felt that she would stay in China for longer periods; our No. 1 villa was very comfortably furnished and with the expected arrival of all the new gear, swimming pool and barbeque; life took on a more rosy hue; well one did dream.

The winter of 1987/8 was extremely bitter, the spray from the aerators in the fish ponds once again froze, any water left outside at night was solid in the morning, one morning we awoke; it is snowing was my first comment; Ann replied " Don't be silly how can you know you haven't got out of bed yet". Very simple; the quietness; falling snow seems to absorb the sounds that abound in the surroundings. Jumping out of bed; quickly dressing, we spent a great deal of the early morning making fresh tracks in the new snow surrounding the villas. It was a magical moment still discussed; there were a few magical moments in China but many oh so many long hours of frustration and annoyance.

One other magical moment comes to mind, it was the previous winter; on the one day a week break; idly walking along the lake side in the Chinese garden attached to the hotel; there was a wall that separated the path from the lake, it was quiet; there was a sound; the tinkling of bells; I stood quietly and listened to this sound entranced by its tune. Walking towards the source of the melody, I discovered that it was the result of the movement of a thin film of ice that had frozen on the surface of the lake; pieces of this thin ice was tinkling against the small stones at the waters edge. A long time was devoted to listening to this natural timpani until the winter sun melted the fragile film of ice.

For some months at the beginning of 1988 now the highest ranking expat the position 2IC of the JV in China. The hope was that this role would continue after the appointment of the new Swedish national who was a manufacturing engineer by profession however this man and wife were very good friends of the Swedish chairman of the JV (also a production man) so this was not to be. One of the roles in a project of this nature is PR; this involved frequent local government contact as well as invitations to banquets when other prospective JV groups were entertained; so time wasting and mostly not enjoyable, it was political to paint a good picture of our experiences; this did not seem to create a problem for the previous Swedish CEO who had such a positive spin on life in general, but as an Australian who speaks their mind it was exceedingly difficult not to tell it as it really was.

A group from one of the large world player accounting consulting firms was visiting China; it was a discovery mission like many at that time. The question like so many others; what was particularly needed to set up an auditing arm for use by the JV organisations. An invitation to join the banquet was extended in both the role of VP of an existing JV and a senior professional working with the local accounting authorities in regard to tax and JV accounting regulations. My experience in system and procedural installations was well known and respected within the Swedish group; the local taxation regulations for JVs now printed in English was a book of about 100 pages with one chapter on a standard code of accounts. This was of particular interest having developed a number of account and product coding systems during the 18 years at Astra A.

One task was to establish monthly operational reports for management, these needed the development of manufacturing forecasts, production costing systems, sales statistics, departmental budgets, actual to budget reports; all of those good figure things that keep management informed on the life blood of the company; a code of accounts very necessary in the new computer world ; question why not use the Chinese Taxation requirements as a base; a long discussion with both the old and young Chinese accountants; who totally agreed.

The first tax return had been submitted; a summons from the local Tax office as in any society required instant attention; the young accountant accompanied me; he now was becoming increasingly proficient in Chinglish; we did not have any other interpreter with accounting translation experience so he was good to have along on this type of meeting. The usual palaver, handing out of cigarettes, a metal lighter with emblem denoting western manufacture laid on the table, a Parker pen ever ready in the hand from the supply in my pocket; steaming cups of green tea, before proceeding to business. The subject; our use of the regulation accounting code; it was pointed out in very critical terms that we had incorrectly interpreted the instructions. Using all calming down powers counting to ten, deep breaths etc I proceeded to try to establish a recognisable logic in their interpretation of the Beijing regulations.

I do not wish to bore the reader with the fundamentals in establish numbering codes but it had been the subject of many previous long meetings including discussions with so called experts in this field. It was a long held belief that in a room of 10 computer code experts there will be 10 different approaches to the main code structure; and many more when trying to establish the sub code structures. Having been the architect in designing a number of identifying coding systems for different applications in Australia; also knowing that all were still being used; even as the business grew exponentially; with transfer from small to larger to larger computer systems. I felt comfortable with my knowledge of coding fundamentals.

Now in late 1987 here in China faced with the ignorance of taxation bureaucrats, a question sprang to mind why is this specie of mankind found in all countries, including Australia. Now mix this specie with the people at this meeting; they did not have a basic education, most had little knowledge of accounting; their main claim to fame was being a card carrying diligent member of the party; blindly following their next in line. Oh the frustration the utter frustration. The interpreter whose father was an educated man; killed during a vilification session, also with two black marks on his records was now trying to be as diplomatic as possible. From his body language it was apparent that he was putting his spin on the discussion just in case they also had a Chinglish speaker. After some 60 minutes of arrogant stupidity, with a smile on my face as another pen was laid on the table, followed by an almost a full packet of cigarettes and naturally a Ronson lighter; with much hand shaking we bid the men good day.

This problem would have to be solved as it would not go away; during the next transit between Singapore and Hong Kong a meeting was arranged with the JV auditor who was had been part of the large trans-national group previously visiting Wuxi. The predicament was explained; they supplied the name of one of the professors of accountancy in Beijing, a man who they thought may have been the originator of the taxation regulation accounting code. Decision next time Ann came in country she would arrange to leave via Beijing, I would accompany her there to meet this professor..

It was much simpler to arrange travel arrangement between cities inside of China with a travel agent outside of China than to try to do so using local resources. Prior to my appointment as a VP in 1988; it was necessary each time you entered the country to obtain from the Chinese Consul in Singapore an entry visa; this application had to be accompanied by a letter from the CEO of the JV specifically stating that you required to be at the JV during a certain period. This visa application usually required a week to be processed; thus each time you left China a letter requesting your return was obtained. The day after arrival in Singapore a visit to the Chinese Embassy was necessary to obtain the next entry visa. Once the position of VP was accepted both Ann and I were granted Chinese residency, and thus received a multi entry visa.

Ann returned to Singapore and arranged the flights, firstly together Shanghai to Beijing, then for her, Beijing Singapore and mine Beijing Wuxi, We had never visited Beijing so took this occasion to be tourists for a few days; sampling the exquisite taste of a real Peking Duck in one of the restaurants famous for this world renown culinary masterpiece; taking a bus tour to a lacquer ware, then a cloisonné ware factory; culminating in a walk on the famous Great Wall of China; (now of rabbit proof fame.) Like tourists; but now Chinese residents we walked on the famous Tiananmen Square, at the time the queue too long to visit the great leader Mao but marvelled at this famous city still operating in 1950s mode.

The visit with the Professor; he advised that he was indeed part of the reference group that proposed the tax code of accounts; further more he totally agreed with my interpretation; his words were "how else could it be interpreted". He would take the matter up at a higher level as soon as possible; there was no further moves by the local tax authorities so assumed this matter was closed.

We departed Beijing; Ann had to go to the international airport; while my departure point was the internal airport. Ann had a great deal of trouble leaving Beijing; at one stage she thought she would have to wait for another 24 hours, you can imagine the frustration, the utter frustration of being in a place where no one speaks your language at all and efficiency in any aspect of living at pre 1950's level. For me a taxi to the internal airport which was part of an air force base; after a great deal of uncertainty there being a complete absence of English of any form; I boarded the correct plane and surprised to discover that it was a converted air force plane; it still had tubular steel, web covered seats; the seat belt was in fact a web belt with a buckle as such that we use to hold up our trousers.

Very aware that China internal air travel; had a dubious reputation for safety; so the teeth were clenched as we took off; when airborne another surprise; 4 boiled eggs, two small cup cakes and a paper cup full of orange coloured water for breakfast. The flight was uneventful; arriving safely at Wuxi airport (also an air force field) here the passengers deplaned and collected their own luggage from the luggage hold of the plane, a driver had been arranged to collect me from the airport so declined the offer of a taxi. The arranged driver as usual was very late and so sat in this small room waiting and watching the military planes on the tarmac. How patient you needed to be with the Chinese drivers.

In due process of time (China reminiscent of manyana time in Mexico) word was received that our new white goods were at Shanghai airport; Ann also due to arrive shortly, therefore kill two birds with one stone as it were, pick up Ann and take delivery of our new white goods, needed two cars to go to Shanghai, should not be a problem as we now had 6 cars in the fleet, 3 Volvos; one for each of the Swedish expats all of whom had returned to European; as well as the original 3 Nissans. Using the in house customs people, all of the required paperwork was in put order; still obviously the Chinese "friendship" approach was necessary. Equipped with a good supply of cigarettes, lighters and pens; electing to drive one car my longest trip so far in China (as yet no licence required; arrived at the airport to collect Ann and our new possessions. After some false starts; there were no understandable signs to point to the freight terminal; we arrived at the hallowed doors of the freight terminal; it was now about 10.00; naturally with interpreter at our side, more searching, the interpreter of no use out of his environment, we eventually found the correct official. The usual offer of a cigarette to the two men at the desk, leaving the packet on the table; using one of the nice heavy metal lighters with logo; lit the cigarettes, and placed it on the table; many new forms to be completed and signed (chopped by them); strange; each new form needing completion the pen passed from my supply would disappear; a new pen or each form. I kid you not.

After completing all of this additional paperwork, two cartons of cigarettes were left on the table with another lighter to replace the one that had strangely disappeared; just as a sign of friendship. We were taken into the large warehouse; to find the man who would find our goods; he would load them onto a fork lift truck and take them to our cars. The man; not one of the two officials leading the way to the goods, indicated that a sign of friendship was necessary to locate the goods, so another carton of cigarettes disappeared like magic into the large pocket of the man's apron; payment made, he showed us the location of our goods and left; the interpreter walked away and found the fork lift driver who only required a packet of cigarettes to deliver the goods to the cars. A pen also seemed to find it's way into the fork lift driver's hand as he unloaded the items onto the ground and got a receipt. Wonders of wonders; all of our items were intact so at 13.00; after three hours of nonsense we loaded the cars and headed off for our 4 hour trip to Mashan.

One of the most stupefying things about working at that time in China was the way that systems and procedures necessary to provide the frame work of a successful business were ignored or even sabotaged, when the architect was absent from the office; for what ever reason; with the consensus approach everything that you did , every small procedure that you wished to established had to have due consultation but turn your back and all would be ignored; it was vitally necessary for your own health and well being that you stayed no longer than 12 weeks (8 for American JVs) in country. This time out was recognized by the US JV's but had not really by our Swedish management; there was an understanding that every 12 weeks you were entitled to have a 2 week break but what was the reason for this down time a question often asked by the Management in Sweden. So the timing of these two weeks were unstructured. In my mind after 12 weeks in China you needed a break but you also needed to go into an environment where things were worked. Just going out to a beach resort gave you a break but you also needed the stimulus of knowing that the work you were doing in China was in deed ordinary; it was only doing what you had been doing elsewhere, a time to reinforce in your mind that what you know works. The Americans did this the Swedes did not.

Therefore; while you sat on the beach being pampered by the never ending stream of vendors of all sorts of physical and culinary delights in some Asian beach resort you knew that what you had achieved in the last 12 weeks would be partly undone when you returned. Systems that were approved, implemented and indeed working would be discontinued during your absence; or a work program instituted to bring about change would be totally ignored. It was difficult to discover why or who issued the instructions to ignore the requirements; when you asked a few people on your return why something was not being done; you would receive a multitude of answers; to the old China hand this indicated that some one on high had decided that the system should not be followed or the new regulation ignored. It was frustration in the extreme.

Immediately on return to China in January 1988 there was an advise that the arrival of the new Swedish VP would be delayed; followed by a question, could my planned outside trip be delayed until his arrival; this was 18 weeks from now. My belief was that I had enough will and dedication to stay the course so agreed to the proposal; at the end of the 18 weeks I was a mess, small incidents became mountainous and the continued lack of cooperation by the new Chinese President who believed he or his masters knew better than anyone else added to the already difficult time of living in China. In many ways the average Swede seems to be able to cope better in these circumstances than the average Australian; they have the ability to bend with the wind, not too care too much if they plainly are being taken for a ride.

Being a Swedish company the natural car selection was Volvo, in fact Astra A had changed exclusively to Volvos in the early 70s, they were seen as such a safer car although very expensive in Australia; notwithstanding as a Swedish company with a fleet rising to 100 vehicles we received special attention; in fact one year we made a larger profit from fleet turnover than we did in selling pharmaceuticals another story. On receiving approval to have a hired car in Singapore for Ann as well as a car in China it was assumed that the order would be Volvo; however their were doubts in my mind on the availability of local service particularly after a couple of hard years use in China. There was an organisation servicing Volvos in Beijing but there was often a long wait until they visited your area for service. The local mechanics were army trained and not equipped in knowledge or tools to handle the more complex vehicles like the Volvo. Chrysler had started a JV outside of Shanghai producing a 4 wheel drive sedan Jeep Cherokee but the report from others in China strongly advised against buying one of these.

From the driving experiences in China both as a back seat driver and the rare times as a driver the thought was that the best vehicle would be a Nissan Pathfinder or a Toyota Land Cruiser; the driver sat high; this had a three fold effect; firstly you were looking down on the bicycles, pedestrians and mini tractors , secondly you missed the full effect of the night driving habits; thirdly when faced with a flooded road you could continue where a sedan would be forced to wait until the water receded.

As a point of interest the night driving habits of the locals were particularly worrying; it appears the common thing was drive only on parking lights; then of course when a vehicle approached you switched on your head lights and flashed high beam, as you can imagine; the result is blind driving for a few moments.

The choice of one of these two Japanese cars was carefully pondered, they both were purpose built for Chinese conditions ie rough terrain, which at that time was the norm in China. From a service point of view both Toyota and Nissan had many vehicles on the road in China therefore servicing was not quite the issue as it was with the Volvo. In Australia the Nissan was considered a more comfortable vehicle in fact it was almost a sedan comfort so it was the preference. The logistics department in Sweden advised that there was a 4 months delay on a Nissan vehicle but an immediate delivery ex Japan on a Toyota. I chose the Toyota knowing that even with immediate delivery it would still take some 3 months before the vehicle would be delivered to Wuxi.

Although 4 additional months does not seem to the casual observer a great deal of time to wait for the vehicle of my choice but at that time it truly was a life time. Look at our position; we were once again at the vagrancies of the factory utilities; one never knew if the next day would be a work day or a rest day, once you had a rest day then work would continue for 6 days or until the utilities broke down again. One of the previous in country Swedes had found a ships provedore in down town Shanghai, it was a godsend; here we could buy western food like bacon and ham, tinned goods from all parts of the world, as well as vegetables out of season in Wuxi. To ease constant work and living frustration it was good to get out of Wuxi for a night to stay in a western hotel surrounded with tourists or other expats; consider the luxury of being able to talk your mother tongue with the Australian expat staff at the Sheraton in Shanghai. So every effort was made to go to Shanghai at least one a month; there were the ever present dangers of road travel and the utter discomfit of the long journey but it was just good to be out of Wuxi.

Without your own vehicle it was necessary to arrange for a driver and car for both the up and down journeys; train travel was an option but this needed at least a three day planning period. The drivers were all party faithful who constituted a law unto themselves; one would arrange with the Administration Manager who controlled the drivers to have a driver and car available at 4.30 on the evening preceding the day that was to be the off day. This would put us in Shanghai at about 21.00. The driver would pick us up at 09.00 on the next day after a nice buffet breakfast, go down town for western food shopping and then return to Wuxi by about 17.00 the following day. There was a street side free market near the Sheraton so staple vegetables could be purchased there before 09.00. All in all it was just so bleeding marvellous to go to Shanghai.

Unfortunately the drivers and the slimy Admin manager had other ideas; we now had two senior Chinese in control of the company, they would determine whether or not you would get a car; we also highly suspected that the drivers were running a taxi or hire car service for the local authorities but this could not be proven. Consequently you would be all set to go to Shanghai at 16.30; we would have packed an overnight bag and ready to escape. The time would come and go; no driver, one would try to contact the Village in Wuxi by phone, this almost impossible, so after a frustrating hour you would unpack and spend another evening playing computer games; cards or whatever. So you can see that the wait of 4 months for ex Japan delivery then the possibility of a further 3 months to get to China to us would have been a life time.

The Toyota arrived; to my horror it was a model special manufactured for China, it did not have the softer suspension that was standard on the Australian models; consequently it handled and rode like a truck. It also had a tendency to slide in wet muddy conditions under brakes but still it was much preferred to drive than the Volvo. In an ordinary sedan like a Volvo you were sitting below the bike riders, you could not see what those very close to you were going to do, the Toyota being much higher gave you a long range view of the road conditions as well as being able to look down on those bikes that you were travelling beside. The mini tractors would career up onto the road from side paths, with a Volvo you would not see them coming but sitting high in the Toyota you could anticipate their arrival.

The other real benefit, night driving; beside the danger of driving blinded by the flash of high beams; somewhat negated in the high cabin of the Toyota, the multitude of bikes had neither lights nor rear reflectors; they were almost invisible on an ordinary dark night let alone on a wet windy night. Pedestrians also walked along your side of the road with their backs to you; in their usual dark blue padded coats, totally invisible in the light from your parking lamps, then blinded momentarily by the on coming vehicles made accidents with other less protected road users a real and present danger. Maybe the reader will understand why the rough riding Toyota; bumping over partially constructed roads was preferable to the soft comfort of a Volvo.

Before the car arrived, rules were changed, now it was necessary to obtain a local drivers licence. Also Ann and I were now Chinese residents, we needed a special license to use local currency. To prepare for the driving test we were given a few sheets of Chinese driving regulations to study, the Administration manager made an appointment with the local police for us to sit the written test and then to test our performance in practical terms. Now recall the previous mention of using the correct translator for ever purpose. It is vital that you use an interpreter who knows the speech terms that will be encountered in the meeting or presentation. We tried to find an interpreter that either had a licence or some driving training, this was impossible. The interpreter we had available to us for official type business was very good in general conversation, however motor vehicle driving and the various terminology used in this pursuit; simple although it seems to us who drive as soon as we possible can; but these special terms did not form part of his lexicon.

Our group of 4 studied the very rudimentary instructions, noting regulations like "no horning near hospitals", horn whenever you are about to overtake another motorised vehicle. Memorising the varying speed limits; through towns 20k per hour, on country roads 50. There was no definition of a country road, everywhere we travelled it was highly populated; farm land yes but highly populated; in NSW the definition of a country road was one without street lights, this did not apply in China as there were very few street lights except right in town. Another one that was difficult to explain; on country roads you must drive down the centre of the road; when an oncoming vehicle appears you must move to the right hand side of the road until the vehicle passes then you return again to the middle. This was a difficult manoeuvre for those who all their life had driven on the left hand side of the road which we all know in Australia is the right side; the automatic tendency is to return to the left hand side. In China like in many other countries the left hand side of the road is the wrong side, the right side is the right side. I have driven now in 28 countries; in fact over time a holder of a licence in 8 different countries; before starting out to drive in another country there is a little poem said to myself; "in Australia the left side is the right side, and the right side is the wrong side, now I am in European China; America, Continental Europe the left side is the wrong side and the right side is the right side. It helped me to remember but one had to be extra careful when entering a road from a car park or garage and more particularly at roundabouts.

The day dawned for our test there were 4 of us plus the interpreter and the police examiner. The examiner wrote about 10 questions on the board and the interpreter wrote his equivalent underneath. We questioned a couple of the interpretations as they appeared weird. The first question; why do you need road rules? The second question; was what would happen if you did not have to have a driving test. We discussed this amongst ourselves and then we remembered that of the 50 pages of instructions almost two pages were devoted to these two questions, it was of prime importance to know that you needed road rules so that the rights of other citizens were acknowledged on the road way, and you needed a driving licence so that you as a person acknowledged that specific rules are required to be learnt so that you could be in command of a vehicle. There were other rules somewhat strange; for example there was no smoking or talking while driving. We wrote down our answers and then the interpreter had to sit and write each person's answers into Chinese. After these answers in Chinese were examined by the policeman; he told us through the interpreter that he would pass us all even though our answers were not as good as he required. Friendship payments ????.

It was now time for the practical driving test. There were 6 people in the car; in the front seat as I drove was the interpreter who sat beside me in the middle, then the policemen; in the rear was Ann plus the other two expats who were being tested. We left the factory area and travelling down the road towards an intersection, the policemen in Chinese told me to turn into the street on the left however by the time that the interpreter gave me the instruction I was past the point at which I could safely make the turn; at the end of the practical test with each person driving for some 10 minutes we all were successful except the guy from the US; he was an ex aircraft carrier fighter pilot but they failed him because he was not forceful enough on the road. A carton of cigarettes and a lighter completed the day, the US driver who had failed visited the police station later in the week with another carton of cigarettes and without further ado was also given his little red book driver's licence.

In China all drivers are re-examined every 12 months, we would attend the police station with an interpreter; the policeman would then proceed to list all of our traffic infractions; yes we were that closely watched. A carton of cigarettes and another "chop" in our book and off we went to break the rules again. China had what many may believe are very stringent road rules, one such rule in particular; at age 60 you are no longer eligible for a licence, just after we left China in 1989 a older Swedish guy who had married a young Chinese girl had his 60th birthday; thus he was no longer eligible to drive; as he was very good "friends" with the local mayor they changed his date of birth so that he could continue to drive. Where there is a will and a friendship gift there is a way.

I keep using the word "chop"; the appointment as head of finance and marketing now presented the opportunity to see where the money was being spent; we were selling our products on the so called open market; as usual in a start up phase funds were tight. All cheques now had to have my signature before they were despatched; in China a written signature is not regarded an authority to charge your account; the cheque must have an imprint of the drawers "chop" or seal; everyone in China has their own seal (chop); my name in Chinese was etched on the end of an ornate piece of jade. A chop can be made out of any stone and the higher the standing of the individual the more costly is the chop. Mine was presented ceremoniously by management together with a tin of the red substance into which you dip the chop before stamping it onto the document. It was a messy business but it worked, naturally the chop had to be kept in a safe place but it also meant that if you were not going to be the in the office for a period of time then you could give your chop to someone who had your authority.

I imagine the saying "chop, chop" meaning hurry up came from the time honoured and still practiced custom of placing a chop on a document; usually on any document there was more than one chop imprint, at least two people had to give their approval; the words chop, chop advised the people to get moving. This multiple chopping or handling of documents is usual in many countries where there is an oversupply of cheap labour. To preserve jobs and create employment; systems are devised so that many people have to approve a document or system before it is fully authorised. The withdrawal of money from a bank or buying travellers cheques is a time consuming process. I described this process when I talked about our trip to Sri Lanka in another book.

In China; as I did during my time as a bank teller; the cashier (teller) would sit behind a screen; the withdrawal form would be passed across; if you wanted to purchase travellers cheques then the first step was to be paid the money; don't ask me why this was so; cheque nicely chopped passed to the teller. Sitting at desks immediately behind the teller was a line of clerks I counted 6 at the Bank of China we used. Each of these 6 people would handle the cheque form, I am not sure what they did; I noted some would make entries on a sheet of paper, others would refer to other records on their desk once they had finished their process they would place their chop on the cheque. You actually left the counter and stood to one side similar the the Commonwealth Savings bank system in Oz in days long gone. Once this process was carried out; your name was called (in our case we were beckoned over as they had difficulty with the name) the teller would dispenses the money; it was now the end of step one. Carrying the money you went to another counter here you asked for and received a traveller's cheque requisition form; you returned to the customer's desk and completed the form and chopped it. End of step two.

This form together with the money was passed across the counter these once again were passed around a line of clerks again 6 in number. On arrival back at the clerk on the counter this person and the person beside them left their stools and proceeded into an office across from the line of clerks. The person from this office together with the two from the counter proceeded into the vault. Eventually emerging with the required travellers cheques; the two clerks returned to their line of desks and the traveller's cheques now made their way around the 6 clerks. After due time and much counting the cheques were given to you to sign; and once again they made their way around the circle. It took some considerable time but eventually you left with the travellers cheques. One never went to the bank expecting a quick exit; as a resident we were paid a proportion of our salary into a US $ bank account, thus every so often we had to go to the bank to obtain local money. We would try to have our driver do this for us as it could take up to an hour before you walked out of the bank with your shopping money.

While discussing banking it is interesting to look at the Chinese business systems used in those days; in particular the invoicing and collection of trade debts. Once again one has to learn things the hard way; a daily cash availability report was implemented; I could not understand why the total of the cheques I had chopped did not approximate the amount that was being withdrawn from our account. I also wondered why the number of cheques I chopped did not equate the number of withdrawals showing on our hand written bank statement, yes 1988, still hand written. A question of the young accountant whose job it was to prepare the report; answer "oh the majority of withdrawals from our bank are "Bills of Exchange".

In Australia our commercial practises moved away from local bills of exchange transactions prior to the 1950, during the late 50s when my position was Overseas clerk at the ANZ Burwood; promissory notes were still a small part of the daily work but today even they have disappeared; in the 1950's there was still a number Bills of Exchange but only for overseas transactions. In China however it was still the way to do to business; the procedure went this way; when the goods were despatched; the seller drew a bill of exchange and attached it to the invoice, this was handed to the bank; it was then sent to the purchaser's bank. The purchasers bank presented the Bill to the purchaser, they acknowledged (accepted) it and were given the invoice and transport documents; in shipping these documents are in fact documents of title to the goods; the holder of the documents actually owns them. The Bill of Exchange now held by the purchaser's bank and at a fixed and determinable future time depending on the credit terms plus 3 days of grace the account of the purchaser was debited and the funds returned to the drawers bank. There was one catch, there had to be funds in the bank;

all of our local expenses for materials was being withdrawn from our bank without having to draw a cheque no wonder it was not possible to relate cheques drawn to bank withdrawals.

In all things; you had to find these things out for yourself, there was no reference books to refer too; certainly my predecessor if he knew would not have told me. Naturally one should have realised that like all other things; China was still living with banking systems prevalent in the early 50s a time when Bills of Exchange were common business practice. Yes no advances in any way since the 1949 communist assumption of power.

While on the subject of money and business practices; in 1988 China was suffering a severe liquidity problem, vendors were supplying goods to the government wholesalers; Bills of Exchange were being drawn but as the buyer had no money on due date they could not meet the accounts. The JV was suffering from the same problems although the Swedish JV partner was still pouring funds into the organisation to keep it liquid; the Chinese JV side were approached as they centrally controlled all of the local pharmaceutical wholesalers; our customers, but to no avail. Another local banking institution was starting up in competition with the one and only Bank of China but the approach for finance was fruitless. Being now VP finance and marketing it was decided to use our accounting and pharmacy sales people to collect monies owing. So instead of selling these people travelled to the major customers and actually sat and waited at the customer's premises until funds were received and they would then return to us hopefully with a bag full of money. It was time consuming and mind bending as they may have to sit for a number of days but at least we were recovering some money from our debtors; at the time there was outstanding some 230 days of sales.

This practice was moderately successful; from employee efficiency it was disastrous; still the flow of funds was not sufficient to maintain our liquidity, some thing else needed to be done. It was suggested that maybe the visit of a foreign advisor would prompt the wholesalers to part with the money; Management approved the plan, as did the local government and police; for in country travel local government and police approval still had to approve your exact itinerary. Ann and I sat in the villa over a glass of sweet Chinese wine and planned the trip. At the time it was not possible to purchase a travel ticket of any type without the presenting to the ticket issuing agency the actual passport of the traveller; local people still had to have a written government permit to move outside of their own region; there was also another regulation that was strictly enforced; it appeared to be connected with the secret police monitoring the movement of individuals. This regulation provided that no travel ticket for inter province travel was issued for a time less than 3 days in advance; this requirement very strict the Manager of the Administration Department advised.

The plan was to drive to Shanghai, take a plane to Chengdu, the capital of Sichuan Province, meet with officials there, do a marketing pitch, collect money and then travel by train to Chunking, do the same and hopefully get more money, a three day travel by ferry down the Yangtze to Wuhan; hopefully more money and then return by plane to Shanghai with own car drive back home to Wuxi. We had arranged with Karen our daughter and John her fiancé to meet in Hong Kong after this trip; they were going to buy their matrimonial rings. With a 3 day delay in each place it was anticipated that this trip would take some 15 days, on our return write a report to management, bank any money, give ourselves a few days to recoup and repack for a Saturday departure to Hong Kong, there we would have a 5 day stay before Ann returned to Singapore and I went back to China. Having by now travelled extensively in a number of countries also travelled within China this timetable should not pose a problem, even the negativity of the Administration Manager failed to see any problem. So the second leg of this trip was arranged and paid for. We were to be accompanied by a new member of the Finance staff who was very good in Chinglish so we put our luggage in the Toyota and bumped our way to Shanghai, there was now a standing arrangement that allowed us to garage cars at the Sheraton provided we spent at least one night in residence; a friendship payment to the garage manager could also get special favours; like car cleaning and minor service.

A CAAC (China Airways Administration Corporation) internal flight on a western built plane was always the key to a greater chance of survival so in the arrangements we tried to make this happen. Second leg after the road trip to Shanghai, plane Shanghai / Chengdu. As was common practice for a visiting dignitary here we were met by a group of people with two cars, there were only three of us but we knew that this visit would be a special occasion for this far flung city; the usual top bureaucratic entertainment reserved for dignitaries would have to be endured. After the appropriate meeting ceremony, Ann and I found our selves in the back seat of a large car together with a local young Chinese lady, the interpreter for the local dignitaries; our interpreter had been allocated to the other car. The top dignitary now sitting beside our driver; during a break in the polite conversation; answering questions such as; why is an Australian travelling on behalf of a Swedish JV?, we asked this young lady what were the plans for the three days; our accommodation already arranged at a new Holiday Inn hotel so we knew that this would be at least of basic Western standard; newly constructed so it should be clean, without mice and cockroach infestations that was a feature much of our travel in China.

Firstly she replied that we were going to have lunch at a restaurant that was very special in Sichuan Province; in fact it was even famous outside of China for its menu consisted of one thousand snakes. "Gulp"' you know gulp was a very common reaction in China; it portrays the drop in the stomach; the quickening of the breath accompanied by the rush of the heart when at a moment in time something is said or happens that makes you wish you were somewhere else. We looked quickly at each other and then resumed a stoic facial expression; it was arranged; so what could we do about it; Ann could opt out; feigning sickness or what ever but my place was in the loop; so in our calmest voices we replied "That sounds nice". Snake had been eaten in Hong Kong, tasting somewhat like chicken or maybe closer to eel but 1000 dishes of snake; the mind was aghast; calmly sitting there in the car with this smiling young lady making small talk but all the time the minds imagining what would make up 1000 snake dishes.

Holiday Inn reception; service of more Western style but still the abrupt Chinese way; still, it was a long way from Shanghai where more friendly tones were starting to be practised; then our room by ourselves and discussed the forthcoming lunch; Ann was committed to giving it a go, so after a strong Dimple, a freshen up; we joined our interpreter from Wuxi; the driver and our new young interpreter friend who proceeded to take us to the world famous 1000 snake restaurant. Imagine our surprise and amazement when we arrived at a grand restaurant that even had signs in English portraying itself to be the home of hot chilli Sichuan snacks, prepared by chefs who were both local and overseas trained and was in truth known outside of China for its 1000 snacks in fact a yum cha type of lunch. In Australia we could have dined out on this story but we were Chinese residents and Australia seemed light years away; drawn together more closely by our many such experiences our faces lit up with a smile as we both enjoyed the hot spicy Sichuan dishes. This dining experience was in truth worthy of international renown, the small delicately spiced dishes kept arriving until as is usual in China you have reached saturation point and then in comes the hot steaming chilli permeated last course; which in Chinese fashion was soup.

Driving through the old streets, we considered how poor the people appeared; Wuxi was beginning to see some fashion creeping into the clothes of the young ladies; but here on the dusty dirty streets; alive with people in all manner of seemingly old clothes hurrying about their business; the many roadside eating places; set up for hot pot style meals; each location would only have one or two tables; each table would have a small wok like vessel on a small coal dust clay cooking stove; the wok containing what appeared to be a mixture of chilli oil and water, this concoction bubbling away sending clouds of chilli smelling steam into the atmosphere. The main element of food appeared to be cabbage although our progress through the ill maintained streets; filled with all manner of conveyances with still mostly humans providing the movement force; did not allow us to get a good look at what people were eating.

That night the usual invitation to a banquet; Ann preferred to stay in the normality of a western hotel room with a room service meal. This banquet was a semi government affair and as guest of honour you were seated on the right side of the top official; the interpreter sitting beside you. This very common seating arrangement at banquets was always very difficult; the host in addressing you; had to in fact to address the interpreter across your face then the interpreter repeated his words albeit in English; then you would politely address remarks to the face of the official, this meant that you had to talk a little louder so that the interpreter could hear what you said and then the interpreter would talk across you to the host. Occasionally there was a host who spoke broken Chinglish; they wanted to demonstrate their skills to the minor officials at the table; then to be able to carry on a conversation in a slow modulated voice was a task that required all of ones attention.

The protocol for banquets required the host to place the first portion of any new dish into you small bowl of rice; they would use their own chop sticks, to us a decidedly unhygienic practice; over time at the Hubin we had convinced the staff that they should provide a spare set of chop sticks for this ritual but this practice was still not common. It is time to talk about some of the dishes that were considered delicacies in China but do not sit lightly on many western stomachs. Over the 4 years when faced with these dishes I had bravely learnt not to "gulp" when they appeared on a rarely translated menu; knowing that they were expensive and very much a delicacy enjoyed by the local people. It is natural when these dinners are paid for by the government and with an honoured guest the officials could and did indulge themselves by having at least one of these expensive special dishes.

The practise of trepanning the head of a live monkey filling the skull with boiling oil and then eating the brains, is not a figment of imagination; it was and probably still is considered a delicacy; I for one find the whole process horrendous, but surrounded by 11 others who were enjoying the occasion it was not polite or political to get up and leave; thankfully this was a one off experience. However another dish always resulted in a "gulp" reflex and unfortunately to my horror was served at a number of banquets where I was the guest of honour. This dish comprised deep fried small chicken;

that was how it was listed on the menu (one was in fact translated into English in my honour); said quickly it seems yummy; however the dish consisted of small; very small chickens that had just completely formed within the egg, before the chicken decided to peck themselves out; the shell was broken and the resultant small fully formed chicken; without any feathers was dipped quickly into boiling oil, they were then arranged on the serving dish with usually 3 to each guest in a 12 course banquet.

The first experience was somewhat daunting; the dish arrived and proudly displayed; upon discerning what they were the stomach went flippity flop. The arrival on the plate accompanied by the smile on the face of the host meant one could not be so impolite as to refuse the proffered delicacy; so there they were sitting on my bowl of rice; the small legs and feet pointing into the air; the head with beak, and sightless eyes looking at me. A watery smile to my host, nimble activity with the sticks, into the mouth and down the cake hole all in one movement; twice more this routine was managed as well conveying delight at receiving such a delicacy; the interpreter telling me how lucky it was to have this dish served; it was served at a number of other official banquets; the modus operandi for consumption was always a quick swallow however it was noticed that the attending Chinese chewed theirs with great relish.

These two dishes were the only ones that caused difficulty in China, later during my 2 year stay in Japan I was feted with a couple of other dishes that were difficult to swallow but more of that in another book. Dishes like duck tongue, chicken feet, all varieties of snake, jellied eel, dog, cat were all part of the Chinese practice of eating every thing that moved and every part of the animal, stuffed pig stomach; a little like Scottish haggis was a particularly flavoursome meal in some parts of China. Quite often at a 24 course banquet (these were made illegal in the late 80s as a decadent waste of money), dishes would appear that you had absolutely no idea what was their main ingredient; the menu in Chinese; not a language that you have mastered, so observe the faces around you, no one is wincing or screwing up their nose; it is acceptable to the rest of the guests; try it and if it tastes okay it is okay. If one later finds out that it is something that you would normally balk at; not because of taste but because of tradition; well that is that. Having eaten in 40 plus countries I can attest that only once have I suffered from an upset stomach and that was in Lisbon Portugal again in another book.

I had been both host and guest of honour at a number of banquets but these were in Wuxi, Shanghai or Beijing, in Chengdu a different kind of host made an appearance; there is in all traditional cultures certain protocols to be observed on different occasions; in China there was a protocol that required the host to visit every table in a gathering; meet the guests and drink a toast to those at the table; as the VP Marketing this honour fell upon me at a number of large medical conferences one of which comprised some 100 tables, 1,200 people; 100 toasts is a lot of drink; another quirk to this protocol; if you clink your glass with any one; protocol demands that you "skoll" (down the hatch in Oz speak) the remainder of the fluid. On these occasions one sipped or pretended to drink if you wanted to be able to walk back to your table after finishing this meet and greet tradition.

These men in Chengdu were hard drinkers; they wanted to demonstrate this fact; unfortunately sitting at a table with 11 others; only one of which had sufficient Chinglish to hold a stilted conversation was a hard slog; particularly when all of a sudden it is realised that during the first few courses a number of them have risen from their seat to click your glass; forcing both to drink the remainder of the glass; often by then it's too late. The Chinese have a favourite spirit called Mao-tai, to me it is a foul smelling acrid tasting liquor; it can leave a residual taste in the mouth for some days after you have been forced to participate in a Mao-tai drinking evening. The evening in Chengdu was a case in point; there surely was a conspiracy to ensure that I left the table almost legless; gamely this attack was survived; next morning putting on my best face but with a head that was suffering as it had never done so before; I arrived at the offices of the No.1 Chengdu Pharmaceutical Wholesaler to meet with some of the men that had tried to drink me under the table the night before.

It was an interesting meeting; at least one of them must have been suffering as much as I; in particular one guy had been a very steady drinker; on leaving he had a great deal of difficulty in making his feet. Another interesting thing noted during the time in China was the suffusion of blood to the face that accompanied most Chinese drinking bouts. One could almost register the volume of alcohol consumed by the redness of the face; this was first noted at the 1986 Christmas party; Chinese beer was provided and a number of the young men would mix this with the Chinese version of "Fanta" a strange concoction but each to his own. The faces of these young men got ruddier and ruddier as the afternoon progressed; it may be that they were also lacing the drinks with medicinal alcohol that was readily available in the laboratory; I shall never know.

One of the main features recalled of Chengdu at the time was the dilapidated condition of the city and its buildings. The building that contained the main offices of the major provincial pharmaceutical supplier was an old two storey wooden building, the rickety stairs told the story of too many years of neglect and the wooden floor was so worn that in places you could see through large cracks; sitting in the usual large lounge chairs I wondered if the chair would fall through to the floor below, the result of this two hour meeting was an undertaking that my honoured visit was not in vain so returned to Ann for lunch and then to fill in time till the early evening of the next day to catch the now paid for, tickets issued and permission given for the overnight train to Chunking.

Remember we were not tourists as Chinese residents we were travelling by normal local transport; the itinerary provided that a train be used from Chengdu to Chungking, this train had an overnight sleeping carriage so this was arranged; naturally any honoured visit is not complete without the customary Chinese farewell; the young lady of the 1000 "snakes" was there to interpret for the local dignitary who was at the train to see us off. As an over night train we were seated in a compartment with the interpreter and another man, the day time arrangement consisted off 4 seats, these were converted to upper and lower bunks with a curtain front during the night; our allocated bunks were both on the lower level, but after discussion we managed to secure the bottom and top bunks on one side thus we could be secure behind our own curtain. Apart from one factor the trip was uneventful; however this factor alone was somewhat overpowering.

The compartment was next to the toilet compartment; the smell that emanated from there was horrible to the extreme; we could not work out why it was so bad; the train toilet was very similar to the ones that were on the trains that as a boy I had travelled on to Ballina; the toilet was a squat not a throne but the drain hole opened directly onto the railway line below. There was water in the tap over the small basin but the smell permeated every nook and cranny of our compartment, the dinner which was served in the compartment by the dining staff was bland and edible but the smell displaced any hunger.

The stream engine pulling our carriages eventually pulled in to Chungking; once again we were met by a group of local functionaries; this city was the seat of Government during part of the Sino-Japanese war; situated in the bottom of a valley through which the mighty Yangtze River flows; it has a huge inversion problem and they say that the sun only shines in Chungking 49 days a year. The combined effects of smog and low cloud meant the Japanese even with total air superiority had great difficulty in bombing the city. Chungking is also known as "the cradle" of the revolution; it was the birthplace and home of the hero of the revolution Sun Yat Sen; we were taken on a tour to this very simple house which is now almost regarded as a shrine to this amazing man. Being certainly no scholar of Chinese history but what I have read is very interesting. On reflection and having had the opportunity to see China grow from agricultural to industrial until 29 years later it has an economy that will soon rival America. To one whom experienced agricultural China the transformation in 29 years is truly amazing.

Chungking; the usual elaborate welcome and banquet; however here we were staying at an old Chinese Hotel and needed to deploy our mice and cockroach barriers before climbing into the high very soft, fluffy bed at night. To counter the entry of these obnoxious pest, prevalent through out the whole country we carried dust excluders to be placed on the floor at the doorway; if there was a balcony another barrier would be placed at that door. A strong pest spray and a jar of very strong "White Cat" brand Chinese detergent to wash the bath or shower was always part of the travelling kit. A supply of food was also carried in case the local dining rooms or restaurants looked to grubby to think of eating there.

Day one; Chungking; the usual meeting that lasted some 3 hours; a banquet; a battle to stay away from the heavy drinkers; then sit and wait for the obligatory three days to expire before we would join a ferry to take us down the mighty Yangtze and through the fabled Gorges; at this time reputed to be one of the scenic wonders of the world but now will disappear. A mighty dam being built to provide the insatiable demand for power required by 21st century China. The obligatory farewell party arrives on day 4 to accompany us to the river harbour; It was astounding to look down 93 steps that led to the large floating pontoon wharf; from this height the ferry looked rather small; we were told that in flood time the pontoon wharf would be at the level where we were standing; the steeps steps were somewhat over the normal 20cm, so assuming that each step dropped 25cm the ferry was some 24 meters below us.

The arrival at the harbour was greeted by an ill dressed crowd of youths who immediately descended on the luggage; we even had to fight to hang on to our most precious over the shoulder bags which contained the important travel papers. The farewell dignitaries also tried to deter this dangerous looking group however without avail; farewell and boarding formalities over, our entourage comprising Ann, the interpreter, myself plus 5 of these baggage carriers each with one piece of luggage walked down the 93 steps leading to the floating wharf where our general purpose ferry was moored. On arrival at the wharf we presented the tickets that had been purchased in Chungking 3 days ago and we and the interpreter, together with the entourage of baggage carriers walked up the narrow gangplank. This gangplank consisted of one wide board with a steel cable hand rail on one side; it was not a walk lightly taken.

At the top of this gangplank we were greeted by the usual green uniformed officials who after minutely inspecting our travel documents spoke to the baggage handlers; one assumed they told them to POQ. Wanting to ensure that each piece of our luggage was placed safely on board we took out some local currency and one by one assumed control of each piece. With the bank depleted by some US $2.00 and unassisted we found our way to the upper deck where our cabin was located. This ferry had 3 above water line decks and at least one below, carrying the luggage up the almost vertical stairs was itself a feat. A sigh of relief; at least the Chinese had not invented a new numbering system; it was only by following arrows appended to chinese character signs; all bar the numbers totally illegible to us that our cabin was found. Once again this was not a tourist boat; we did see some very luxurious ones as we moved down stream but not for us as residents; in China service was a word not yet introduced into their lexicon.

This ferry did not have a first class section, we were travelling 2nd class; this constituted a small top deck cabin about 2.4 meters wide and 3 meters deep there was no window but we entered straight from an out side deck viewing area. In the cabin against each of the two long walls was a narrow bunk. Between these bunks on the bulkhead furthest from the door was a very small sink with a cupboard underneath, although each of us was travelling with one suitcase, (no wheels yet) a brief case and over the shoulder bag there was barely enough space to stack our luggage and then sit on the small chairs at the foot of each bunk.

The "Friendship Store" at Chungking had renewed our stock of Dimple but as there was only the usual pump vacuum flask of boiling water present in the cabin and there being no chance of some ice or even a glass of potable water; so we forsook our glass of nerve calming amber fluid and went out on deck to watch the departure from Chungking; the ferry our home for 3 nights; next locate the conveniences; goodness gracious; a white ceramic throne; next door a squat; for the locals, we affectionately named it "our" toilet; luckily it had defective plumbing as a result the water continually flowed into the bowl. Considering the rather disgusting state of the squats next door we considered the discomfort of getting the bottom slightly wet was a minor matter at least the bowl was always clean. Showering was an exercise to be carried out in the middle of the night; no wall separating the shower heads, they reminded me of my time in the army and its all in together showering facilities.

Together with another high ranking cadre we were the only 2nd class passengers as we left Chungking; our interpreter as was decreed by the Chinese Administration Manager travelling 3rd class. At a river city stop on day two 2 other westerners joined the boat; they were from the US of

A looking at a JV opportunity. Ann had the female shower room to herself during the whole voyage this was just as well it also had no separation walls. The ferry was a vessel about 30 metres long; as 2nd class passengers we could go anywhere we pleased; just after leaving Chungking we decided to inspect our temporary home; in the front of the deck below ours was the second class dining area and immediately below on deck 1 was another very large dining room.

Deck 2 also contained the 3rd and 4th class cabins; these were 4 and 6 berth areas; 3rd class was private with solid walls as distinct from 4th class which had open metal grill walls. Deck 1 had dormitory like accommodation for 5th class passengers and then 6th class a general area where those that did not require or could not afford a sleeping berth sat or lay on the deck. These ferries were part of everyday travelling life on the Yangtze; they stopped at all mid sized towns carrying cargo and passengers; we were only allowed off the ferry twice during the three days and nights of the voyage; these two stops introduced us further to inland cities in China in 1988. These two cities were very old; all building were of unpainted grey wood and even the ones that were substantially constructed showed signs of age and lack of maintenance; really, dilapidation would be the key descriptive word to use. People went about their daily life with a sort of numbness written all over their faces. Human pack animals; carrying large loads on their head or back; laboriously pulling or pushing all manner of wheeled conveyances; the misery portrayed humanity trying to survive for a better future yet not knowing when or how it would come.

On day 1 the interpreter informed us that in the 2nd class dining room' meals could be ordered from a menu and there was a charge per dish; the other dining room on deck 1 provided free meals for those on board but there was no choice; you were presented with your own bowl and it would be partly filled with boiled rice, the cook beside the rice dispenser would then ladle some concoction that filled the bowl to the top, then you sat either at long metal topped tables or return to your bunk to eat; if you were still hungry you could have another bowl. One visit to this dining room during a meal time showed that the stew like substance being served also featured on our menu; however in the 2nd class dining room there was a menu that featured at least 30 dishes, the tables only seated 4 at a time; the per dish charge was miniscule, three dishes plus rice would provide more than enough food for us 2 this would cost about US 50 cents. The food was very bland, each dish similar tasting; in fact even similar in appearance so at the first stop where we could go ashore; a jar of chilli condiment was purchased to give the food some zest; we ate alone; the interpreter was very careful not to take any money from us; living all the time on his US 50c per day travelling allowance.

This refusal to allow us to pay any costs always occurred when we travelled with local Chinese; at a later time after gaining the trust of the young accountant; he told me that after a trip with a foreigner a full report had to be prepared and submitted to their work "danwei" and this report had to contain all monetary dealings by the westerner; if money was taken by the local person then that sum had to be paid into the control groups fund. So why take money when they would have to pay all of it to someone else. The written report must contain details of whom we met, what was said and any other pertinent details; it was further stated he even had to report on how Ann and I treated each other; in other words he was to spy on us; a copy of this report was also sent to the Secret Police in Wuxi.

Our time on the ferry was purely devoted to watching the ever changing scenery along the banks of this sometimes wide; sluggishly flowing; other times narrow, and then racing; river; shortly after leaving Chungking we were impressed at the way the farmers (nee peasants) had cultivated the steeply sloping hill sides; sometimes there appeared to be only two rows of grain per terrace level; farming every inch of available soil. The hill sides were often so steep that it looked like you would fall down many meters if you over balanced, surely they must have one leg shorter than the other to farm those fields.

Steaming around a river bend; one would behold a break water protecting a small harbour, concrete barges lined up along the inside of this man made harbour, some filled with bulk material being unloaded by a line of labourers (aka coolies) carrying bamboo baskets in whatever fashion was comfortable; others were being either loaded or unloaded with crates, boxes and bags of all shapes and sizes, human labour the only power, millions of workers who for countless ages had been plying this mind numbing back breaking work for a pittance. No end in sight, a time to work and a time to sleep before another day; more of the same so life went on; at the end of it's span however short or long a grave on a hill side bemoaned by relatives as they also braced for the daily round eternal.

No wonder in Chinese history there has been the never ending story of a rise to power by a peasant then the dynasty becoming corrupt until there is another revolution by the peasant class who seize power to change lives and then over the fullness of time corrupting power once again forcing a revolution of the peasant class, the history of China and its many dynasties; all arising by a revolution against corrupt power. For three days we made our way down this mighty river; life was cheap in our new country of residence, mid morning on day 2 in a wide sluggish part of the river we passed the body of a man, no effort was made to retrieve this floating object; although it created a noticeable interest for the 4 foreigners, the Chinese cadre on deck displayed no emotion.

Nearing Wuhan the river opened out into a huge inland lake, cruising along at full speed when all of a sudden the ferry slowed and turned around; a short while later now steaming back up river; later the interpreter advised without any emotion that a person had fallen over board; the vessel went back over its tracks to see if the person could be found but after about a kilometre there was no evidence so it resumed its journey.

Imagine a similar happening on Sydney Harbour or any water way in Australia, the ferry would have searched until it was relieved by a marine rescue unit; it would be the full time topic of conversation and indeed it would be in the news until the body was recovered. A 10 minute break in the down stream journey was the sum total of our awareness of the loss of a human life. I wonder would it have been any different if it had been a westerner that had fallen over board. One should not dwell on those thoughts when you are so far away from your own culture and tradition; particularly when the vessel on which you are travelling has no visible signs of rescue equipment, no life rafts, life buoys or even life jackets to put on in the event of an emergency.

We passed through and were truly amazed at the scenery in the so called Gorges; now to be covered with water forming part of a large hydro system but then it was a must see on a visit to the Middle Kingdom. The journey was now near the end; just before the large city of Wuhan travelling on a body of water that could be described as an inland sea; but was in fact a large water retention area behind a huge dam. To reach the next river level the vessel had to negotiate a large lock; we were the first ferry to enter the gates, soon 2 others followed, one was a tourist ferry filled with Europeans, deck chairs and glassed in viewing areas; a big difference to our open front deck where standing was the only way to see the never ending changing scenery. Our ferry was some 30 m long; now there were three of this size tied along the inside of the lock; the huge gates closed and then we slowly sank to the next level of the river some 40 meters below; the lowering was accomplished in the space of what seemed a few minutes; it is imagined that going up stream the time would be a lot longer. This lock was a great display of yesteryears engineering; the dam was built many years ago; again imagination took over; the methods used to construct this huge dam and lock system could also have been used by the pharaohs in ancient Egypt.

Wuhan an ancient city and a very important city in Chinese history, smelled and looked like it had 100 years before, the same seething mass of humanity in their old clothes; some more patches than original cloth; going about the daily grind, shop, labour, eat and bed, the majority living in an average space of less than 2 square meters per person; the footpath was their social club, laundry, wet cloth hanging space and relaxation area; lounge chairs, small bamboo stools, wooden blocks taking up the length and almost the breadth of the pavement at evening time as the residents enjoyed the last vestiges of sunlight, then after dark; a black and white TV would be arranged sitting on a ledge where it could be watched by the footpath loungers. This scene was replayed in every city, town or village that we visited during the 4 years living in China.

Wuhan; another welcoming committee, still no western hotel another old Chinese Hotel, the same ritual on entering the room, spay around walls with pest spray, clean the bathroom with white cat cleaner, arrange the mice and cockroach barriers, check for bed bugs, ensure that your emergency food supply was off the floor and then relax. Night one the banquet, more sipping of Moa-Tai protecting the glass from the quick clink, another room filled with large lounge chairs another round of talking and promises; the official line, yes money is tight but some will be at Wuxi on return; then a small lecture by officialdom how the freeing up of private enterprise was creating huge problems for the government, this official's line was that this relaxation from the central control was very bad, it was however giving some with adventurous spirits the opportunity to possible become the new rich in China. How right he was, how much he was negative to this possibility.

Ann and I; now wanting desperately to get home to Wuxi, we had been travelling for 12 days; living out of suitcases; eating all manner of food; relying on emergency supplies when the meals were suspect, our only communication between each other; no outside news; no television; it felt like we were in limbo. Our wish was to get to Wuxi; write the report for management; but of over all importance we needed to repack for our trip to Hong Kong to meet Karen and John; there were now only 7 days before we were due to depart for this exciting some what emotional trip.

Wuhan meant another 3 days wait; so with our travel arrangements secured permits given we settled down in the seedy dirty hotel to wait out the time; by now we were well and truly out of tourism mode; hotel laundry took 2 days and even that was not sure, the supply of clean clothes after the boat trip was dwindling; the water in our hotel room was of uncertain quality and cleanliness; like the water at the Hubin, it would sometimes leave brown stains in the clothes; all in all we just wanted to be back at the villa. Pressure was put on the interpreter to see if we could leave before the 3 days had expired, but there was no chance; on the day scheduled for our departure the whole city was covered with dense smog, the result of an inversion layer of low lying cloud. Arriving at the airport with usual "goodbye" entourage and were told that the daily flight to Shanghai was cancelled; the aircraft could not land. After some trying negotiations we secured seats on the next day's flight and then returned to the hotel. Next day the same storey, now it was becoming a little desperate. An enquiry regarding a train was rejected, however we were advised that there was a flight late that afternoon which they we were assured would operate; this was a Russian design Chinese built aircraft so with grave misgivings we felt that another day was a safer solution. The next morning after a 2 hour delay we lifted off in a MacDonald Douglas MD 9 built in China and arrived safely in Shanghai, now we had only 2 days to spare before leaving for Hong Kong. Just time to finish the report, do a large laundry load, repack for Hong Kong.

The new Swedish VP had arrived; he was a production man, however as he was the best friend of the incompetent reigning Swede in charge of the Swedish JV; he assumed the top expat position. As an Australian even with 2 years in country experience they felt the appointment had to be a Swedish national; the Swedish non confrontational (they have been neutral for 250 years) approach certainly was more acceptable to the Chinese who were getting away with what would be called fraud in a Western organisation but was called consensus aka "friendship" in China.

Burning the midnight oil and our laundry working over time we managed to complete the program, repack, take the bumpy road to Shanghai, negotiate the airport people wall; then the officials and oh happy day join our daughter and her fiancé in frantic Hong Kong for 5 glorious days, it was so enjoyable; introducing them to eastern food, watching their excitement as they shopped for rings; Ann who had already ventured into the jewellery exotic area was well qualified to assist them in their purchases. Five days passed so quickly they flew out to Australia, Ann flew to Singapore and I returned to China; the land cruiser waiting for me at the Sheraton and a load of work waiting at Mashan..

One of the requirements for accepting the position as VP was that each of the three expats families now living in the villas would be provided with a driver and a cleaner; the Chinese side refused this saying it was against the original "spirit" of the JV agreement; all of the top management irrespective of nationality where all to be equally treated. The Chinese side (this was how we spoke about the two nationalities in the JV) management were to have the same employment conditions as the Swedish side management. We had three villas, they were also provided with a residence at the village built for our employees in the city. Our in country pay was US $1,000 per month so was the pay of the two top Chinese; if they allowed each of us to have a cleaner and a driver; well so should the two Chinese; it was pointed out that they had immediate access to a driver and a car where they lived. Our three Nissan cars were garaged there and the drivers lived there, also neither of them was prepared to learn to drive so we should have at least one driver that would be available during work hours for our wives.

Grudgingly this was agreed provided we paid half, OK. This left on the wish list the provision of a cleaner for each villa.

This was a huge stumbling block; why should we need a cleaner, were not our wives accomplished in this small task; a different approach; of course the real need was for some one to keep the villas clean during the absence of our wives or when we left for our regular R& R. This made some sense to the Chinese in control and they agreed that they would employ a young lady from the nearby village and we the residents of the three villas would pay her total wages. So now the three villa families shared a driver and a house keeper.

The driver was a particularly nice guy; he would travel into work each day by bus, and then using our cars do any driving, sometimes shopping or other errands as required by the villa's residents; this meant the two new lady residents one Swedish; the other American did not need to go through the licensing dramas; Ann already had hers but was not particularly keen on testing her newly acquired, drive on right side, skills. Eventually the Swedish lady obtained her licence, driving occasionally, then she had an accident; not her fault; this caused a great deal of local angst; so slowly the driver became part of our families, eventually his daughter studied overseas and he was invited to Sweden. The young lady cleaner however was a different story. She eventually became dysfunctional and put off but that was after our time.

Now to have a housekeeper even on part time basis was a real bonus, the air was so polluted that after an absence of two weeks with the house shut up; there would be an oily scum on all flat surfaces greeting you on return; this oily scum would take some effort to remove. Now just before departure for either R&R or in country business you would prepare a list of jobs for the cleaner and this list would be supervised by one of the other villa ladies so on return the villa was clean. There are a number of stories worth telling about experiences with this cleaner. Firstly she was a farmer by trade; coming from the nearby village; riding her bike to work every day; she lived with her parents, in an apartment in a large cinder brick building, quite close; she was about 17 years old. Her cleaning experience if any was negligible; her learning curve was literally from the ground up; part of her duties was to do the large linen washing, sheets towels etc; we had a nice front loading washing machine for this purpose; in the early days she would sit and watch the clothes go around, remember her washing experience up to this time was beating clothes on a large stone in a pond that fronted the farm where she lived.

One day Ann discovered her trying on her underclothes; on return from a trip it was found that she had tidied up the kitchen food cupboard, every tin was lined along the shelf in height order, the same went for the bottles and the packets, it looked neat but it is not the way we keep a pantry cupboard. During her so called work day it was necessary to keep a close watch as she would join her friends at the factory to sit and chat. We sometimes wondered if it was really worth while.

The construction quality of the villas was poor, one never knew when something could occur; interesting, in hind sight but frustrating at the time; sitting one day in the office, our driver appeared at the door; in his very broken Chinglish he asked that I come to the villa immediately; immediate thoughts; something has happened to Ann; so dropped the task and walked quickly home. Ann had been cleaning her teeth over the wash basin in the down stairs toilet; the basin had fallen to the floor; this broke the copper water pipes both hot and cold, now water was gushing all over the floor. A plumber quickly despatched from his usual slow morning to turn off the water and replace the basin; at one time or another; the same thing happened at each villa. Heating pipes would get a hammer in them so nerve wracking especially at night when trying to sleep, it would continue until the plumber arrived to cure the problem. Taps would stick, open or closed; pipes would burst, there were never ending maintenance problems.

On this particular day the burst water pipes had caused a secondary problem; the floors were polished Chinese wooden parquetry; it had a rather uneven finish having been sanded in a rough way but it was serviceable. The flooding water caused a portion of the floor to lift, a call to the building maintenance people and two men appeared; it was always necessary to watch the maintenance people closely; they tended to wander through the house idly looking; touching ornaments or whatever took their fancy. These two men laid out the individual slats of wood in the correct pattern so that once they dried they could be replaced into the original position. The next day was our cleaner's day, she saw the tiles arranged on the floor; picked them all up and placed them carefully into a plastic bag; the close arrival of the maintenance men saw an eruption of the so called inscrutable Chinese demeanour, ever laying that old adage to rest.

The swimming pool and barbeque arrived from Australia the pool marked for customs purposes as a water tank; the many packages were delivered to the villa area; the American couple (Davis and Wendy) and their young son were anxious to have it installed; in the present hot prevailing conditions it would be well used. Having installed one before I was in charge of proceedings; first gather the necessary installation equipment; this type of above ground pool installation is not rocket science but can be hard work; after consultation with other expats living at the hotel it decided that it would be fun for all to join in a Sunday working bee; with a lot of hands it should easily be erected in one day. The BBQ installed; using scrounged bricks thereby enabling us to give our helpers a rest from Chinese cooking, pork chops for the barbeque prepared for the occasion.

Digging equipment was required; the pool site had to be level; a quantity of sand next on the list; this proved most difficult; we had no government allocation. As usual a friendship payment produced the desired results. next step; shopping for shovels, picks and mattocks. Under Chairman Mao's great leap forward program, each area had to be self reliant in all things, so the acquisition of the metal part of the tools was easy; it was the wooden handles that proved to be difficult; this at first was a surprise, but in retrospect it was realised, that all of the hand tools used by farmers; no mechanisation at this time; were furnished with rough wooden handles. Not to be out done; there were some wooden packing cases and branches from an old tree in the villa compound; so we fashioned the handles. None of our volunteers had been engaged in physical labour for some time; the day was very hot so there were many drink breaks (cold Chinese beer) consequently the construction process was completed by the light coming from the adjacent villas. There was no theodolite to ensure that the site was level so a long length of plastic tubing was used as a water level, this tubing was obtained from the laboratory. During the next few days after work; the final touches were completed then the filling process commenced.

This filling process can be tricky; it is necessary to ensure that the plastic liner does not get wrinkles, we were successful so now we had a pool and BBQ area, how homely it appeared inside the villa area, an oasis away from the outside world just a fence away; the purchasing officer at Astra A made a mistake sending a diatomaceous earth filter instead of a sand bed one, this was to create some problems however using all DIY skill the plumbing complete and the pool prepared for use. The day came for a test swim, the word had spread in the neighbourhood about this pool so many of the locals had to come and see it for themselves; considering their situation it was a luxury beyond belief; it was however very unnerving for us to have people peering through the brick fence or even standing on a ladder to look over the fence as we enjoyed a swim. This pool with BBQ became a focal point, enjoyed by the villa residents and many other short stay visitors who were accommodated at the hotels.

During 1988 a very concentrated marketing campaign was started; it is known that the sale of prescription drugs is very controlled in Australia; where the government has a prepared schedule of all pharmaceutical substances then rated them, for example Schedule 4 must be prescribed by a medical practitioner; in China no such system had evolved; the JV product range comprised large volume infusion products as well as tablets; most of the tablet products in Australia would have required a doctors prescription; not so in China; all products were freely available from the pharmacy. Market research showed that in the pharmaceutical market 50% of sales were the result of a doctor's prescription; 40% were self prescribed and 10% recommended by family and friends.

As VP Marketing; sales strategies needed to be formulated to increase the public awareness of our products; there had been foreign marketing advisors employed by the JV almost since its inception, one such was a Hong Kong Chinese, she was a very capable person and appointed on my request as she spoke Mandarin, thus allowing her to freely communicate with people at all levels. The strategy was to introduce a more western approach as far as training and selling were concerned; she was tending to ignore these strategies even though agreed upon by the local Chinese product managers some of whom were trained in Sweden; she also largely ignored the advice given by visiting marketeers from the parent companies. She would take matters into her own hands; eventually she decided not to return to China.

The Chinese side had appointed a party member; a very much up and coming cadre as the Chinese Marketing manager reporting to me. As a party member he naturally interfered in every way even though he appeared to have little knowledge of the industry; so it became more and more difficult to work. The market was 50% self prescribed so it was decided to advertise the non hospital product range both on radio and TV; yes TV. As VP marketing and as well Company publicist a TV report on the joint venture had been arranged. The only station was the national one, so it would be aired nation wide a number of times. All facets of the project were covered and all foreign permanent staff featured at least once; in my case appearing as the CFO discussing various aspects of the formation from the Swedish side; now however we needed to have a more product specific promotional series; over time all members of the marketing team formulated this campaign; both for TV and radio..

Using an interpreter the local radio station was approached, an arrangement completed for the cardio, respiratory and pain control preparations to be promoted just after the morning weather report; this was considered prime time listening; the affect was monitored at retail level in the area. This campaign saw a marked lift in market penetration in the local area, the decision was made to broaden the approach and create a national sales force. Next the TV campaign, once again research found a local production company based in Shanghai. After many hours of negotiation and a number of visits to Shanghai the shooting and production was arranged. One product was a dispersible aspirin tablet similar to our disprin. The marketing people were firmly of the opinion that the dispersible feature; not available in local products; was a serious promotional point; this soluble type product would be particularly useful for young children; so let's promote this feature. Project next to hand, write a script and shoot a TV advertisement showing the preparation being given to a young child. Being in China meant you had to be multi talented or at least appear to be.

Discussions with the TV producer, and a decision ; we would use the master bedroom of our villa as the location; actors were engaged including a young mother with her baby; they all arrived in a series of buses; the usual (not to me but to them) pre-shoot discussions and dialogue rehearsal now ready for action. The scene was set; for the benefit of readers the bedroom was not a large room in our terms the master bedroom in a modest villa; so now it was very very crowded with actors and crew. For some 3 hours they tried to shoot a successful sequence; the small child totally refusing to co- operate; ultimately we had to abandon the shoot. Two other successful TV promotions were produced on both a respiratory and a cardiac product; these were shown nation wide resulting in a very positive affect on our sales.

Wuxi had discovered the benefits of international business partnerships; the number of expats rapidly increased; a new hotel built in the city by the local government featured an external lift was well as a water feature that continuously jetted water coloured by multi coloured lights; it was impressive; to the locals it was a must see feature and every night crowds gathered to watch the lift going up and down the building and marvel at the water spectacle. To us the wonder was a clean new inner city hotel, could now used as accommodation for our many international visitors, locals expats also took the opportunity to use the dining room which served both Chinese and Western dishes, it was a welcome addition to home cooking. Unfortunately one of our best interpreters was allocated to this hotel as an assistant manager this ad hoc allocation from one job to another a very frustrating feature. We would train they would transfer. As local residents; our frequent arriving visitors felt it necessary to repay our lunch time hospitality thus we were often invited to join them for at least one dinner; this was a very welcome break although driving the 10 k from home to the city could be an exercise in patience, however it was something to do other than sit at home working, writing letters, making small talk or playing computer games.

During the first few months of the hotel's opening, residents and visitors and guests had to run the gauntlet of local parents trying to arrange for their children to be taken on a ride in the external lift; the security guards stationed at the door were working hard to prevent the locals from entering into this newly erected but still to us westerners, somewhat old fashioned hotel. Now the board meetings were held in this hotel; us usual in China at that time, after just a few months the slowly deteriorating standard of cleanliness was obvious; the carpets in the hallways showing signs of bad cleaning practises; air conditioning either too hot or too cold or just ineffective; marks on walls where the bell boys had hit them with loaded luggage carts not cleaned off; the fire escape stairs littered with paper, drink cans and cigarette butts. The local government contact advised that a Japanese JV were also about to construct a new hotel opposite the fading newness of the Chinese Hotel, this opening was much looked forward too; under Japanese management it would have a very high standard.

Now because of the proliferations of JVs a critical shortage of trained people as translators, drivers, even cleaners, became obvious. We were experiencing more and more instances of the removal of people that we had trained, they were being removed by the authorities and reallocated at a better price to the authorities to the new JVs. Naturally a friendship payment would open the doors for the new JV's to be allocated our trained people, one sad loss was a nurse that had firstly been trained in China then trained in European, she was particularly close to all of the expats as she spoke very good Chinglish and was vital on a number of illnesses occasioning hospital care. This lady (her father was a victim of the Cultural Revolution) had assisted me after I had developed a growth on my hands and fearing skin cancer approached her for assistance.

Ann and I together with this nurse, in the rough ride land cruiser, visited the local hospital; what an eye opener this first visit. A spittoon was placed at each door and if the hallway was long another half way; the patients in the wards visible as we walked through the corridors; laying on beds, cots and stretchers all dressed in their own clothes most without sheets or blankets; relatives feeding them home prepared meals; a long walk and we arrived at room about 5 meters square; in each corner was a desk; three chairs; one behind the desk, two more for visitors; the lady doctor, in a white/ grey doctor's coat, stethoscope around her neck invited us to sit down, she examined my growth, took a bamboo knife device from a jar on the table and scratched the surface; she spoke quickly to our nurse and took out a small book and with a ink stained finger dipped the pen in the ink yes ink well and dip pen in 1988 China. She wrote, the results of her examination; it was simply an old age blemish; blotting the page she handed me the book and we departed.

The young nurse was always practising her Chinglish, she formed a friendship with the expat wives quite often visiting for a morning or an afternoon cup of tea; on one occasion she explained to Ann that her father had also been a doctor; he had practiced the art of hands on healing, she also

126

gave Ann some essential oil; showing her the various spots on the body that could be rubbed with this oil to have a healing effect. On one of our rest days Ann experimented with this oil; rubbing it onto the various spots as recommended by this nurse; later in the cool of the evening just before dusk we rode our bikes along the levee that ran alongside the lake and then ventured on foot onto a path almost covered by long grassy weeds.

On arrival home Ann began to complain of a rash developing over her body, she was covered with hive like swellings; the itch became progressively unbearable during the night and at one stage it appeared that the lining of her throat was also being affected. Gloves on her hands prevented her from breaking the skin but our worry was the throat closing up. What could we do, the neighbours were away, we were alone in the villa compound, phoning was impossible; although we had the number of the office at the residential units past history showed that the person who answered would say "Wei" (hullo) and that would be the sum total of the communication.

It was a terrible terrible night; the next morning as soon as the buses arrived we got the nurse and travelled once more to the hospital; walking along the spittoon lined passage ways; past the wards and into the consulting room. Again sitting before another lady doctor behind a similar desk; once it was established that Ann was the patient, our consulting area was besieged by both doctors and patients from the other consulting tables in the room. Red hair acted like a magnet to the Chinese people, here was a red haired patient we must look at this strange apparition. The doctor prescribed an anti histamine which quickly alleviated her suffering but two things were decided on the way back to the villa, firstly we must establish a medical emergency routine, and secondly ensure that we have a bigger range of medical care products on hand at all times, there was already a supply of analgesics, tummy upset palliatives, water purifying tablets, bandages, cough and cold medication, ointment and salves but we needed to expand this list.

A meeting of expats and local officials was called to discuss what could be done; a large number of expats had decided to leave their JVs and return home mainly due to Government interference, constant spying and bungling, now I had a new role; JV representative to the local government. Local officialdom had arranged a meeting of all the expats in Wuxi to try to solve the difficulties being experienced by these constantly demanding foreigners; my mother tongue English so all agreed that I should hold this position. At first I considered it to be a feather in my cap but soon realized that it would be a dubious honour. One big concern was medical emergencies such as we had experienced; a meeting with a local bureaucrat was arranged, as usual after a long negotiation, disappearing pens and lighters; it was decided that all expats could use the special now very old, medical facility that had been built for the top 4 levels of cadres, this was outside of the city but on the way to our villas at Mashan. To control entry all expats were issued with photo identity cards; this facility was available 24/7.

In China some 20% of the population suffer from hepatitis C, a deadly form of the disease; even within our work force this percentage existed; all staff was examined annually particularly for this condition; during the 4 years in China a number of deaths of employees occurred from this deadly killer. All expats were now able to go to this special hospital facility for the annual check up. As the marketing director of a pharmaceutical company and one who had now devoted two decades to the industry this old but very efficient hospital facility was extremely interesting. As befitting its standing and the standing of the people who were hospitalised at the facility it was far above the standard of the hospital for the ordinary people.

It was very scenically located overlooking Lake Tai; the equipment was not what one would call modern but was very efficiently and well used by professional people, a complete tour of the facility was arranged, they had a very large Chinese medicine pharmacy as well as a smaller western medicine pharmacy. The required annual physical examination took 8 hours; covering all physical aspects; as a chronic gout sufferer they also prescribed both western and Chinese medication together with a diet translated into Chinglish; a quick perusal and it appeared that it would be better to forgo eating totally; most of my existing diet was deemed taboo.

The gout attacks were becoming a real problem, there were weeks when it persisted the pain was acute as anyone who have suffered this curse will attest. Well outside of your comfort zone; suffering extreme pain; life becomes very dreary. One instance is very vivid it had lasted for what seemed like weeks; thankfully for the emotional state; Ann was in country. An attack struck again in the left knee two days before her departure for Singapore, Her flight was mid afternoon so departed Mashan just before sun up; in case of traffic; the Toyota was a manual drive car and every time a gear change was required the pain was unbearable.

Driving for over 9 hours; always a mind bending experience even when well; now with gout; well it is a day that is etched in the memory! Approaching Sou chow, about 90 minutes from home, 4 trucks each loaded with similar goods, travelling in close convoy, not an unusual occurrence; these trucks only able to travel at 25k and maintained a very close a station almost as if they were linked together. There was absolutely no way to pass; the road from Sou chow to Wuxi, as in most of Jiangsu Province is flat; except where they pass over the numerous canals. Approaching Wuxi is a small rise near the river, the bridges over the canals all up and down; with some very steep grades. Thus at every one of these canal bridges these old trucks would lose speed and then go down through the gears to make it to the top of the rise; of course at this speed I had to do likewise. Behind this convoy now for some 2 hours; now at last arrived at a place on the road; only 10 k from home where a small bridge is crossed and after about 25 m the road became part of a brand new 3 lane wide road.

At last I can pass this convoy and in 15 minutes lie down and take away the excruciating pain. Oh no! The convoy of trucks stopped just before the bridge; all of the drivers and their offsiders jumped down and lined up to urinate into the canal; the oncoming traffic was heavy; my vehicle with about 50 others now trailing were all prevented from passing these 4 trucks to reach the 3 lanes now in sight; the drivers and offsiders now considerable relieved rejoined the trucks; the convoy started again; in 25 meters after 2+ hours I could pass and make my weary pain filled way home; driving in China had little to recommend it.

There were no road maps available to find the way around the country; when arranging to drive to a new place it was necessary to obtain detailed directions and landmarks; on my first solo self drive trip to Shanghai I had a rough road map drawn by one of the Swedish guys; the first road travelled was part of the main roadway system, as such it carried a lot of heavy traffic; close to Shanghai where Jiangsu provincial area met the Shanghai city outskirts was a check point (our named check point Charlie). All vehicles were required to stop and present travel authorities; we were known by most of the check point guards and so were usually waved through; one of the Chinese drivers told us that this route was a long way around and suggested another route; he drew a map containing landmarks and particular street directions this road was then routinely used. In some places it was a better road than the highway, in others narrow and winding; its benefit; it entered the city via the airport road, much closer to the Sheraton Hotel than the old route. Returning home it passed the new Japanese Nikko Hotel and residential complex here we could buy western items such as milk and fresh orange juice; both a welcome change from powdered milk and orange concentrate mixed with pre boiled water. The Nikko also enables us a last toilet visit before departing for the now three plus hour trip to Wuxi; incidentally of course on the way to the Sheraton if a comfort stop was urgently required after the long trip from Wuxi, the Nikko toilets were some 30 minutes earlier than the Sheraton's.

Prior to April 1988 I had only driven myself once to Shanghai to pick up our white goods; immediately after delivery of the Toyota alone in country I decided to drive to Shanghai; this required the negotiation of the city proper. At that time we only had a choice of 3 petrol suppliers between Wuxi and Shanghai. In fact Shanghai only had one such supplier. This was close to city centre, always a necessity to fill up the tank before the return trip. It was difficult enough being a passenger in the city but far worse driving yourself; the winding, narrow streets, all filled with bicycles and pedestrians with only the occasional car. The old; very old buses ramming their way through the maze of narrow streets, forcing a way through the other street users; passengers crammed into these smoke filled human sardine cans, all overflowing, some brave souls holding onto the rails fitted at the doors coming very close to be knocked off their precarious perch or knocking bike riders as the buses rumbled along.

This first trip in my car (truck); I had an arrangement to meet the American and his wife at the Sheraton; he had borrowed one of the Nissan company cars while his car was being repaired after a collision with a truck. We would return in convoy showing him the new way to Wuxi; they had recently arrived as part of the replacement group; so this was one of his early trips to Shanghai with wife and young son. After an evening relaxing in the Sheraton; all together enjoying the relaxation away from Mashan; me resting from the mind bending experience of driving myself. Next morning shopping at the nearby department store and markets then I knew it was now necessary to brave this strange city to get petrol.

The American with his family had taken a taxi shopping; during the previous evening they had met a Japanese girl in the Sheraton western dining room; the blonde hair of their little boy always attracted a lot of attention, after discussion they found that she was employed as the head waitress in the Japanese Restaurant soon to be opened in the new Japanese hotel in Wuxi. Enquiry at the desk to speak to the American co worker, this young lady standing close by heard me, to her an American and an Australian voice are very similar so spoke to me; she was waiting for the American couple who had offered her a lift to Wuxi; according to the desk captain they would not return for over an hour at which time we were returning to Wuxi.

She was there patiently waiting with her luggage; I suggested that if she wished she could accompany me while refuelling with petrol, this would also introduce her to down town Shanghai. A great treat for a new arrival; so she joined me in the Toyota. Her Jinglish was understandable; no real communication problems; to assist guests the Sheraton had prepare a very rough road directory of Shanghai; so there was no lack of confidence to buy petrol and return to the hotel in time to meet with the Americans and return to Wuxi in convoy. Ha; Ha; Ha; no trouble to find the petrol station or even acquiring and paying my first time for the petrol,; it took some time as usual there was a large queue. A strange enforced rule existing then in China; no one other than the driver could be in the car when it entered a service station; so the Japanese lady had to alight before I entered and stand outside. The same rule applied to bus passengers, so it was not unusual to see many people standing waiting outside a petrol station. Unbeknown to me she left her purse in the car. Once filled, next step pay the bill; someone during my absence stole her purse. She discovered the loss some minutes after she rejoined the car so we had to retrace our steps to the gas station. No purse; no pass port all her travel papers gone it was a trying emotional time for her and also me; trying to find the way back to the hotel I got hopelessly lost.

In later years there have been occasions to be lost in other countries, a good street directory guides you on the way; Shanghai with no street signs that I could read, no person that I could communicate with, battling some of the 5 million bicycle riders; the streets all looking the same it was frustrating in the extreme; after some time I discovered we were driving around in circles; eventually a familiar street that would lead to the Sheraton, for some 90 minutes we had been lost; the American with wife had departed some 45 minutes earlier. As they were due to depart the car had refused to start, examination showed a flat battery; the ever pleasant Sheraton garage manager (the recipient of many friendship payments) used jumper leads to start the car; they had then left for Wuxi.

The garage manager; a skilled mechanic, was concerned that the battery was failing; he suggested that we should try to catch them in case they stalled the car and it would not start. Accompanied by a very teary dejected Japanese girl we departed and proceeded to break all of the speed limits in an effort to catch up with the other vehicle, this was not achieved until we arrived at the employees village in Wuxi; here the car did stop and refused to start. We then left the car and travelled together from Wuxi city to our villas in Mashan after firstly depositing the very forlorn Japanese lady at the yet to be completed hotel. Over the next 18 months there were many trips to Shanghai and never once again got lost, recognising on the next visit where the mistake was made in the old French Quarter and very soon knew the city as well as Sydney or Singapore Island. .

Driving in China during 1985 to 1989 was a real adventure; one never knew what would be seen or how long it would take to arrive at the destination. There was only one petrol supplier between Wuxi and Shanghai and the supply was not always reliable; coupled with the fact that you could wait for up to an hour and find that this day they were only serving even numbered cars. Expats had special number plates mine was # 5 this enabled the police to recognise the city of residence and also that the fact that it was a foreign driver. There was an unspoken rule among us foreign drivers, if there was an interpreter in the car often in my case then the interpreter was to act as if they did not know Chinglish; the decision was based on the fact that none of the police could speak even a rudimentary English, thus with no chance of communication we could pay the on the spot fines; at that time reputed to be a feature of police salary.

The speed limit through towns was 20k, on the open road 50, the police were equipped with hand held speed cameras, like all speed police they would hide in the bushes that grew along the canal banks then literally bounce out of the weeds or from behind the trees that lined all of the roads and wave you down. You would then go through a pantomime; he explaining that you were exceeding the speed limit and you telling him that you don't understand; eventually they could grab open the door and point out the legal speed on the dial, hopefully by then you had the friendship payment ready; they would slam the door shut and wave you on. One day with an interpreter I did an illegal turn in Shanghai, unfortunately the interpreter was too keen and so was fined US 20c.

I was pulled up number of times; at the next regular visit to the police station; it was interesting to note; the occasions when I did not have the friendship payment ready by the time the door opened was the time that the police; during their 30 minute lecture advised that I had driven dangerously. Still during the 2+ years of driving there was only one accident involvement; a girl on a bike ran into the side of me at an intersection she was unhurt and apologetic so off we went. Often we shopped at the Friendship Store in Shanghai for western goods; also the shipping providores both shops also close by the famous Bund; shops at the bottom end of Nanjing Lu had great bargains however the return journey to the hotel through the old international quarter was a test of endurance. Each time we visited Shanghai this torturous drive was suffered; however it was interesting to see as 1989 drew to a close the changing difference in fashion and clothes now worn by the local city dwellers, and displayed in the shops..

How I recall the famous Nanjing Lu; it was just wide enough for two cars; footpath had a 1.5 m steel barricade to deter pedestrians from overrunning the road; using the up and down single lanes of the road would be bicycles, man drawn carts, plus other cars and buses; added to this congestion was the overflow of pedestrians all of whom wanted to move faster than the ones walking behind the barricade. You dare not stop, if you did you would be surrounded by a packed body of people, unable to move again; sitting high in the Toyota was good; you could see over everyone; in a sedan like a Volvo and a Nissan you were below the bike seats; therefore easier to bump another road user; the trick was to engage low gear and then keep moving very slowly; in the smaller back streets which made up most of Shanghai it needed a lot of patience to keep moving in this sea of humanity and conveyances. The city itself was not then very big geographically and you could drive from one side to the other in a matter of 40 minutes, when I returned in 1992 and 1995 the city had expanded dramatically, today 28 years later a modern thriving city of some 20 million..

Across from the Sheraton was the main sports stadiums; in the many hours spent overlooking this large complex it was interesting to watch the local people arrive and depart from events; there was an army unit based nearby and they drilled on the grounds regularly. In mid 1988 I had occasion to visit Shanghai Hospital No.1 to meet with the head of thoracic surgery. Not as a salesman; but as the head of marketing; trying to arrange a series of seminars for cardiologists to take place in Shanghai and Wuxi. Astra is very strong in cardio products and wanted to arrange this visit as a sort of gesture to both their Swedish doctor friends, as well as to create new Chinese doctor friends.

China was at that time probably more so than now; an exotic destination. Therefore to give a person a free opportunity to travel such a vast distance from European and then visit this exotic country; was an opportunity for Swedish doctors to hard to resist; even if some of them had to do a little lecturing as they went on sight seeing.

This particular Chinese professor of thoracic surgery was of considerable importance; he had performed the first heart transplant in China, a quiet unassuming person; easy and interesting to talk with. For me whenever an opportunity presented, there was always a question about the Cultural Revolution; it appeared to be such a devastating time in China's history. This extremely modest man, called it "the great chaos"; all of the schools and universities were closed; the professional, academic and any other educated people were publicly criticised; victimised and quite often died from mistreatment at the hands of the Red Guards and the population in general. .

A book worth while reading covering this chaotic period it is called 'Life and Death in Shanghai" written by a lady who had spent time in Canberra with her husband. If interested at all in this chaotic period the book is a must read. The doctor in Shanghai would have been in his late 40s during this period, he was called upon to repent his sins; then soundly victimised by the Red Guards (mainly students but also some radicals and even the general public); then he was shipped out to a rural location; there led to a wooden shed; and shown 10 beds with a dividing wall; at the other end was another 10 beds, the other person; also called doctor; was following one of, now very old Chairman Mao, creed of learn by doing. The other doctor had no formal training; he had read some books on medicine and surgery but now he was looking after 10 ill people; even worse the highly qualified surgeon was not supposed to interfere in his work in any way. Somewhat scary don't you think.

In our organisation we employed; as Product Managers; people who had a medical degree yet had not attended University; their degree may have been gained through the Television University or at some higher level of education but without any practical experience; they were recognised as doctors, they were addressed as doctor but without any real GP skills; they commanded a reasonable salary although a driver was still better paid.

Although crime was supposed to be very low in China; the first thing that was built before any construction work began was a hand made brick; cement rendered wall, quite often with broken glass or razor wire at the top; there was such a wall on three sides of the villa compound; the fourth side defined by a canal; occasionally boat people stray along this canal, it went no where; on seeing such a nice level grassed area they would decide that it was a nice place to anchor and spend some time; these unwelcome visitors although harmless, forced the building of our own bamboo wall; there was a door which was supposed to allow us access to the canal for fishing or just passing the time watching the rank water. This placid water often became extremely infested with blue algae, creating a vile smelling emanation. There was also a large double gate at the entrance to the villas all for our security; this gate was always supposed to be kept locked a large padlock was there for this purpose, it was rarely used; the reasoning; there were 24 hour security guards in a guard house at the factory entrance and this entrance was adjacent to the villa compound, so why should we carry this large key.

One evening, returning from a dinner in the city we were shocked to discover a man asleep on the front door step. Regularly, as we drove, we saw single men plodding along pushing a barrow with all their humble possessions; even very occasionally you would see a family; man woman and child. This man was apparently looking for some where warm to sleep and found our door. The guards were alerted; on arrival they commenced to beat him unmercifully; eventually we intervened; the man had done no harm, he was now almost unconscious. Chinese cruelty is very obvious; at times sickening; unbeknown to top management the person in charge of security decided to employ the use of a dog. One day we noted that a large german shepherd was tied to a part of the fence near the guard house and the guards were continually tormenting it; using an interpreter they were asked to desist this treatment of the animal but this had little affect, for some weeks this animal was badly treated until one day it was no longer there. We conjectured wrongly or rightly that he probably became a meal for the guards although the eating of dogs was illegal at that time.

Many instances of this cruelty could be cited, one day travelling to Shanghai we passed a man on a bike; attached to the back frame by their legs were a number of live geese; one had wriggled until it head was reaching the ground, the head rubbing on the roadway was slowly being abraded away; another day and we saw a bicycle with 4 live goats each hung upside down by their tethered back legs from poles fastened across the front and rear of the bike. Many other instances of this type were witnessed the rider paying no heed to the suffering of the animals.

In the summer of 1988 a blue slimy algae grew in all of the adjacent drainage canals, this affected a number of things, firstly it created a problem with our factory water supply; resulting in loss of production for a number of days, but worst of all was the terrible smell emanating from this multi hued goo; the canal beside the villas was severely affected; a ducted air conditioning system had been installed in each house, however in our villa the installation of this piece of Swedish equipment had been mishandled by the Chinese engineers; therefore it was useless, this meant that there was no air filter effects to mitigate the smell; for over two weeks this horrible stench was endured until at long last, rain came to wash out the canals. Some nights for me, a visit to one of our 2 neighbours who had a working air conditioner gave some relief.

One evening sitting on the back step enjoying the dusk; suddenly the lights went out in the villa, first check the fuse box; no problems there; at the time Ann and I were the only two residents in the villa compound. The trouble must stem from the company power station, this station comprised the equipment to transform the high voltage supply that entered the factory and reduced it to the particular voltages required for the factory and villa needs. For some reason the special over load switches had been tripped; There were three, on duty engineers trying to correct this problem; those familiar with this electrical equipment will know that to reconnect the mains supply to the local transformers requires extreme force; the head engineer believed the fault was isolated and sent everyone outside while he pumped up the connecting switch; with two almighty bangs it connected then disengaged again. After about 2 hours that comprised a number of loud; dangerous and abortive attempts the supply was reconnected and I returned home to bed.

We were not so lucky on another occasion; it was extremely cold, the heaters in the villa operated by hot water from the boilers; their main purpose was producing copious amounts of steam for the factory. The two boilers were very dirty coal fired monsters, once again a walk to the boiler room; using the best sign language mimed that we were freezing; in his best sign language the chief of the night shift said there was nothing he could do about the situation. We would have to put up with it until morning; we went to bed; put all on all the blankets and doonas as the sleet and rain beat on our windows. The next morning after arrival of the factory workers; I again made contact with an engineer who spoke a brand of Chinglish; he advised; in the boiler room are a number of pre-determined worker positions, all highly skilled. In fact each demands special understanding of a boiler's functions. One of these specially trained men had failed to arrive at work; this man's special function was turning the tap to allow the hot water to flow through the pipes into our heaters; the day shift had closed down one boiler for maintenance, the night shift had made the second boiler operational but because the tap turning man did not arrive for work then we were unable to have our villa heated.

This specific; functional operational exclusivity was a feature of the employment situation, there were just to many people who were desirous of working for foreign JVs; the local government received a substantial up front fee for every worker they allocated as well as a continuing weekly payment, this amount was the difference between the JV rate per week and the amount the worker actually received; the system thereby encouraged the allocation of workers even if they were not yet required. The hope was that the continued growth of the JV would warrant more and more bodies. Jobs were often found for these people by the Chinese managers sometimes unknown to the foreign JV partner's staff.

This fact was discovered when an issue was raised regarding who actually paid the wages to the workers; every month a cheque was made payable to the Chinese Union. It was this local government body that actually paid our employees. As stated before it was JV policy that the two Chinese top managers were paid the same scale as the expat top managers ie US $1,000 per month, for us these funds were paid into a US dollar bank account however the Chinese executives were paid in cash. The payroll system went this way; consortium staff would calculate the amount each worker was entitled for the month at JBV rates, a cheque would be drawn for the total amount; this cheque was drawn in favour of the local so called union; this controlling body then paid the individual workers including the top Chinese execs at Chinese rates, even though the JV was paying the top local execs US $1,000 they were in fact receiving the equivalent of US $250 a month, the same thing happened to a lesser extent with each of the workers, the local government pocketing the rest; this was pointed out to the Swedish top man and he told me to attend to my own business.

By late 1988 the free enterprise movement was burgeoning; the China Daily English language newspaper reporting on the burgeoning ranks of Chinese millionaires; one in particular from fresh water pearl farming. These stories also told how these millionaires were reportedly contributing to all types of charity concepts; from our view point; sitting among the graft and corruption we wondered what friendship payments were being made to ensure that their wealth was not totally frittered away.

The decision to hold a medical seminar was given approval by the local government. The Chinese marketing staff recommended a well known conference centre in a so called "free zone" near Guangzhou (Canton); this centre was chosen as it gave the doctor attendees from all over southern China a chance to shop in a place where all types of goods were readily available in both FEC and Yuan. A group of overseas lecturers were invited from Sweden; also a given a Swedish version of friendship payments. Our local marketing group would arrange the function, invite the local cardiologists while Sweden would arrange the speakers; the arrangements meant our staff would travel by plane to Guangzhou, stay overnight ; then proceed the next day to the conference facility. Permission was given for the locals to travel outside of their allotted zone and of course our travel arrangements also required approval to purchase travel tickets.

As usual travelling with the local Chinese staff; arranged by the Admin Manager one had to accept the arrangements; in Guangzhou the accommodation was in a very old; very dirty; seedy hotel. Guangzhou had a lot of first class western hotels but they were too expensive for our budget; the admin manager also hated the expats and would do anything to show his power over them and also his power over his work mates. This power display was rampart among party members against non party members.

There were a few hours free in this burgeoning city, so for a short time we acted as tourists; our travelling companions looked in awe at the array of items freely available in both currencies. They could not afford anything but the smallest of these tourist trinkets; their pay scale was significantly less than that of the Guangzhou free zone. The next morning we all boarded a hired mini bus and began the 4 hour drive to the conference centre. There were 8 of us in this mini bus together with the driver; now for the first time in China we saw farm animals in the fields; in Wuxi and surrounds all physical effort was human; here there were cattle and horses replacing the two peasants pulling a plough, or a cart loaded with produce; also amazing was to see the roads lined with Australian gum trees. Arrived at the conference hotel; then for the next 4 days the only specific job was to officiate at the opening, closing and banquet functions; there purely as a figurehead; Ann and I sat around and looked at each other, read books played cards; very boring, four days conference over; the team boarded another bus for Guangzhou.

The day was hot, the non air conditioned bus had lost its shock absorbing characteristics some months before and they had not been replaced; the seats were typical Chinese, hard vinyl clad bench seats with little if any padding. For 4 hours bodies were subject to a battering that at times was excruciating, this physical torture;   made worse by the fact that we knew there was no accommodation arranged at Guangzhou, nor did we have any flight bookings for our return to Wuxi. On our minds also would there be the usual 3 days requirement similar to our previous long journey. Was it possible that our flight could be arranged to leave as soon as we arrived in the city.

By mid afternoon very bottom sore, hot, thirsty, hungry and tired we managed to get accommodation at another very seedy hotel; the sales manager went off to arrange return flights. To our relief on return he reported that our departure would be after lunch the next day on a CAAC flight using American design planes. In the fullness of time we returned once more to the comfort of our villa by the canal.

During these travels we discovered a number of interesting aspects of the travelling habits of our local sales staff; one was the amount of luggage they would carry for a week away. Expats would have a brief case, an over the shoulder bag plus a mid sized suitcase; packing all of the possible emergency needs plus more clothes than absolutely necessary just in case there were no laundry facilities or the water was too dirty to wash even our smalls. Our travelling companions; always men, would travel with a small brief case and a small imitation leather overnight bag. This bag would only be about 30cm in length and 20cm high; we assumed it carried nightwear toiletries and maybe a spare shirt and undies; it certainly would not hold anything more; they all travelled very light.

The difference in food and eating habits was also noticeable; we travelled with Wuxi locals and then mixed with the locals from the area. One habit in particular is worthy of note; in Wuxi when prawns are eaten, the local diner would take off the head and then place the rest in the mouth, after a deal of chewing and tongue movement the shell was taken from the corner of the mouth, it was quite a delicate manoeuvre; those in the south however; removed the shell with their fingers before popping the delicacy into their mouth, just as we would. Cuisine was another large variance; in the far north pasta was the staple diet, as you moved south rice and pasta became equal and then further south rice was the staple diet. Moving east from Sichuan to Shanghai on the coast, chilli slowly lost its influence; round full bodied sauces taking the place of the hot chilli pepper elements; moving south arriving at Guangzhou the meals were much subtler, each course building on the taste of the other; dumplings, boiled or fried were a major food item in this southern area.

Language; another feature, although Mandarin was the official language; local dialects were widely used, from the Cantonese of the South East with its very pronounced 8 vocal tones compared to the 4 tones in the dialect of other parts of the country. During the few days in Guangzhou, our staff from Wuxi struggled to make themselves understood and even more so to understand the local people. One could see that to unite China one official language was very necessary. Although many countries have different dialects in different regions; Scottish brogue for example; non would be more pronounced that China.

August; moon cake festival time and cause for celebration; the company held a party where "moon" cakes featured and a concert took place. Now days in every August, the time of moon cakes, Ann and I reflect on this special festival and in particular on these special cakes; actually cringing as we remember the gifts and then having to consume large quantities of these "rock like cakes" during this particular time of the Chinese year. There were a number of festive occasions when concerts would be held; the expats required to take a part and provide at least two performers.

The dour Swedish contingent were quite notable by their absence in these festival functions; thus it fell to me to make up the numbers; it was good fun, singing songs like Waltzing Matilda and "Click go the shears boys"; all of the performers in the company and there were many would prepare small skits, play the local stringed instruments or just sing to a tape. With only a small number of Chinglish speakers my renditions were met with a polite applause; however being on stage before the assembled company meant that I became a well known figure to all employees and therefore could always count on a nod and a smile on frequent walks.

As head of Administration as well as marketing, the dining and kitchen staff was functionally under my control; modern Swedish equipment had been installed however the main utensils used were rice cookers and woks both Chinese manufacture. One day a staff delegation visited my office and complaining about the quality of the food; this was passed on to the Chinese head of the dining facility; the reply centred round the funds available to them and the persons responsible for the supply of raw materials. Later that month another complaint; Ann was in Singapore, so I started having lunch in the staff dining hall. The daily menus required at least a choice of three dishes, I found that even though the menu listed three different dishes all of the food looked remarkable similar; the company brochure stated that every day a meat, a chicken and a fish dish were to be available at the canteen. During the survey I found 3 meat dishes one day and three chicken dishes on another the only discernable difference was the sauce that covered the small globules of meat; to further cap the problem off the rice was of such poor quality that one ran the risk of breaking a tooth on small stones the size of a rice grain that had not been washed out in the rice washing process.

Again it was suspected that the staff were lining there own pockets; buying inferior food and then charging for top quality produce; plus of course the usual percentage above the market price that any Joint Venture would normally pay. This assertion was conveyed to the Chinese President who severely refuted my suggestion of corruption but after the investigation the quality improved. The hygiene in this beautiful Swedish stainless steel lined kitchen was appalling; one day what looked like a path leading up through a crack beside the exhaust fan was observed; using an interpreter the obvious question was asked; "What was this dirty mark" Answer; we had a very bad infestation of mice and they used this path to return to their nests in the ceiling". A placing of mice traps was immediately ordered as well as the possibility of poison; once again action taken but only after enquiry; it was obvious that to the Chinese management who ate in the dining room and the kitchen staff felt that mice were an acceptable part of a kitchen scene.

Keeping fit by riding my bike in the country side and discovered a number of local businesses in the immediate vicinity;, there were two local barbers who ran their business beside the road in good weather and under a piece of canvas if it was wet. At the exorbitant price of US.50c I could get a hair cut as well as a shave; a local tailor would make you any item of clothes from material supplied and a shoe manufacturer prepared a special mould of my feet so that he could supply me with shoes. All of this at prices that would equal in Sydney the cost of a small bus ride. One day saw a dentist setting up his foot operated drill and special dentist chair beside the canal in a small village, passing by I saw that he had no customers but on another day he was peering into the wide spread mouth of an elderly resident; another find was a local market; operated every morning from 7am to 9 am; beside a large canal in a small village; here locally grown produce was sold; as usual a local official controlled its activities and collected a friendship payment from the stall holders.

This river side market became Villa 1 source of local fresh food; it was only a few minutes away instead of the minimum of 30 minute drive to Wuxi; here there was no parking problem or parking fee. In 1987 we parked for free anywhere but now a number of local entrepreneurs in Wuxi were collecting parking charges in the area near the free market. Part of a local community just outside Wuxi; on the way into the city also decided to build their own bridge with lead up road; it reduced the travelling time by about 10 minutes but more importantly it was a wide good smooth concrete road; compared to the narrow tarred road that was the norm into the city and surrounding country side . To cover the cost of this local construction the village officials charged a toll; to us it was no money but to a locals it was a considerable impost, this road, never congested was our preferred route into city centre the other way often choked with traffic.

One must remember that car ownership was almost entirely foreign; so locals did not pay to park at the market, although they did at the bike parks at the bus stops. As the only westerner using the riverside market I would be greeted on arrival by the local official, he would be my shadow for the duration of my stay. Quickly recommending stall holders who were selling the things that he thought would be on my list for the day. This market only sold local produce so it was seasonal, pork, live chickens; ducks; quail were always there so were eggs. potatoes, onions, tomatoes capsicum, cauliflower and multiple choices of cabbages only available in season; there were also stalls selling locally made iron items of all types; knives of all variety, woks, hand tools hammers etc, all made in a local iron foundry.

This official, a smiling man in his mid 40s of no great physical stature but large in power had a small understanding of Chinglish; by sign language and broken words over quite some time he explained that his son was very small, then asked if we had anything that would make him grow; the man also suffered from asthma so gave him some medication that we made; we would walk along the canal inspecting the produce and when I displayed an interest he would tell me the price, then collect the money and the goods were placed in the bags that I carried; I never saw him actually pay any of the stall holders but that was not my worry; he seemed to have the situation under control. With the new freezer we were now buying vegetables in season; after blanching, placing them in the freezer so we could have a constant supply of frozen goods just like at home, this was also done with cuts of pork in winter, stockpiling this staple meat to last us over the hot gruelling summer period.

One of our JV partners did have a human growth drug in clinical trials, but after a brief discussion with the Medical Manager in Sweden over the phone it was decided it was too risky to let him try the product. We did continue the supply of asthma products for which he was exceedingly grateful. Whilst talking about international phone calls in 1989, the local Wuxi government installed radio telephone equipment at a nearby site specifically to provide a better service to the JV, until then the telephone line cable wound its way to the city on all manner of posts, sticks; sides of houses; trees and any other protuberance that would keep the cable above ground level. Naturally this cable suffered many breakages. This microwave link transmitted the JV calls to the large manual Wuxi exchange.

Mobile phones were still some 5 years away, ISD was just beginning to make its presence felt in Australia but China still some 40 years behind had manual exchange operators. To call overseas you dialled the exchange operator and they would connect you to another operator in the country you were calling; that operator would connect you to the person you were calling. This process may take minutes or it may take hours depending on the international phone traffic. In China there was a further reason for the delay in connection; all incoming and outgoing calls were taped; in fact all of our incoming and outgoing mail was also opened and a copy made. Big brother was always watching you.

How vivid is the recollection of trying to establish an international phone call, not often; as they were costly and so frustrating to arrange. Firstly their were few Chinglish speaking operators at the Wuxi exchange; when you received the typical "Wei" answer from the operator; very slowly you asked did you speak English. On most occasions there would be an audible click as the operator hung up; dial again; and again until maybe you were successful in getting a Chinglish speaker; or other operators got fed up answering the phone and called an operator with some Chinglish; there had to be an important reason to call overseas with all of the angst that accompanied this function.

It was Ann's birthday, she was in Singapore; being apart so much we did make a very real effort to keep in touch particularly on special occasions like birthdays; returning from the office at 17.30 immediately went to the study to place the call; there was a possible 5 hour window before it would be too late. After 5 attempts to get a Chinglish speaker I gave up; cooked; ate some dinner, cleaned up and sat once more in the study to try again; again no luck; however it was a special occasion not to be missed so decided that no matter what happened; that night birthday wishes would be the goal. Leaving the study; and returning; but now equipped with a bottle of scotch, some ice made with boiled water; a glass with cold water, some local shelled and roasted peanuts (home cooked) in a bowl on the desk; now ready to restart my sole task for the evening.

After some more operator calls, reached a Chinglish speaker, and asked to be connected to the Singapore number; she responded saying that first she wanted to practice her English; always willing to oblige we sat and conversed in banal terms for about 5 minutes; again asked if she would connect me to the Singapore exchange; once again she said that one of her co-workers was also trying to improve her English; frustrated but willing to fill in some time I agreed; another few minutes and requested again to be connected; this time a little stronger. The line went click and the connection was broken; poured another drink, ate some peanuts and tried again, same deal different operator, once again we conversed, once again my request to be connected was met with a disconnection. This performance continued until 23.30 when I gave up hope; knowing that this evening no overseas connections would be permitted; it was apparent that the recording equipment was either being used elsewhere or the operator who did the recording was absent; if they could not record the phone call then it would not be connected. Another instance of the frustrations of residing in this society, how did the people who lived their lives in this environment survive?

Ann enjoyed her art; the possibility was discussed of finding an artist in Wuxi who would give her and the other ladies if they wished; art lessons in the Chinese vogue. We had on a number of occasions visited the special artist's street in Soochow to purchase some of their works; at the time the prices were very reasonable priced particularly if you visited outside the tourist season, our driver Mr. Wu who was extremely obliging found that the professor of art at Wuxi University was prepared to give private lessons provided we provided transport to and from the villas and I would take a class a week in oral English. This appeared to be a small price to pay and so started 3 months of classes at the University. The mixed class of about 20 people were studying International trade and were all hoping to be given a job with a JV or even given the opportunity to live in a far off country.

The level of written English was very acceptable, my role was to improve the verbal skills; to do this and be interesting; debating in English became the teaching style. It was insisted that only English be used for communication during 90 minute classes starting at 19.00; dinner at home and then drive into the University it was no big deal; the road between Mashan and Wuxi had been improved; the challenge was enjoyable what is more it passed some lonely time; an opportunity also to learn more about this burgeoning country at grass roots level. Of many hours with this group I recall with great clarity two debates that opened my mind to reality.

The first was a debate titled "Are the sexes equal in China today". There were a number of women in our JV organisation who held senior positions; a much larger percentage than at the time in Australia; in fact the original chair person of the JV was a Chinese lady; the general party line portrayed; there is no difference between the genders. So much for the general party line; the strong female debating team brought forward some stark facts, the baby bonus for a boy is more than for a girl; the cost of schooling is greater for a girl and the pass mark for most subjects was higher for a female; how true these facts are I cannot verify but certainly the men's team did nothing to dispute these apparent realities.

The next subject of interest was an article that I had read in the China Daily; it featured the affects of tourism on the general community. One team took the stance that tourism was good for the economy and China in particular; the other team, dissented, the arguments were very compelling and very much against the over all concept of tourists in the present staggering economy. Sure the whole group were united in the need for technology from the more developed world but almost as one they were against the tribes of people invading their country from a curiosity point of view; the one baby; one couple concept entered this debate rather strongly; this situation was not raised at all in the debate on equality. The dissenters explained that the reason for the one baby one family hinged very much on the ability of the country to sustain the population from its internal agricultural output; there was in an public area in Wuxi a large wall used to depict the disadvantages of the "Han" race having more than 1 child; it showed how strongly food production and population were inter-connected; it went so far as to depict starvation unless the general public adhered to this restriction. This public area showed over time how the population had increased and how this had reduced the volume of food production as farmland was made over for dwellings.

The dissenters also pointed out that the horde of tourists; demanded food quantities and variations far in excess of the local population, thus causing shortages and increases in price that severely affected the local population. The best quality was being used to feed the tourists; also the waste that emanated from the tourist dining rooms; whole armies could be fed on the food thrown away. One person further went on to argue how local prices of all goods had risen due to the tourist influx; this due not only to tourist demand but also the people working in tourist areas were very well paid in comparison to other local jobs; one person stressing that the people involved in these well paid jobs were party favourites. The person who raised this particular point did not press it too hard; once again realising that they could be severely reprimanded by taking this line in front of a westerner.

It is worthy of note that the one child per person only related to the "Han" tribe. The greater population of China are of this ethnic origin. There are other family number rules for ethnic minorities as there are for people living in extreme conditions; this regulation has caused a lot of discussion in many places I for one feel that the concept was to be applauded, although I did not agree with how it was controlled nor do I find tolerable the idea how the Chinese tradition of a male child was still being followed with rather serious consequence on female babies. There is on going evidence of these practices continuing and eventually there will be a serious disparity between the genders in China. Another effect can be seen on the single child, this child is doted upon by 6 adults, there are many journal articles explaining how this is having a serious physiological affect on the children themselves.

The painting professor held his classes in the villa, his teaching methods very much hands on; he of course did not have a personal space problem and with three well endowed western ladies his hands some times strayed from the original task, this is how it was reported to me. He was an artist and he did some particularly fine painting for us including a portrait of our daughters from photographs. He did however require payment at the end of this work; the request was not onerous to us just a Japanese Colour TV; once again into the smuggling mode we presented him with his wish and his lessons ceased. Naturally this gift was to be a secret but I am sure that he would have needed to make friendship payments to a number of people before he could keep possession of the new box.

During 1988 we took a trip to Thailand a very common R&R spot for expats in China; a week in a resort town after 12 weeks in China was the opportunity to relax and do nothing; we tried Puket; although the beaches were nice, the people obliging, the accommodation 5 star and the scenery relaxing it was not our scene; we did try another resort on the Thai west coast but once again not for us. Returning to Singapore from one of these trips; during the flight Ann discovered that she had left her travel documents in the toilet area in Bangkok airport. The cabin crew were advised and they immediately contacted their agents in Bangkok; we could do nothing except continue the flight. On arrival at Changi Airport we approached immigration with trepidation and advised them of the situation; Singapore Airlines staff also told them that a search had been instituted and the bag had been located with the travel documents intact.

The immigration officer however refused Ann entry; the Australian Embassy was contacted but it was late Friday evening; they advised that all of the staff that handles these matters had left for the weekend. Ann had no choice but to wait in the airport until her documents arrived on the early morning flight from Thailand. She was provided with a small cell like room but not permitted to wander around the airport precincts without a guard until the documents arrived. A bottle of champagne and a snake skin were her only companions for the evening. Her documents and bag arrived in a locked safe on the first flight the next morning, after some formalities she was re-united with them and cleared both immigration and customs where I was patiently waiting.

On return to China we were invited to attend an engagement party at the Tai Hu Hotel, the expat logistics manager his contract complete was returning to European, and, shock horror to the Chinese side; was becoming engaged to one of his staff. A true uniting of East and West, but oh so frowned upon by the local Chinese management coupled with the local political leaders. As expats we rejoiced for them but knew that their troubles were just beginning; it took them a number of months before she could join him in European. Her relatives, like us were extremely happy for them; they could see an escape for her and money for them; but the parents and her immediate superior in the JV lost privileges and were also forced to write letters of self criticism and denounce themselves in front of a large group of peers.

The year of 1988 drew to a close; arrangements made to return to Singapore and then Dural; any type of travel arrangement was difficult to arrange within China the phone system was still unreliable, the booking clerks un-cooperative, on arrival we always had a return booking with a paid ticket; in those days you had to confirm your booking no later than 3 days prior to departure; mostly this proved extremely difficult; Singapore Airlines had opened an office in Shanghai and were always helpful; consequently we always tried to fly SIA but with only 3 services a week it was not always convenient.

Ann with her comings and goings was more flexible so could usually arranged to fly with them however for me it was not always possible. Mostly my route took me through Hong Kong flying Cathay then onwards to Singapore, this flight I had arranged with my secretary to send a telex to Cathay reconfirming flights however on arrival in Hong Kong they advised that the connecting flight was full and as they had not received a reconfirmation my departure would be delayed for at least 24 hours; after a great deal of angst a seat on a Thai flight was arranged this went via Bangkok to Singapore. On Ann's arrival in Singapore a few days prior she had been told that all of flights to Australia before Christmas were over booked although it may be possible to get a flight on Boxing day; panic set in; not to have Christmas in Australia was unthinkable.

We were very frequent users of Singapore Airlines; they were, after all the world's premium airline. So armed with the record of all our flights we approached the office in Singapore and managed to get one seat on a flight next day; They could also arrange a flight to Jakarta on the same day, this flight would connect with a Garuda flight from Jakarta, to Denpassar, Perth and then Sydney. There was no choice; Ann took the Singapore Airlines 7 hour flight while I took the round about 14 hour journey. It was all worthwhile; to be back in Australia; in our well christmas decorated Dural and with family around; this is how Christmas must be enjoyed.

It was always a strange feeling returning to work after Christmas in Australia; Ann preferred to spend more time with the family, therefore I would leave after my 2 weeks holiday break and 7 public holidays added; why 7 public holidays. I worked under Swedish conditions, in European if a public holiday occurred on either a Tuesday or a Thursday the Monday or Friday were counted as holidays; theoretically at Astra everyone worked an additional 8 minutes a day to account for these extra days; also I figured that working 6 days a week plus being on hand 24/7 living in the villa; would allow me the same days off. Anyway leaving the nice hot summer days of Sydney to return to the bleak winter days in China was not something to be enjoyed, it was the job so it was done.

1989 the overall position in the company was deteriorating, in the JV letter of understanding it clearly documented that the imports of a one of our competitive product from Japan would cease after our production could meet the national demand; this did not happen. Now we were in a very competitive situation; another sticking point was the subject of foreign currency parity; this issue arose whenever a new forecast was prepared. The Swedish JV partners were trying to solve this import/export imbalance; doing much to create a market for products manufactured in China however this market was not eventuating. A large shipment of one of our tablet products was sent to Sweden for repackaging; this approach failed as the unions in the factory in Sweden where the production of this volume would have occurred black listed the shipment. They would not even allow recovery of the main substance; the tablets were dumped; new estimates were continually being called for and it was almost a full time job to provide up to date forward estimates as circumstances altered almost daily.

To counter the Japanese imports I put a radical idea firstly to my assistant Marketing Manager (the new young party official) then to top management. The basic philosophy in China was what could be termed the fear approach; if you did something wrong then you had to atone for your sins at the very least this meant writing a report on yourself. This report had to contain criticism of your actions and thoughts; if it was not harsh enough to fit the apparent crime then you had to redo the report. There was no benefit for excelling even in the selling game; once it had been proposed that if a sales rep failed in his target he would be penalised by not sharing in the next round of salary increases. I proposed that we set a basic achievable unit sales target and then set a sliding scale bonus to be awarded for every 10 units over the basic target; a rough analysis of sales showed where our products were being used so a different basis could be set for each area.

For China at that time it was a very radical approach; grave problems were put forward at a meeting to discuss this proposal; it was a hard sell to the other members of the top management team. The Chinese side did not believe in this type of reward system and the Swedish member was a production guy who also had problems with this bonus marketing approach. It was estimated that an attainment of the set targets in the first quarter of implementation would increased our sales by some 10 %, it was so successful that we doubled this to 20%. Production were more than able to meet this demand increase and management in European congratulated the field force; Chinese Management however were less than impressed, then there was a grave reluctance to pay the bonus. At a meeting after the event I asked one of the area sales managers if the bonuses were received, yes he said, they were paid out in special bank bonds maturing in 5 years; so much for a system that rewards good performance.

In late January of 1989 Ann returned to China, one of the Swedish JV companies were heavily into antibiotic products; they were trying to sell a large quantity to the local Harbin Government; the city of Harbin is located inland in what used to be called Manchuria south of the Russian border but north of the Russian port of Vladivostok. During the Sino-Japanese war this city was the centre of Japanese medical experiments similar to those carried out by the Germans; Sweden decided that I should go to this city; fly the flag and hopefully win the contract. The Swedish trained Chinese sales manager who was originally going to be appointed national sales manager but had been replaced by the allotment of a young card carrying dilettante. The Swedish trained guy , was to accompany me, he would also act as interpreter he spoke good Chinglish. When Ann and the Swedish VP heard of the trip it was arranged for both Ann and his wife to also make the journey our cost of course.

In the negotiations in late 1987 one condition of employment set a specified sum as a travelling allowance for the 2 year term of the contract. Therefore we had a ready supply of funds to go in and out of China; this allowance was approved and in fact all future secondments of staff included this sum in their remuneration packages. It was a substantial sum, but it allowed the two ladies and other in country employees to see more of this exotic but harsh nation. All was arranged; on the night before the flight to Harbin we departed Wuxi together with the Hong Kong Chinese marketing lady who was returning home. The Toyota was a very rough a ride, after a convincing argument we took the Swedish VPs Volvo; the boot fully loaded with luggage as three of us we were going into unknown territory with extreme winter temperatures.

Warm clothes, for me suits for the ladies good banquet type clothes, medicine, cleaning gear, toilet shower sanitizers, mouse cockroach barriers ; back up food all included in our luggage; China was not a place where you could visit a super market to replenish your tooth paste or buy some biscuits and cheese. With 4 in the car and the large boot of the Volvo fully laden we set out for the 4 hour trip to Shanghai. Just after passing Soochow a little over an hour into the trip and we ran into a pea soup fog; the car was so heavy in the boot that the lights even on low beam rebounded straight into my eyes; high beam was useless; it pointed to the sky; the fitted fog lights gave me a viewing range of about 20 metres.

Forward momentum was reduced to a crawl; bicycles, pedestrians, mini tractors, trucks and buses would suddenly loom up out of the pea soup fog; the road was full of pot holes with many detours around road repair areas, non with forewarning notices or red lights; roads works were common as the various communities along the road battled to maintain a poorly constructed surface now carrying three times the traffic that it was designed for. At one stage progress was limited to the speed that we could travel while the front seat passenger directed my steering by looking at the side of the roadway; over time we had survived some horrendous car trips but from a driving point of view this trip surpassed all others. Arriving at the Sheraton 6 hours after leaving Wuxi; tired, worn out and somewhat dejected at the life that we were supposed to live.

The next morning; a CAAC flight to Harbin landing in the sunshine at 18 degrees below; the usual greeting party with flag waving school children then hustled off to our decrepit Chinese Hotel, the large rooms, in fact as an honoured dignitary, a suite grandly furnished in 1940s décor; a brief outdoors sojourn while we were regaled with the customary welcome at the airport made us realise that we did not have head protection to counter the prevailing minus temperatures; so with interpreter we found a shop that sold the typical fur head wear of the region; now with some modicum of comfort we had some time that day to enjoy this new city.

Walking along the streets we were struck by the Russian influence; the shops and restaurants decorated with carvings and where we had lunch; a must have dish was what we would consider to be Russian borsch soup; here so far north pasta was the staple food and although plain it was ample. Strolling along and saw an old lady struggling across the road on her very small, almost baby sized feet. She had been subject to the feet binding tradition that was banned by Mao in 1949; this practice was cruel but it was meant to separate the peasant woman from the high class lady; this was the only evidence we saw of this past somewhat barbaric Chinese practice.

The usual official meeting held sitting in large lounge chairs, cigarettes and green tea to everyone before the meeting got underway; as usual lighters furtively disappearing into pockets; what a game we played. Then the translated discussion on price, quantity, supply and shipment, these discussions mostly centred around my local sales manager; in point of fact I was there only as a figurehead; aware of all the details but it was better for the locals to discuss with locals, in this way also I would have no knowledge of the friendship payment agreed upon.

We had arranged a medical conference in Harbin so a lot of our Chinese staff would arrive for this and the banquet afterwards, it was a grand affair then the usual days to wait before returning to Wuxi; these free days were nice from a tourist view point but frustrating as far as work was concerned. This was Chinese Spring Festival (the Communist name for Chinese New Year) so one night there was a visit to the big trade type gala presentation; all of the local industries putting on somewhat garish displays. Harbin is the location of one of the world's famous ice carving competitions; with temperatures sinking to minus 35 it was an ideal location. At the hotel our interpreter had been told that every morning the local residents meet in the town square and instead of performing Tia Chi as they do in other parts of China they dance; this we had to see. At 7.00 the next morning, clambered out of the nice warm high fluffy bed and dressed for the cold. Joined by the Swedish VP's wife we strolled along the city streets to the square beside the frozen river; sure enough before our eyes was a large number of people of all ages very warmly clad in an assortment of heavily padded clothes, hats and gloves, dancing to the tune of a loud speaker of dubious quality; it was amazing to behold. We walked amongst the dancers trying a few steps ourselves much to the amusement of those around us.

These people of all ages gathered every morning to dance; at one time in China it was obligatory for everybody to take part in community exercises; in some cities this practice still persisted with the whole populace out on the streets doing their exercises but I had never before seen people dancing;

imagine the scene; snow and ice covered the ground beneath our feet, the old wooden or brick two story building, with ice hanging from the guttering, snow mantling their roof, steam breathing from the mouth of every participant as they laughed and joked among each other while deftly keeping in time with the music.

Later that day we made a tourist trip across the frozen river to a small village, the mode of transport was horse drawn sleds; the equipment, horse harness and drivers all bore witness to the lack of resources that was a feature of all China. The sleds were very old, they showed signs of repairs over repairs; the harness made of leather, rope; even string; anything to keep the conveyance running; the drivers all in clothing that had been mended, patched and mended again; padded coats with the stuffing showing through the cloth; these men did not laugh and joke they went about their business in a morose way. We enjoyed the sled ride and wandering around a small village that was; just as it has been for many decades; but at the end of the day you wonder what motivated these people to get up every morning and exist.

That evening we visited the ice carvings, what a wonderful exhibition. These ice carvings are not your restaurant type of decorations although in the hundreds of carvings that we saw; there was the occasional swan or fish but in the main they were much larger structures. Electric lights had been frozen inside these structures so that they glittered and sparkled like a fairy land. The main carving as far as Ann and I were concerned was a very good replica of the Sydney Opera house, it was large enough to fit at least 20 people inside and was so detailed that you could make out the individual tiles on the roof. Our group wandered around the exhibition which covered about 1 hectare and marvelled at the spectacle, the freezing air forgotten in the wonderment.

Back to the hotel our three days up and we caught another CAAC plane to Shanghai, recovered our car from the Sheraton and drove back to Mashan. Construction in Shanghai was booming, 24 hours a day 7 days a week work went on, new hotels, apartment houses rose where before there were people's farm land and hovels. A driver told us of a new road into Shanghai that reduced the time spent travelling in the city proper, a small map was drawn and we started to use this road; it passed through an area where corn was the main crop not rice. There were no canals to cross and the road although narrow was well constructed, it bypassed a number of the towns where there were serious traffic bottlenecks, these were old dilapidated towns; where new factories were springing up; the infrastructure struggled to keep abreast of the new industrial need for transport and workers. Now we were witnessing the beginning of the surge of China into the 20th century at grass roots level.

Sitting on our balcony at the villa we could see the main road, every day teams of young men about 10 in each team, travelled the road coming from a concrete factory some distance from us; each man would be in control of a pre cast concrete cassette. These were beams of prestressed concrete some 5m long, 50cm across and 20cm thick. The beams were carefully balanced on a two wheeled pneumatic tyred carriage. They would push these beams along the road to building sites in the city which was some 10 k away. Although the road was predominately flat at each canal and there were many, was a bridge, these bridges were higher than the normal road level to cater for the transit of canal traffic. These raised bridges were often quite steep, a situation I often cursed during my daily run; they were too steep for one of these men to push his cassette up and down; as they approached these bridges they would assist each other to get their loads over the bridge; up and down; in our area there was probably on average a bridge every kilometre, this labour must have been very hard, balancing as well as pushing these large objects some 15k; During the day these teams would return, trundling their two wheeled carriages before them as they went to pick up another cassette and begin the journey again.

Seeing the on going construction; now scattered all round the country, the majority of it done by manual labour it reminded me of the stories that dad told of the hard days toil that he had to contend with during the so called 1930s great depression; indeed in many ways China was just emerging from the 1930s. The police still rode motor bikes with side cars that were reminiscent of the one owned by dad and which in the early 40s carried his family to town.

During 1989 we visited Kunming; positioned just above the Vietnam border where the majority of the people in the street were of an ethnic minority; they still wore their traditional garb and with determination tried to sell their handicrafts to the few foreigners that arrived in that city. Close by was a tourist attraction called a forest of rocks, it was interesting to spend one of the two wasted days meandering around this interesting geological formation. These forays into other provinces and cities interesting though they were; had a negative affect on the resilience of the body and mind. Travelling not as tourists with the attendant safety requirements of the local bureaucrats but as Chinese residents; staying mainly at Chinese hotels at budget prices, accompanied by our local managers we were however treated as visiting VIP's with the usual children waving flags welcoming ceremonies, but never the less always travelling on planes hopefully of US make, steam trains; decrepit buses often in cars that would be deemed un roadworthy in Australia, the public transport forms often crowded, mostly grimy and dusty, it was a far cry from tourist conditions.

Life was settling into a pattern, monthly meetings requiring the preparation of reports, the Chinese accounting staff were catching up with western reporting requirements, and were keen to learn more of their craft. Although most of the factory technical staff had been sent to European for training this had not happened with the Finance people; I proposed that the top two people in the accounting department should be exposed to the Astra financial procedures and visit another subsidiary for a week of familiarisation. Knowing all of the financial managers in the region as well as the CEO's a visit could easily be arranged, also I was aware that the CFO in Thailand spoke mandarin as did at least one other member of his staff.

This proposal was made to the local management; the idea was accepted then a request was sent to the Swedish side to determine if they would pay the expense involved as this would entail foreign currency. Approval was given and the funds made available into my account, the head of the finance department now spoke good Chinglish; we had spent a lot of time together and I had gained his trust;. as discussed early in this tale, he had some bad black marks, one of which concerned his father killed during the cultural revolution so he was not a party member and prepared to buck the establishment; up to a point. The lady his assistant, had very little Chinglish; was a party member, thus very uncooperative; and was the accounting department's in house tell it all. In the department was another lady; she also tried to communicate in a positive way and was infinitely more cooperative however I could not pass over the 2nd in charge; knowing the ramifications. When both were approached with this opportunity it was as though they were being offered a house of gold. These two extremely excited people then had to arrange their travel documents; this took some weeks allowing time for the tickets to be sent in from Hong Kong. As reported before; in Sweden when travelling there is a very adequate daily allowance paid to a traveller in advance. This allowance covers all incidental travelling costs; the amount dependent on the country to be visited.

With costs an issue for the two travellers accommodation was arranged at a local non tourist trap hotel in down town Bangkok; this hotel was used by our expats when they travelled to Thailand for R&R at their own expense; this was not a 5 or even 4 star tourist hotel but one used by local travelling Thais. Over lunch on day one each very exited traveller was given their 6 day travelling allowance in cash; to facilitate better bargaining in Bangkok this sum was 50% in local and 50% in US currency. This large amount of money shocked them but they made no comment, it was arranged that the hotel room cost would be on my account so instructed them that any mini bar, in room dining as well as laundry was on a separate account which they would pay from this daily allowance.

153

Knowing that we would have lunch provided and also some dinners by the Astra Thai people; this daily allowance would more than cover costs particularly since we were staying at a local hotel, here laundry and in house meals were far less expensive than the 4 plus star hotels used as the basis for calculating this daily allowance.; my feeling was that this would enable the two lowly paid Chinese to have money to spend on gifts etc and still retain the equivalent of one or two months wages when they returned home.

At dinner that night needing a break from Chinese food they were invited to join me in the hotels western restaurant; their eyes were big and shiny; filled with wonderment at bustling Bangkok; to me it was very east Asian, to them it was a brave, exciting almost surreal adventure. The lady in her early 30s had a lot of difficulty with the different eating utensils; the young CFO experienced no difficulty at all in using his knife and fork. The lady trying to act as if she knew all about these new eating irons decided that her bread roll should be eaten with the knife and fork. It was difficult not to correct her, yet unkind to let her display her awkwardness; during 1988 there was two of these familiarisation trips they improved the understanding of the accounting people in reporting and control methods however each time the awe and wonder of a new city so obvious on the faces of my travelling companions that it re-ignited in my mind the first time I travelled overseas some 19 years earlier.

That is racing ahead; during this first visit, I again arranged to meet with the two after dinner to get some feed back on how they were enjoying the travel and office experience; in particular how good was the level of communication between them and the Thai staff. After establishing that the trip was proving successful then asked where had they eaten that evening; both quickly answered; they had not eaten dinner at all; the Astra provided lunch was very sufficient; something was not right; I knew from other trips with the CFO that he had a prodigious appetite; lunch as big as it might be would not suffice for dinner as well; however I also realised that the lady was the accounting departments "spy" so left the matter. The lady retired; so invited the guy for a drink; during the next 30 minutes it was discovered that before leaving China they had both been instructed that their daily allowance was US $1 and that they were expected to return the difference between this $6.00 and the US$ 240 that they would have in their pockets when they returned home.

Although our stay was at a local Thai hotel and street vendors could supply a nice meal for almost no money US $ 1 was totally insufficient for 3 meals a day. The young man was also a recently a proud father; he wanted to bring presents for the baby. My resources were far greater than his so I gave him what to me was a small amount of money but to him was untold treasure. He of course had to be

154

circumspect on his gift buying as the lady would quickly report him if she saw him spending more than the very little he could afford. This recalls an earlier conversation; we had an appointment in Shanghai; he travelled with me in the Toyota; on arrival at the Sheraton he informed that he was not permitted to stay at this hotel nor was he allowed to stay at the less expensive Chinese hotel which was part of the Sheraton complex. His accommodation was some 2 k away in a Chinese hotel one which would not have qualified for any of the western hotel star grades.

He was invited to dinner; once more he demurred saying that he had relatives in Shanghai and would dine with them; he would how ever join me after dinner in the new disco that had opened in the Sheraton; arriving at 20.00 we sat and watched the few westerners enjoying the music; we spoke about his living conditions; he said that things were far better now that he was working for a JV, an interesting point was made when one considered his level of salary plus the various allowances, his ability to save was far greater than mine expressed as a percentage of total earnings. The quality of living of course was far less but the percentage he could save was far greater.

In early 1989 unrest amongst the non party members in our organisation became obvious, there was more candour in conversation with locals and the number of expats in Wuxi increased dramatically so did the number of new JVs. Our personnel manager a party faithful chief advised that we were to receive a large number of new employees; at a top management meeting there was considerable dissention between the two expat VPs against the 2 Chinese executives. We now had both the Chinese President and the Chinese Chairman of the Board as full time players in the Management team. As professional managers neither the Swedish VP nor I could see how these new people could be employed nor how the additional costs could be justified with the present turnover. It was an impasse. In due course the new employees arrived. Now on some production lines two people were doing the job meant for one, there was another sign that my days were numbered, I expressed very strongly that this was not a JV but part of Corporate China. The Swedish guy of course with his consensus attitude let it flow.

Just after this rather strong conversation I was told that the guy in charge of Personnel had been relegated to a lower position and would leave our employ, a new person had been appointed. The personnel officer had been quite outspoken against some of the happenings in the company; he was a person that was trusted to give both the party line and his own view point. Both myself and the Swedish VP tried to get this situation reversed we were successful in a way; he remained in the Company at a far lower pay and in fact had no duties. Apparently too close to the westerners.

After only a comparative short time in operation, factory maintenance now became an issue; particularly with the utilities equipment that was mainly of Chinese origin; this subject had been raised before and the Swedish VP was successful in convincing our Swedish masters that it could be timely to have the whole question of preventive maintenance formalised. A Swedish expert in this field was appointed and arrived in country. This man had a Vietnamese wife and children it was very difficult to get permission for his wife to join him, on consideration we felt that this was done to ensure that he would only stay for a short time and thus curtail his activities.

On arrival we were both involved in a maintenance survey, my involvement necessary, it was to be a computerised maintenance program record, as the resident computer expert and the originator of the request for better maintenance it demanded my full involvement. With this man's expert knowledge coupled with my local experience he validated my fears that utility maintenance was not being undertaken even close to the degree required to supply the complex western manufacturing equipment. This was very evident particularly in the basic areas of incoming and outgoing water treatment, steam generation; ground water handling, all comprised Chinese supplied equipment 40 year old design but new manufacture, the level of preventative maintenance was almost non existent. Something needed to be done to counteract the obvious degradation of this old fashioned equipment.

We prepared a joint report on these matters and had it hand delivered to Sweden; knowing if we posted this report it may not arrive at its destination; if we gave it to the Chinese top management they would ignore it; preventive maintenance was not a traditional practice in China in fact it was little understood; a walk around any local factory was sufficient evidence of this lack. Some time after the report was despatched we were advised that the Chinese Maintenance Manager had been found in the possession of a Swedish pornographic magazine; he was to be reduced in rank within the city hierarchy; after sessions of both self and public criticism he may be dismissed from the company.

The expats found this difficult to understand; firstly this man had been trained in Sweden, the equipment was installed under his jurisdiction, now some 3 years after this man had returned from Sweden this book is discovered; all Swedish people knew that this material was readily available; in Stockholm at that time it appeared as if adult book shops were more numerous than ordinary book shops; why was this magazine just discovered? Where had it been over the past 3 years and how come this discovery came to light just after our report had been delivered to Sweden. Once again a valuable employee; trained in Sweden in his chosen field victimised by the local system just after a confidential report to the Swedish JV. This man after the required lengthy vilification procedures was relegated to the ranks then sat in his old office all day doing nothing.

Another Board meeting; another set of forecasts; another series of reports; further discussions on possible actions; all concentrating on the foreign currency parity problem; a marketing seminar had been arranged in Inner Mongolia unfortunately I could not attend as another set of new figures were required. As an input to this next meeting a long report was prepared on conditions within the company, particularly the affects on the expats performance and party interference in the day to day operations; This action culminated in the Manager (totally inept) of the Swedish JV arriving in Wuxi a few days before the meeting; his story was that he wanted to investigate the matters raised in my confidential report, all of the in country expats were extremely pleased as they were very anxious to add to my written list of perceived grievances.

In a move that still has me pondering on this man's human resources (or should I say Lack thereof) judgments; Why was he ever was put in charge of this JV; the Swedish boss invited the Chinese Chairman of the Board to take part in all of the expats meetings and to listen and comment on the grievances. To say that we felt betrayed was to put it mildly, at the Board Meeting the Chinese side accused me of a number of crimes against China including having Chinese girls in my room when I visited Shanghai and of trading in Foreign Exchange Certificates. My boss from the UK now in charge of the Astra operations in China also held a similar opinion of the Swedish JV Manager; soundly disputed the allegations and the request for me to be removed from the JV was rejected out of hand. It is worthy of note here that the Chinese Chairman now fully in charge of all day to day decisions was totally inept as a Chief Executive.

This was the beginning of the end as far as the employment of expats was concerned; from then on it became obvious that our days were numbered. Significantly at this time there was a growing civilian resistance against the 20 million people who were in control; as always resistance of this kind starts in universities and academia. A much loved and respected country wide university lecturer was now being derided and ridiculed in the government controlled media, but the voice of the masses was rising. Our organisation had more than the 20% average number of party faithful, this fact became very evident at this time; previously our employees refused to acknowledge either that they were or were not party people; another of our Swedish trained top assistant managers was under extreme fire for supporting this university professor now being maligned. This manager had already published a text book on the different types of pharmaceutical hygiene classes, stressing how they should be used rigorously in the pharmaceutical manufacturing processes; he had admitted to me that he had been a Red Guard, one who had travelled the country vilifying the educated class. A bright dedicated hard working individual; but now considered to be unfit to lead his department. Once again we tried to have this decision reversed but with our power of decision making diluted by the inept actions of our Swedish principal and the local Swedish VP we bowed to the inevitable.

The local China Daily was now vaguely discussing the prospect of some changes to the present central control system in the next four yearly People Congress; although we were circumspect with whom we discussed these matters the feeling among the expats was that there may be movement towards a more open society. Some of our Chinese assistant managers who were particularly friendly with their western managers were becoming confident that party influences may be weakened; those expats that had been in country for some time however realised that 20 million controllers with a high degree of autonomy coupled with absolute power would not relinquish this power without a big fight.

One afternoon sitting on the balcony overlooking a fish farm we noted a man arrive at the farm house pushing a wheel barrow with what looked like his worldly possessions; next morning returning from the morning run the man was seen levelling an area on a bank that retained the water in one of the ponds. That afternoon sitting on the balcony winding down after the usual mind bending day it was noted that he dug 4 holes and inserted 4 nondescript wooden poles; It was assumed that he must have been given a job by the farmer; it was about this time that people started to travel with fewer restrictions. There was now grotesque beggars in the street leading to the city free market, this was very strange; begging was considered a crime against the state. The next day; seated again on the balcony I saw he had created 3 walls using bitumen impregnated paper sheets and using the same material he had created a roof, now he had a small shed no more than 2 meters by 3 meters. That evening as Ann and I sat with a glass of sweet Chinese wine, we noticed a light in this shed. The next day using the same material and some wooden slats he created a door and using leather straps had swung the door to the frame; he now had a house with a door and earth for the floor.

A few days later it may have been a week or two, a lady and a very young baby arrived at this house; the man and his family were complete in their castle. One late afternoon we walked around this small house just for curiosity sake; the man and his wife and child were enjoying the afternoon sun sitting on small bamboo chairs at the side of the pond. As we approached the lady got up and with hand gestures invited us to join them in a glass of hot tea; the glasses were in fact old jars so we declined but did manage a look inside this 6 m2 home. A two tier bunk bed was along one wall; hooks with their pitiful clothes partly covered another wall, the usual clay stove with two woks, a door less wooden cupboard held their eating dishes and meagre food supplies with a tin saucepan sitting on a small table where they ate if it was raining; otherwise they ate outside beside the pond, this constituted their castle. In winter it will snow and in summer it can be very hot but this was their home and they seemed to be happy. There was no toilet or washing facilities; we assumed that they used the facilities at the farm house. Often of an evening sitting enjoying our glass of Chinese wine we would ponder on this young couple living some 50 meters away in circumstances that we would balk as housing for a dog.

There was a strange situation in the manufacturing division; one adviser was from the US of A; all expat managers were required to have a Chinese secretary to assist in translations; interpretations, the usual typing and fetch and carry functions that go with this position. This man was very kind to his staff but she for a reason that I am still unaware off decided that she would go on strike. This happened in very early in 1989, her boss did not know the reason; it certainly had nothing to do with him or his actions as she was always very friendly and courteous to him and to all the expats. But she refused to take part in any work; she would arrive in the bus from her home every morning come into his office where she had a desk; then sit all day doing nothing; at the end of the day she would cover her typewriter and depart for home. This lady was somewhat of a rarity she was divorced; in the China of 1989 this was very much a social prohibition. I am not aware of the true circumstances and can only surmise; however certain facts emerged; a very good Chinese interpreter had joined the company in 1987 he had formed a close relationship with this lady; the story goes that at one time she was very much in favour with officialdom as she spoke very good Chinglish, this new relationship however caused her to discontinue the relationship with the other top managerial person in the organisation; to counteract this persons displeasure she decided not to work.

In mid 1989 my secretary approached us for a $6,000 loan to enable her to visit Australia for 6 months to study English; every local you spoke to wanted to leave China and go to the gold lined streets of the US, Canada or Australia. Male expats were heavily targeted by young ladies in Shanghai who saw a way out of the daily grind of Chinese life and particularly the controlling officials who could make life so unpleasant; they saw an easy path to a better life. Many married men succumbed to these relationships, particularly those older guys who did not have a strong marriage at home; later experiences would show that many of these young lady and older man relationships foundered after the girls were successful in getting another countries passport. But that is life.

Ann and I looked at our fiscal situation, yes we had the funds but would we ever see them repaid. The numbers did not seem to stack up; firstly she was earning about US $ 60 a month, living with her parents so she had no expenses as the various allowances included in her package would have been sufficient to feed and cloth her; the young secretary had been working in the JV for 3 years so she could have saved some Aus$ 3000.00 however she needed Aus$6,000 just for to pay the private education institution in Australia there was still her air fare, daily living in expensive Sydney. Once she arrived in Oz legally she could work for 20 hours a week, but from that she would need to pay for her accommodation, travel and other living expenses. We questioned her at length and on the side she mentioned that her mother and fathers parents had some gold that they would contribute but we found this rather hard to understand, so we refused her request.

Jumping some months; our contract for China was not renewed; we left in November 1989; on returning to Australia for Christmas this young lady rang and advised that she would arrived in Australia in January 1990 with a 6 months student's visa; she overstayed her visa and Bob Hawke's amnesty for the so called Tiananmen Square refugees of which she had absolutely nothing to do with; gave her the opportunity to obtain Australian citizenship; she now resides in Wuxi and has her own company advising Chinese how they can become Australian citizens. To continue in this vein, a slightly different approach was made by the American's secretary who was on strike.

Apparently to be admitted into the US of A from China you had to prove that you had some US$ 12,000; this lady did not ask for any money for herself, her request of the American guy was that he visit his local bank manager and arrange a loan for that amount in her name. She would not touch the money but with the funds technically in her possession she would be issued a working permit. Just after arrival home the American guy arranged this with his banker and this girl followed; she spoke good Chinglish so was employed very quickly and then her new husband our interpreter joined her in the US and the last I heard some 6 years ago they were living happily ever after, she worked for a university translating he as a taxi driver.

Two other approaches from top people in the pharmaceutical industry to foster their daughters or sisters to come to Australia was made to me and they let it be known that they would do anything to get at least a student's visa, one guy even brought his sister to the Sheraton hotel to meet me on the pretext that both wanted to improve their English; he left when I went to the bar to buy some drinks and it was obvious what the game was. On my return I chatted with her for a while and then drove her home.

I would go to Shanghai every second weekend, just to get away from Wuxi and boredom. All of the villa residents lived in harmony; the swimming pool; outdoor barbeque we lived a good life, but Wuxi had only just started the rapid building programs that Shanghai was experiencing, so it was good to visit Shanghai to get a bigger picture of what was happening in China. The tremendous construction and business expansion was all built on foreign money, prices were going up, there was more and more JV's; more expats all wanting to live in comfortable surroundings; thus fuelled the housing and population boomed.. This boom created rich Chinese mostly party faithful they also wanted better housing and so it snowballed. With this financial explosion came the good time people, a number of places in Shanghai now catered for both locals and expats; intermingling became more open, young Chinese women and men frequented these places, the girls arriving with the young men but were really there to find a way out of China. One evening I was with the USA expat sitting having dinner at one of the new ornate places where western food was served; there was a mixture of ethnicities in the room but predominately people from occidental countries. We had a bottle of French wine on the table and discussing the way Shanghai was changing and how this would affect us, it was a quiet night; we were enjoying our surrounds.

A Chinese couple enter the room accompanied by a young lady she looked to be her mid teens, all three were very well dressed and the young lady particularly fetching. However she was obviously distressed and the couple kept her very closely under control; they ordered meals and just as the entrée was served an older man joined them at the table. This further distressed the young lady however after discussion she departed; obviously quite unwillingly; with the man. We agreed that we were seeing the beginning of prostitution in down town Shanghai.

The contract was finishing at the end of 1989; we looked at our travel allowance to discover that we had a substantial amount not spent. Mainly due to the fact that I was often forced to stay in country longer than the normal 12 weeks, coupled with the fact that our home was in Singapore therefore not as expensive a travel as the guys who returned home to Europe or USA. So with this money we decided to take the trip of a life time and do a safari tour in Kenya and Zimbabwe. As the Europeans usually holidayed in July and the Americans in August we decided to book our tour for late May early June.

A requirement in travelling to and from Africa was a yellow fever inoculation. To be safe we tried to have this injection brought in from Australia however this was not possible therefore grudgingly forced to use the Chinese made product; the common usage in China was multi use needles not single use needles as in Australia; distrusting the hygiene procedures involved in multi use needles we did manage to have disposable syringes brought in from Hong Kong. Were we a little paranoid? I think not.

China to Hong Kong; Kia Tak airport to connect after the obligatory 3 hour stop spent in one of our favourite first class lounges, yes we were going to travel top of the range. Then British Airways to Abu Dhabi connecting with Kenya Air at the time Abu Dhabi was a new airport in the United Arab Emirates. Connecting with Kenya Air; on joining this flight it was obvious that we should have taken the long way round via the UK but after surviving CAAC we settled down to enjoy the flight along with the other 20 passengers; Ann and I the only two in first class on an old Boeing 707. Reminding me of my first flight in 1969 20 years ago. The in-flight service even with these few people on board was somewhat perfunctory however not to worry we were out of China and now had 14 days of excitement before us, also we were travelling first class to ensure that our travel allowance was fully utilized.

Arrival at Nairobi airport and met by our travel guide; a quick city tour before arriving at the hotel, thus we arrived quite late in the evening to book into the Hotel Intercontinental; but after our usual "Dimple" with ice slept soundly. We were awoken at about 6.00am by a demonstration outside the hotel by a large group of young people, they were marching up and down in front of the of hotel screaming obscenities and calling on the rich bosses to leave their girl friends in bed in the hotel and face the mob. This was a shock to the system; we viewed this scene for some time from the room balcony; it was not a nice welcome to what we hoped would be an exciting 14 days seeing wild animals in fields; not wild people in the streets.

09.00 picked up by our guide in a specially equipped mini bus, our 5 day safari began. Although the bus was equipped for 9 passengers ours only contained 6 so there was plenty of room; this space to move around was an important feature when we got to the game parks. Driving out of Nairobi we realised that our experiences on roads in China were to be replicated in Kenya; the traffic rules appeared to only exist in print and the roads were very badly maintained. A track is the word brought to mind.

Our first night was at the Tree Tops Hotel. An actual hotel built in the trees beside an animal watering place. To reach the hotel one walked for some distance accompanied by a white hunter with gun bearer. He explained very clearly that we were in lion country and it was dangerous to be outside of the party which comprised some 30 people all staying over night at the hotel. This hotel was the one where the present Queen Elizabeth was staying when she was told her father had died and she would be crowned. It was the same location but the original building had burnt down some years hence so we could not claim to have walked the same boards as the present Queen of England. Our first night on safari was awesome; sitting in the lounge, a Dimple in hand listening to big game hunter stories and his reminiscence of the quantity and quality of animals of yesteryear.

As the night progressed we watched from the safety of the glassed in balcony while the large array of wild animals joined each other at the water hole. Wild elephants; almost within stroking distance, lions, hyena, the stately kudu, the bounding springbok, and many more varieties drank at the water hole that night, it was almost too exciting to go to bed but we knew that there was a long distance to go tomorrow so reluctantly left the animals to themselves and retired to the small but well appointed room in the trees. We had been warned not to open the windows; the monkeys were friendly but mischievous, but even without aircon the room was comfortable.

Next morning; again accompanied by the hunter and gun boy we returned to the bus and journeyed to the famous flamingo lake. Indeed a sight to behold, pink flamingo covering this large water area, one could walk within 20 metres and those nearby would wheel into the sky like a pink cloud; a sight never to be forgotten; two of our travelling companions were from the UK and the other a Dutch couple; over the time we formed a tight knit group. It was interesting to arrive at a particular tourist wildlife attraction; a pride of lions for instance; to be joined by other small kombi like buses all similarly equipped with a large sun roof so that all 6 could view and comment upon the wild life scenes. Sometimes the occupants of up to 10 of these buses would be looking at animals in their natural habitat only before seen by us in zoos or TV; sometimes, and what we liked best was to be the only bus.

The next evening we stayed in lodge type accommodation, very comfortable except it had no security fence; surrounded instead with a wall made up of a thorn covered bushes. Once again warned against wandering around in the dark and leaving the windows opened; we took a walk in the afternoon within the immediate grounds but felt relieved when we re-entered the building; our driver in the mornings appeared somehow detached; and suspected he was a drug user; the driving, considering the road and traffic was not erratic but this knowledge made us little uncomfortable; we did not mention this to our fellow travellers, not wishing to alarm them. This was a special day; right down amongst the animals, elephants, giraffe, lions; we were so excited to be so close to all of these majestic animals but the thrill of the day was to see two cheetah actually engaged in a hunt, the coloured streak as they sped after their prey and the anguish for the hunted animal were emotional incidents not to be forgotten.

That evening we pulled into a tented camp site; we had been assured that we were travelling first class so were somewhat dismayed to find that this tent camp was beside a river and without any fences; on entering, however; we found that the camp was indeed surrounded on three sides by a thorn bush fence, the other side was the river; showed to the tent; our misgivings as to comfort; disappeared. The tent was entered from a 3 step balcony, inside were all the modern conveniences one found in a 4 star hotel room. Ensuite facilities and comfortable lounge chairs dispelled the feeling of camping; there was a warning that crocodiles were present in the swiftly flowing river so care should be taken walking of an evening in the confines of the camp.

Dinner time; Ann decided she would not accompany me to the dining room; however while enjoying the company of the other travellers and the wonderful meal of local cuisine; Ann made her way into the dining tent. There was no immediate explanation for her change of mind and she did manage to eat some of the local dishes on offer. On return to the tent she explained that she was sitting comfortably reading when a loud splash rose from the river nearby, fearful of the local aquatic carnivore she decided to seek company.

After a hearty local breakfast of mealy, eggs and bacon we rejoined the coach proceeding to a Masai Mara village; passing on the way through a village that is located right on the equator, this was a nondescript village comprising a few wooden structures mostly shops however we were warned by our driver not to take any photos; the villagers were very anti tourist. It was a special feeling to stand in both the northern and southern hemisphere at the same time; we left this village with a strange feeling as the people did visibly display an animosity that we had not previously experienced.

The visit to the Masai village was indeed special; they are amazing people; in this village they specialised in small bead work, famous for the region; we sat watching the women sitting on rough stools making these intricate ornaments; an invitation into one of the houses; completely made of cattle dung mixed with straw. There were no windows to let straying wild animals enter and even in the bright sunlight of the day the single large all purpose room was pitch black; there was not any noticeable smell from the walls as we conjured up in our minds what it would be like living in these conditions. The local chief regaled us with some stories and we rejoined the bus just as another group of tourists arrived.

That day during a visit to a local wild life reserve we were sitting looking at a herd of very large elephants; our vehicle was travelling very slowly away from the herd; the six of us looking behind saw the leader of this herd a very large male elephant with trunk held high thundering down towards us on the track that we were travelling. He looked exceedingly angry and certainly did not take kindly to our presence; the driver was in one of his own private reveries and it was only our loud shout that alerted him to the danger; the bull was almost upon the back of the bus before the driver reacted by a quick speed increase away from the danger. He was apologetic but in our minds eye we could envisage a badly crumpled bus lying on its side, while yonder bull wrought his spleen on us and our fragile conveyance.

During this day we were privileged to see a leopard enjoying a quiet afternoon nap in a tree, with a small dead buck hung from a branch, although camouflaged by the fur's spots blending into the foliage it was still possible to see the golden eyes surveying us from the safety of the tree. At Ann's insistence a hot air balloon ride had been arranged over the nearby part of the Serengeti, close by the Tanzania border with Kenya, this adventure provided for a 1 hour balloon ride and then a champagne breakfast in the veldt. That evening at our hotel we met with the balloon pilot and his wife; they were desperately trying to migrate from Kenya and had tried to come to Australia but at the time helicopter pilots; his other paying job, was not a profession Australia had need of, so their application was rejected.

The dawn of a new day; and a new adventure; Ann had already taken a balloon flight and was excited to revisit the experience. It was a perfect day for ballooning; joined the tour group and crew for the departure location. The usual pre flight preparation with the large balloon laid out on the ground before the burner slowly filled the seemingly fragile canopy with the hot air that would lift the basket and its passengers into the sky. Soon to be airborne over the wilds of Kenya drifting for a time over the border into Tanzania; looking down from a height that enabled one to get a feeling of such a vast expanse, continually seeing various groups of wild animals below us, undisturbed as we drifted silently with the prevailing wind currents. What an experience, it was worth all those lonely frustrating hours in China.

Flight over; back to reality; we lurched and bumped our way back to earth and to a standstill. A lovely breakfast spread out before us on a trestle table, the local food accompanied by some cold bubbling champagne; yet surrounded by a countryside that was filled with what to us were wild exotic animals; guns were in evidence but not required. Leaving this hotel and our balloon friends behind we travelled over more open country watching the almost extinct white lipped rhinos walking majestically in their habitat; continually surrounded by their bird friends and then the unforgettable hippos as they sported themselves in a wide wild river.

Another hotel; here entertainment was provided by a group of Masai dancers; their spectacular leaps to the tune of drums were truly amazing; how these spectacular people have tried to resists modernisation is a complex and moving story; well worth the listening if you have an opportunity. Then the long bus trip back to Nairobi and the Intercontinental Hotel; departing in the morning for Harare, Zimbabwe and another Sheraton Hotel. As some of the trip in Zimbabwe involved flying on small aircraft we were advised to restrict the size of our luggage; so repacked and deposited a suitcase of surplus clothes with the hotel. The next morning we departed for the great Zambezi River and the Victoria Falls; our first two nights were at a hotel within east strolling distance to the falls; this provided plenty of chances to watch this majestic river tumble and swirl into itself. The spray from the falls wet everything and every body within a 100 meters of the river's edge; so it was always necessary to don wet weather gear just to walk onto the numerous viewing platforms. Once walking from the hotel to the river we met a group of local youths selling their stone carvings; we purchased one called mother and child which still has pride of place in our home. One of these boys; really young men; actually offered to swap Ann's blue jeans for one of his painting but she gracefully declined.

The next day was partially spent on a "Falls Cruise" this was somewhat spectacular, travelling on this large river that rises so far up into the African heartland then makes its way to the sea. On the vessel we met a number of Americans couples; two of the ladies were in fact Australian by birth and were two of the many thousands of WW II GI brides who followed their husbands back to the states. Interestingly at the hotel there were photographs of the old Catalina Flying Boats that regularly flew from Australia to England; this town was one of the technical stops for these slow ungainly amphibious aircraft slowly making their way across the world; these planes took of from Rosebay in Sydney in the infancy of overseas air travel.

The next day we boarded a delightful little plane a BAe 111; it looked so small yet it had 4 small pure jet engines; apparently they are very reliable and able to land on a road if need be. We returned to Harare and the next day took a safari through a game park. It was very disappointing and we were glad of the decision to do a long safari in Kenya; later we were told that Tanzania is better than Kenya for the variety of wild life.

That afternoon on return from the safari, sitting and watching CNN news, hoping to catch up on the world trouble spots; but confronted with the news from China; large groups of people were demonstrating in Tiananmen Square; they reported that all of China was in an uproar; people demonstrating against the establishment. This was dumbfounding news; we had an inkling of the rebellious passion that was building within the consortium organisation but we did not think that this anger was so widespread; or; that it would lead to such widespread disruption and chaos. We sat and discussed our present position for many hours, it was decided that we should try to immediately return to Hong Kong.

It was obvious that our in country people would need to take action and leave the chaos and devastation that we saw on TV. Our place was with them; or at least close by; ready to assist in whatever way was possible. An unsuccessful attempt to contact China, it was the weekend so impossible to make contact with the executive in Sweden. A hurried change to flight plans; necessary to return as soon as possible to Nairobi, then Kenya Air to Abu Dhabi; BA connecting flight to Hong Kong, booked a room at our HK home away from home the Sheraton on Nathan Road. A visit first to the concierge to pick up the stored luggage; strangely for some reason or another they had stored this in the freezer. To day we cannot explain why but when they were delivered to the room they were all frozen stiff; everything needed to be hung and defrosted before we could re-pack them. Next morning we returned to Nairobi to link up with the Kenya Air flight the following afternoon.

Now extremely anxious to get back to Hong Kong; but wait we must for the Kenya Air three times a week service to Abu Dhabi the next afternoon. A walk around down Nairobi town; it is one of a very few cities visited where I felt extremely afraid. As a smaller man it was a vulnerable feeling in a city filled with tall powerful local residents, male and female; needless to say it was a quick walk and soon returned to the Intercontinental. We had arranged to visit a famous local BBQ restaurant that evening; this eatery sold flesh from all manner of wild animals. It is not only famous locally but it was mentioned in many Kenya travel brochures available in other countries. This was a once in a life time opportunity; it became a quiet affair; our minds more on the fate of our friends in China; we did however try small pieces of a number of wild animals finding the flesh quite strong and gamey to the taste.

Our last evening of a wonderful cut short adventure, reminiscing over a final drink in the bar before retiring. This bar was much darker than other intimate bars we have in many hotels in many countries, enjoyed. We sat in a banquette style area across from the circular bar; Ann was carrying her camera, so took the opportunity to take a photo through the reflections of the mirror behind the bar. The camera flash drew an immediate response from a large man in another banquette. He was angry and extremely abusive of our photographic actions; he demanded the camera and suggested that we were unwelcome in this establishment. The situation was tense however we refused to surrender the camera and signed the bill then retired to our room very nonplussed at this whole affair. We have since travelled extensively; never once being told that photographs are not allowed in ordinary public places yet we were told twice in Kenya, once at the equator and again in the bar..

The next afternoon; still feeling concerned regarding the previous evening's confrontation we arrived at the airport and joined the 20 odd passengers travelling to Abu Dhabi. The usual check in, immigration and customs procedures; here there was a restriction on the export of local currency so an extra currency inspection; being accustomed to the rigidity of the Chinese functionaries this added dimension was just another queue to join; then wait and wait while the over zealous officials go through their paces.

On scheduled time we were invited to board the 707 aircraft and once again had the pick of seats; settling down in the first class section along with only one other passenger. Departure time came and went; our pre flight drinks and glasses long gone. After a delay of some 30 minutes it was advised that the plane had a crack in its windscreen so the flight would use another 707 plane at another gate. This naturally did nothing to waylay our apprehension of flying Kenya Air but as sheep we followed the ground crew official to the other gate and once again settled into the seats. Another pre-flight drink as we waited for the announcement that we were ready for push back; again; the advised altered scheduled departure time came and went; again our pre-flight drink glasses were empty.

The planes PA system called our attention and advised that the original plane's windscreen had been replaced so we could now rejoin that aircraft. Once more this small group of passengers accompanied by an official traversed the departure area to the original gate. Boarding the aircraft; another pre-flight refreshment and at long last we departed. When our trip was organised in Singapore to connect with a BA flight in Abu Dhabi to Hong Kong it required a 5 hour stop over; we had discussed how this time could be utilized; now after this delay the 5 hour transit time had been reduced to 2.5 hours; Abu Dhabi air port was rated a 45 minute transit time so this delay did not pose a problem; there would still be time to look at this wonderful new airport and maybe sample the business class BA lounge. The flight continued; first class food service, champagne for Ann, a white wine for me; the inner person satisfied; a game of cards and then settle down for the next 3 hours before Abu Dhabi. We had just managed to get comfortable in the half sitting half lying position that one is forced into on long flights on a 707; when the captain advised that he had lost his weather radar; there was the distinct possibility of storms ahead so he was returning to Nairobi.

Now wide awake, we called for a glass of juice; followed by a whisky poured from the large bottle; not one of those miniature things, this goodly portion was one of the few bright spots on the flight; so far. We then did the time calculations, 3 plus hours for our return flight to Nairobi, provided no storm; an hour while they transfer the luggage and passengers; providing they have a plane available that is airworthy; then 5/6 hours to Abu Dhabi. Yes the connecting BA flight will be long gone. Then questions come to mind, will Air Kenya arrange accommodation in Abu Dhabi or will we have to sit in the airport hopeful that 2 seats would be available on BA.

Everyone knows; the bleakest picture is painted in an unknown circumstance; it was too much to conjecture in our still rather somnolent state; as one does when one is travelling into the unknown; we sat and waited the outcome of the new day. Nairobi, new flight number; another old tired 707 and back in the air. An uneventful flight and we arrived in Abu Dhabi; Kenya Air ground-staff was very helpful, they had arranged accommodation for us at a hotel in an area near the airport; all passenger's passports were taken; and we were escorted to this small hotel surrounded by sand and aptly named "The Palms". Now we were assured of seats on the next days British Airways flight; so rested easy until we were picked up the next day for our flight to Hong Kong.

Arriving at Hong Kong as fast as we could we hurried to the Sheraton on Nathan Road to meet up with the remainder of our friends from China. They told harrowing stories of how they drove in convoy from Wuxi to the new Nikko Hotel near the airport; then went to the airport sometimes in dangerous situations and after some days arranged flights; the American couple with their son had broken the golden rule; "never come into China without a return ticket"; they could not find an airline to sell them a ticket from Shanghai to anywhere. Qantas who had sent planes there to evacuate Australians agreed to take them to Hong Kong provided they signed an IOU to pay the fare once they reached Hong Kong. This they did. The group spoke of burning buses lying on their side; trains set alight and demonstrations surrounding them. The peoples' anger was not at the expats; they felt no personal danger from the crowd; the danger coming from the People Liberation Army; young soldiers who fired indiscriminately into the crowds to regain order. One must remember that Shanghai has always been a radical city; it has always resented the fact that it is not the capital city. Consequently the demonstrations in Shanghai against the central Beijing order would have been on a greater scale than the Beijing demonstrations.

With our people safe and in a country where communications were easy we were advised by our masters in Sweden to return to our home countries until they were assured that we could return in safety or they that they had decided to pull out of China. We returned firstly to Singapore; then after it appeared that we would not be returning for some time we obtained approval to return to Australia. After a pleasant 3 weeks we were advised that they had been assured by the Chinese JV partners that it was safe to return to our jobs; this return of personnel would only be those who were essential to the Chinese operations, wives and children would not return until full safety could be assured. It was summer holidays in Sweden the Swedish VP asked me to return with the two production managers and keep Sweden advised of the situation. A contact with the Australian Diplomatic post in Shanghai made them aware of the position; there was no Swedish diplomatic post so the Australian official noted my Swedish workmate friend's location. The American was covered by the US Embassy. The Swedish VP would remain in Sweden on holidays until mid August.

The two production managers, one US and the other Swedish and myself arranged to meet in Hong Kong to travel together back to China; three cars had been left at the Sheraton so we could enjoy an overnight stay; if we considered there was no immediate danger to ourselves we would each drive a car back to our Chinese homes. With some trepidation we arrived on a CAAC flight at Shanghai airport; all other airlines had cancelled their services. The plane was less than half full; the formalities at the airport were quite strict; in fact it took as long to get outside with our luggage with this small number of passengers as it usually did with a full flight. A Sheraton hotel limo now readily available at the airport took us to the hotel and we met again over dinner to consider the position. The consensus was there did not appear to be an immediate threat so we would proceed to Wuxi the next day in convoy as planned.

During the road trip and on the next few visits to Shanghai we found that the presence on the road of PLA (Peoples Liberation Army) troops very disconcerting; they were young men; we knew that if they stopped a vehicle and an occupant tried to flee that there would be indiscriminate fire from the rapid fire weapons these men held ever ready. An uneventful trip to Mashan we went to our villas and agreed to go together to the office/factory. Here we were greeted like long lost friends by the non party people but there was a depressed air about the whole establishment; the party faithful were of course beaming as they knew their control over every body was intact and they could continue to wield their absolute power.

The local non party people in quiet tones in sheltered spots told us of the carnage that spelt the end of the affair; tales of one of the local bank employees sitting in an office on the first floor of his bank visiting Beijing on assignment; killed outright by a single bullet fired at random. Many deaths as the PLA fired indiscriminately into the demonstrators as they marched in the streets; one of our employees a lady aboard a bus, the tyre blown out by a demonstrator's crude bomb; assisting the other passengers and driver to change the wheel, so they could continue on their assigned route. The PLA shooting them as they sat. One of our very good translators who always had a radical approach to the political situation marched in Beijing and died for his point of view. I acknowledge all of the thousands who died and suffered during this event, they were the martyrs to the corruption of power that still exist in China although not to the same extent as it did in the 80s and early 90s.

Counting the safari I had been out of country for almost 7 weeks; it was frustrating to find that most of the control and reporting procedure put into place had been countermanded; the end of month reporting schedule ignored and the actual against budget functional managers meetings; a monthly event disbanded. Apparently it was thought that I would not be returning; as the appointed expat representative to the local Wuxi government, there was an invitation to bring those few expats that had returned for a celebratory dinner at a local city restaurant the following week. Considering the feelings of 75% of our people; who were not party members I agreed on the express understanding that it was to be a welcome home celebration, without political overtones and that there would be no media presence.

We three from our organisation plus only two others from another of the many other JVs; met outside the entrance to the restaurant at the appointed time. Not only was the print and radio media there but also a crew from the local TV station with full outside broadcast facilities; leaving the other 4 expats outside I entered the main door and advised the restaurant staff that we would not enter until all the media had left. One of the official party; a Chinglish speaker asked me what was the problem; I politely (for me) told him about the express agreement; there would be no media presence; he glibly advised that the media were there purely as a restaurant promotion it had nothing to do with our presence. He was cordially informed that once the media had departed we would enter; now there was a Mexican standoff. Eventually the print, radio and TV media people departed and we joined a very cold looking group of officials to celebrate our return. We enjoyed ourselves and it must have cost them a fancy (for China) figure as each of us was the main guest at a table holding 11 other top officials from the local government. Situation 60 diners; 55 very disappointed at the lack of media coverage; attended our welcome home party. It was no wonder that I was not the flavour of the month in Wuxi.

This August summer was very harsh; for over 28 days the thermometer did not descend below 28 degrees. During the day it hovered in the top 30s; sometimes the low 40s; at night it descended to around 30, we lived in the land of fish and rice; fish ponds were just across our wall, the lake 100 metres away, the humidity was 100%. The swimming pool was a relief however the temperature of the water slowly rose until at its hottest it was 35 degrees. There was a rule in China that once the temperature reached 39 degrees then all factories and schools closed, as our factory was fully air conditioned this rule did not apply; it did however apply to office workers; however these people would have been just as hot at home as in the office so they elected to continue to work. In my office was a small window unit that would maintain the office temperature at around 28% but even the effort of using the computer would elicit a flood of perspiration. To use a pen and paper was accomplished only by placing a towel under your hand and arm to mop up the sweat.

The workers asked and were given permission to stay overnight in the factory corridors so that they could sleep; the conditions at home made sleeping next to impossible. The Sheraton Hotel employees were also given permission to occupy the staff hallways in an effort to provide a better sleeping environment. Earlier it was mentioned that the central air conditioning unit in our villa was wrongly installed so it did not function. To ensure that the Chinese could say that the villa was air conditioned; thereby saving face regarding the faulty installation; they had installed a small system in the upstairs master bedroom. On return from work I would take a swim and then have a quick dinner before retiring to the bedroom where I could sit in the 28 degree comfort which was the best that the small unit could manage and that only after I had fully insulated the return cooling liquid pipe to improve performance.

Again my thoughts went out to the man, wife and small child 50 meters away. The town's people were sleeping on the footpaths, some even taking their beds out beside the road ways where the passing vehicles created an air movement. One couple with their infant child sought relief from the heat on a bridge over a canal; during the evening they were run over by a lorry, the driver failing to see them asleep beside the road. These 28 days were one of the hardest that I have lived through, it was made all the harder realising the situation of the millions of people who were suffering this heat wave in circumstances far worse than mine; the end of course came with the rain and as usual in China the mighty river flooded. Down town Wuxi was awash; with the land cruiser I could still travel but the sedans were useless until the waters receded.

The Swedish JV was unravelling. Mainly due to the merger of one of the companies with a non JV rival; the two large Swedish pharmaceutical companies were more interested in doing their own thing outside of the JV; management decided that only production expats would remain in China; my time was drawing to a close; just before Ann's last visit we were told of a new highway that had just opened linking Wuxi with Shanghai; again we had our driver draw us a map showing how to access this road and from then on we drove to Shanghai in comfort. Shanghai this run down dirty city as we knew it was now quickly becoming another Hong Kong, an under ground railway under construction, hotels were proliferating; the building boom was intensifying, the young ladies formerly dressed in unfashionable odd coloured clothing were now dressed in the height of fashion. The China we knew was disappearing; all that remained for us to do was to pack our belongings, return to Singapore and await a new posting.

One of the features of departing from China was the Customs inspection of all of your belongings before shipment home. In particular it was forbidden to take unregistered antiques from the country; over time we had shopped for interesting artefacts but always at licensed dealers; although once during a visit to Macau we had purchased some antiques but these were never taken into China. As a memento of China one of the local ceramic factories made a special vase showing our villa; other than that, all we were taking back to Singapore were legitimate items. Regulations required you to pack your belongings into the final packing cases and then a team of Customs officers would attend your home. They would have you unpack the goods and then under their scrutiny repack all of the articles back into the crates. Once they were satisfied that you were not taking anything out of the country you would seal the crates, they would then place their special seals on the crates leaving you to arranged transport, the usual officialdom; mind bending exercise.

We followed the rules; had all our belongings packed into two large crates, a team of 4 customs officers arrived 2 men and 2 women; they were invited into the kitchen and sat at the table with the paperwork; lighters and pens disappeared as did cartons of cigarettes, after the paper work was finalised we adjourned to the crates sitting in the drive way. The process was commenced; one after another; take out the articles undo the packaging; show the contents to the customs officials then repack each article; then eventually repack the crate; halfway through crate two there was a conference between the customs officers who invited us to stop our unpacking and just repack what was on the roadway. The customs inspection was over; our crates properly sealed and they all departed. A few days later after a large farewell party we also departed China for Singapore.

In my later role as an International Consultant I revisited China three further times; once accompanied by Ann. We were amazed at the speed of modernisation, a new airport terminal, uniforms of different types for the various functionaries at the airport, no longer the flimsy three copy incoming forms, no customs check on departure, What a difference a few years have made. Motor bikes now replacing the bicycles, no helmets the riders and their passengers every bit as non concerned as before on bicycles but now at a faster motorised pace; as a consequence a large increase in serious accidents. The city streets; where once our cars were an oddity; now filled with cars of all makes and models. Nanjing Lu still a narrow important street with modern shops and lit by neon signs now grid locked with cars instead of people. The Sheraton has reverted to its Chinese owners, the service dropping accordingly. The disco now filled with young Chinese women who wanted to discuss price before asking will you buy me a drink.

The large intersection outside the hotel; during our time cluttered with human powered carts and mini tractors all loaded with farm produce for the market; now covered by an overhead road leading to the city centre. The famous Shanghai Department Store No.1 once dirty and dusty with spittoons in each corner; a modern shopping complex; the concrete floors and wooden counters replaced by marble and stainless steel. From the cash only economy the ubiquitous credit card had made its way into the economy in late 1987 now there were large bill boards trumpeting their advantages. The cathedral near the Sheraton; once again became a place of worship; shining like a beacon to the Christian community; what a transformation. The goal of 4 square metres per person by 2000 was realised, the "honey pot" replaced by water closets, and the majority of the residents have running water. Shanghai now a city to rival Hon Kong; China an economic powerhouse.

But scratch the surface there are still only a small proportion of the 1.3 billion people Party card carriers; this small minority still hold unlimited power, executions are a daily occurrence and human rights are a figment of anyone's imagination.. Since 1989 I have worked in 30 countries resided in 8 visited 47 and driven in 28; I have lived and worked with many nationalities all with diverse and interesting customs but for me I am still fascinated by China, with its multitude of survivors; I am still awed by the total power and corruption of a small minority but I am humbled by the power of its billion plus people

Printed in the United States
By Bookmasters